The Psychologist

Saundra L Williams

ISBN: 9798869276612

Dedication

In memory of my dad, Albert R. Duckett

In memory of my mom, Gloria Duckett

In memory of Vernice Austin

In memory of Loretta Coleman

In memory of Lisa Davis

In memory of Sherelyn Fleming

In memory of Francine Harper

In memory of Benny Napoleon

In memory of Willa Mae Raines

In memory of Geraldine Powells

In memory of all the beautiful pets who, while on this earth, provided so much love, tenderness, and joy for us owners: Jonathan, Jennifer, Hercules, Goliath, Sophie.

Dedication

Acknowledgement

I acknowledge all those whose names I borrowed to use as characters in this novel. I needed to name my characters and fondly thought of you. I hope you will find it complimentary that I was thinking of you while writing this novel. Greg B., Gwen D., Della P., Janet L., Rubye W., Larry C., James H. Thanks to Tequella for patiently reading my first draft and to Carol for reading the second. And to my husband, Herman, who always supports every endeavor I undertake.

CONTENTS

About the Author

Saundra L. Williams is happily retired after serving as the President of the Metropolitan Detroit AFL-CIO labor union organization.

The author holds a Bachelor of Arts degree in Labor Studies and a Master's degree in Business Administration/Human Resources. Saundra resides in Auburn Hills, Michigan, with her husband, Herman Greene, and her latest cat child, Kimberly Alice.

She has an adult son, six grandchildren, a grandson-in-law, granddaughter-in-law, three great-grandsons, and one God-dog. This is her second novel. Order her first, Love & Espionage, Unmixed via her website: saundrawilliamsnovels.com

PART 1

Chapter 1

Shay Jackson, a woman of composed nature, now stood frozen, holding on to her kitchen island as she listened to the news broadcast. Her eyes scanned the bold text that lit up the screen.

Shay's eyebrow was raised in anticipation as she patiently waited for the picture to confirm if it was really who she thought the news was about.

Shay's mouth dropped open as the picture was finally displayed on the screen. It was her. She inhaled sharply, finding it difficult to breathe. Moving forward, she found the remote and turned the sound louder.

"I didn't mean to hurt him," the young woman on the TV kept pleading through sobs. "I didn't mean to hurt him."

A uniformed police officer led her away in handcuffs. Shay found herself moving closer to the TV.

"This is Greg Bowens reporting live from Bonner Memorial Hospital," the reporter stated in a monotone voice, "where Mrs. Willa Raines was just led away by police, suspected of stabbing her husband, John, who has been admitted here at Bonner Memorial with what we are told are non-life-threatening injuries."

Shay couldn't believe her ears. She wanted the reporter to stop, but he just kept going,

"The victim was stabbed multiple times. At this time, we have no motive for the stabbing. We will have more for you as the story unfolds. Greg Bowens, here, Channel Four News."

Shay blinked twice, experiencing an involuntary shiver. She pulled her soft white fleece robe, a gift from her husband, tighter around her slender body for warmth. Now feeling lightheaded, she realized she had been holding her breath. She forced herself to exhale and felt her head clearing instantly. How could this be?

Shay continued to stare at the TV long after the young woman's tear-stained face had disappeared from the screen. Her eyes were glued to the screen, she couldn't look away.

Sounds were blaring, and other faces now replaced those that had previously appeared. Shay could not focus. Oblivious to her cocker spaniel, Pam, rubbing against one side of her leg and her cat, Kimberly Alice, rubbing against the other, she wondered again, how could this be?

How could this have happened? The young woman, certainly a little disheveled and now wearing a blouse clearly stained with blood but recognizable, nonetheless, was Willa Raines.

Mrs. John Raines had appeared in the office of The Relationship Fix Group Inc., with her husband, John, just a little more than three weeks ago. Shay had provided counseling to both.

Shay distractedly leaned down to pet both animals as she thought about the history of The Relationship Fix Group Inc., run by Shay Jackson, her husband, Jeff, and their partner, Sam Roberts. They prided themselves on providing caring, compassionate, and useful service to those who required the intervention of professional psychologists trained to listen, guide, and mediate issues between couples, both single and married, gay and straight.

The building in which they were housed was located in the Renaissance Center in Detroit, Michigan. Often counseling was provided pro-bono for those without the financial means to pay for such a service, as all the partners realized that finances often were the root cause of the problems between couples.

Consequently, The Relationship Fix Group Inc., also known as TRFG, was always willing to help.

Never had they ever encountered something like this, though. This was beyond bizarre.

Shay forced herself back to the present to enable her to pull the pot in which she was boiling eggs off the stove. Like a robot, she turned the stove off, carried the pot to the sink, and ran cold water over the eggs.

She found herself attempting to unsuccessfully peel an egg with one hand while, without thinking, simultaneously popping wheat bread into the toaster placed to the left of the sink.

Placing bacon on plates for herself and Jeff, she now used both hands to peel the eggs before putting them into a bowl. She pulled the toast out of the toaster and buttered it while still in a daze.

Shay carried the two plates to the French doors leading to the enclosed sunroom. Pam and Kimberly Alice followed, looking up at Shay for their usual treat, which did not come this morning.

Shay pushed one door open with her shoulder and walked toward the round glass table where Jeff was now seated reading the morning paper. She put the plates down, picked up the coffee pot, and started to pour herself a cup.

Jeff looked up at his wife just in time to pull her hand, holding the coffee pot up just seconds before the coffee would have overflowed onto the table.

"What's wrong, Shay?" Jeff asked. "You look as though you've seen a ghost."

He took the coffee pot from her ice-cold hands.

"I just saw a news broadcast," she said shakily. "The couple I told you about a few weeks ago, Willa and John Raines..."

"I remember," he said, nodding his head. "The husband cheated continuously, right?"

"Yes. At the last session, I suggested he go to therapy for sex addiction. I guess he didn't follow through on his promise even though he swore on his mother's grave that he would contact the sex addiction counselor immediately. I gave him Anna Blake's name and phone number. She's the best, you know."

"Yes, I know," Jeff responded. "I've referred her a time or two myself. But how do you know he didn't take your advice?" Jeff asked, wrinkling his brow.

"Because she stabbed him. I just saw the police lead her away from Bonner Memorial in handcuffs," Shay said now shaking visibly.

"What? Who stabbed him? Who is she? You don't mean his wife?"

In a daze, she said, "Yes, his wife, Willa, stabbed him. According to the newscaster, she actually stabbed him multiple times."

"Multiple times," she repeated incredulously.

Jeff rose from his seat and put his arms around his wife, gently pushing her down into a chair.

"Are you sure it was her on TV?"

"Very sure. She actually looked much the same as the last time I saw her. She was sobbing hysterically, just like she did during our counseling sessions. Only this time, her tears were captured by a TV camera. I just can't believe something like this could have happened."

"I guess killing the cheating spouse is always a possibility. It's really too bad they couldn't have worked it out. But he probably deserved to die," Jeff said stoically.

"Oh, he's not dead. The announcer said he sustained non-life-threatening injuries."

Jeff's eyebrows rose, but he said nothing.

Jeff glanced at his watch and hurriedly began to stuff his mouth with food. Shay picked at her food, pushing it around on her plate, first one way and then the other. When she noticed Jeff had completed his meal, she collected the breakfast dishes. She walked to the sink and raked her food into the garbage disposal.

Eating was not on her mind this morning. Jeff followed behind, assisting with putting the dishes in the dishwasher and tidying up the kitchen.

"I guess my day is free. The only couple I scheduled today was John and Willa. I thought I'd give them some extra time. I thought they could use it to talk about the results of his sex addiction counseling. I suppose that visit is no longer pending," Shay said, her voice sounding weak.

Jeff put his arm around his wife's shoulders.

"I have a few errands to run before my first client at two this afternoon. How about we have dinner out tonight? We could go to Como's in Ferndale," Jeff said, attempting to cheer his wife. "You always like walking through the area," he said, reminding her how they normally enjoyed strolling through Ferndale, a suburb of Detroit.

"I do love Ferndale," Shay admitted distractedly.

"You seem a little off-kilter by the news of the stabbing."

"Yes, I guess I am a bit dazed after hearing the news. That's sweet of you to suggest dinner at Como's. That would be great.

"I'm sure things will turn out as they should. He probably won't cheat again, I'll say that."

Shay shook her head. “I’m not so sure. He actually has an illness. I’m still hoping he’ll check into the sexual addiction clinic I suggested. He promised he would. So, yes, I guess I am a little thrown by these developments. As long as we’ve been providing counseling, I’ve never seen anything like this happen. Our clients normally either work things out or, in rare cases, they divorce. Nothing this dramatic.”

“It sounds as if their relationship was dramatic,” Jeff said. “It appears these two just don’t need to be together.”

“You think?” Shay said, managing a brief smile. “You haven’t heard the entire story. I think we were interrupted by a phone call when I started to tell you and Sam about this case.”

Shay, Jeff and Sam often discussed difficult cases with each other. Frequently, one or the other would come up with something creative to try that helped to resolve whatever problem they were discussing.

“Oh, I remember, I told Sam about this, but you took that call and didn’t hear it all. At the first visit, Mr. Raines confessed that in just one month, he’d had sex with more than thirty women. Often, he had sex with two women in one day, one before arriving at work and the other either at lunch or after he concluded his day.” Shay began to recall all the details as Jeff took a step back.

He nodded wordlessly, trying to take it all in.

"He confessed that a couple of times, he'd had sex with three women in one day. Oftentimes the sex occurred in the vacant houses he showed his clients. He's a very busy real estate agent, it seems."

"So, he's a real estate agent, huh? I was wondering where he'd find the time for all that sex and work too. That's unbelievable," Jeff shook his head. "And he said all this in front of his wife?"

"Well, not all of it. Once I got the gist of what his problem was, I asked to meet with him separately. He had perfect recall when it came to starting to name all thirty women. I stopped him." Shay paused, shaking her head again. "I told him I really didn't need all that information. He actually seemed proud of it. Said he was often aroused and had to relieve himself.

Jeff began to shake his head at the craziness as Shay kept going,

"He said this as if it were his right to satisfy his appetite anywhere and in any way possible. He said it as if he believed it was not a problem. He told me more than once that the women were willing. It was never rape or even persuasion. Most had offered without his having to even ask."

"That sounds crazy. Maybe it's best you don't have to deal with it anymore," Jeff made a disgusted face.

"That's our job," Shay reasoned.

“I know. I was trying to show you the better perspective.” Jeff smiled, revealing the chipped tooth that Shay had affectionately noticed on their first date, before saying, “Gotta go. I’ve got something to take care of before my clients arrive. I’ll see you tonight around eight for dinner?”

Jeff looked back at the distracted face of his wife and continued to console her,

“Try to relax and get this off your mind. Don’t worry. Everything will work itself out for the wife, I’m sure of it.” Giving his own wife a wide smile, he kissed her.

“I certainly hope so,” she said uncertainly.

She couldn’t help but attempt to smile as she looked at her husband. Shay watched Jeff as he strode toward the door.

“I love you,” he said, turning and smiling at her. The look on his face showed the admiration and heartfelt love for the woman he’d been privileged to marry.

Chapter 2

Shay could not imagine her sweet, unassuming husband ever doing anything remotely resembling John Raines's infidelity and wild escapades. In fact, she and Jeff had only one problem in their marriage.

Sighing, Shay decided not to dwell. Most important was that Jeff was kind, considerate, generous to a fault, and always loving. In all their years of marriage he had not changed. He'd never raised his voice to her and he made her laugh. What could be better? she thought.

With Jeff gone, the house seemed unbearably empty and quiet.

Shay poured herself another cup of coffee and headed back out to the sunroom. She felt the morning sunshine providing warmth to her body as the hot cup of coffee warmed her hands, still ice cold.

Shay set the coffee down on the small table next to her favorite lounge chair. She sat down slowly, enjoying the plump cushion as she looked out at the Detroit River. Water always calmed her. She was grateful that Michigan's frigid temperatures had now thawed.

In February, chunks of ice had floated by, offering a chilly and dismal view of what in summer was a beautiful body of water. Now, things were thawing nicely.

Both animals waited patiently until she was seated. Then Pam put her large wet mouth on Shay's knee as Kimberly Alice sprang up to jump into Shay's lap. She absently rubbed them both.

Jeff and Shay had purchased the home they were in just three years ago. There were no children, just the two of them rattling around the house with their two animal babies. But they loved it. There was plenty of space for Shay's entire family, who lived in Virginia, to come and stay during the holidays.

There were five bedrooms with attached baths, a huge great room, a library, and a huge state-of-the-art kitchen. There were floor-to-ceiling windows in every room, all with exceptional water views.

Shay loved the fireplace in the master bedroom best. On Thursday evenings, when Jeff always had late-night volunteer work, she'd snuggle up under the covers in her bed with a good book. She was currently reading Love & Espionage Unmixed. The more the story unfolded, the better it got.

Shay realized that she and her husband were blessed. She thanked God each and every day for the life they led. They traveled, dined with friends, golfed, skied, scuba-dived, and watched old movies together. They loved each other's company and were almost inseparable, except for one problem.

Again, Shay put it out of her mind. Nothing going on in her marriage was comparable to those she counseled. Today had to be especially trying for the Raines family.

Chapter 3

Shay closed her eyes as she envisioned her session with John and Willa Raines only three weeks ago. Gwen Davis, TRFG's reliable office manager, had announced the couple's arrival.

Gwen was not only the office manager but also a long-time friend of Shay's. Shay, Gwen, and their other BFF, Saundra, had been the three happy musketeers for more years than Shay could remember. She recalled vividly Gwen showing the Raines in, asking if anyone would like coffee, water, or a soft drink, and then quickly serving the drinks before the session started.

Willa was at least initially smiling, even though John looked mildly irritated and no happier to be there than he had on the first visit. Shay knew, however, that Willa had staked all her hopes on these sessions, bringing her and John closer. Willa seemed extremely happy that John had agreed to return once more.

Shay remembered that after the first session with Willa and the session alone with John, he swore he would not return. He insisted he did not need counseling. Shay admitted that she was glad that he had decided to return, as John needed counseling more than anyone she'd ever worked with (although she didn't tell him that last part). And Willa deserved a try at saving the marriage.

"Let's start where we left off last session," Shay had said when John and Willa were both seated.

Shay remembered the conversation almost verbatim.

"Mr. Raines, as we ended our last session, you said you love your wife. Yet, your wife discovered that you've been having sexual relations with at least three other women. How do you think those relationships impact your marriage or your wife's desire to continue this marriage?"

"I guess I never thought about it," He shrugged.

"She's always home with the kids, and things seemed to work better when I came home later. I—I mean," he stuttered, "Whenever I'd come home before she put the kids to bed, she'd be busy. The kids would yell, and the house had toys all over the floor. So, one night, I stopped for a beer and didn't get home until after ten p.m. By the time I got there, the kids were already in bed, the house looked cleaner, and she was in bed and looking kind of sexy. So I started staying out later and later."

"Mrs. Raines, did you ever know that the noisy kids and toys all over the floor disturbed your husband?"

"No, he never said anything," She sat twisting her wedding ring. "He'd just eat his dinner and then go into the bedroom and close the door. I tried my best to rush the kids through dinner and clean up the dishes and the toys so I could get into the bedroom with him. But it's not easy to rush three young kids. I thought John just went into the bedroom because he was anxious to have sex with me. We always made love at least twice. I probably wasn't a very good partner because I was so tired from dealing with three kids all day long. I once apologized for refusing when he wanted to make love yet a third time."

"What was his response when you were too tired and refused to make love three times?" Shay directed her question to Willa.

"I only refused him once. When I did, he hit me pretty hard across my face," She absently touched the spot as she spoke. "After that, he left the house, and I didn't see him again until the next evening. So I never refused him again."

"Mr. Raines, do you remember that?"

"Yes, but I don't recall hitting her. I just remember leaving the house."

"What did you do after leaving?"

"She knows I have to have sex, and if she isn't going to give it to me, I will find it somewhere else."

Shay watched tears well up in Willa's eyes and decided to change the tone of the session, "Mr. Raines, what do you think your wife should expect from the husband who says he loves her?"

Once again, he shrugged.

"I can answer that," Willa spoke up. "He only seems to care about what he expects, and he expects sex all day and all night. When he doesn't get it from me, he goes elsewhere."

"Is that true, Mr. Raines?"

"I just said that, didn't I? She knows I have to have it. She knows that. She's always known it, even before I married her. She knew I used to bang several women every day before we got married. She knew one woman was never able to satisfy me. Willa knew about them all before we got married. She seemed okay with it then."

"Is that true, Mrs. Raines? Were you okay with Mr. Raines's sexual exploits with other women prior to your marriage?"

"I wasn't exactly okay with it before we got married, but I tolerated it. Then he proposed. I assumed he had decided I was the only one he needed."

"Mrs. Raines, did you have a conversation about this where Mr. Raines told you that you would be the only woman in his life?"

"Well, no, but who does that? Why did you propose if you didn't intend to give up the others?" Willa looked accusingly at John.

"I told you, I tried. But I was drawn to them. I ended it with two women I'd been sleeping with before we married. But I found myself having sex with two new women I had met within a week of our marriage. And when those relationships ended, I returned to the first two and continued with yet a third woman. I just couldn't help it." He lowered his head.

Willa opened her mouth as though to speak, but only sobs came out.

"I'm sorry, Willa. I didn't mean to hurt you. I do love you. But I've had three and sometimes four and five women all my life. Sometimes I'd even have sex with two or three on the same day. I can't seem to help it," John said once again.

"I am always aroused when I look at women," He added as he lowered his head again.

Willa now sat sobbing openly. Shay held out the box of tissues.

"There was one woman in particular who started calling our house looking for him," Willa said through her sobs. "I thought she was related to his real estate agent job. I mean, I thought maybe she had hired him to sell her house or find her one. I figured that it was all innocent since she was calling him on our house phone instead of secretly on his cell phone."

"Did you ask him about this woman?"

"Not at first, but when she kept calling, and he kept leaving to meet her after each call, I asked him why she was calling him at home and not in the office."

"Mr. Raines, tell us why this woman called your house when she could have called you at the office or on your cell phone."

"It was kind of the way we'd planned it. I was only thinking of Willa. I thought she would be okay if I said a client was calling and needed to meet with me."

"When you say the way we'd planned it, you mean you and this woman?"

"Well—yes." He lowered his head again.

"And you didn't think Mrs. Raines would get suspicious when the caller was the same woman all the time?"

"No, because Willa knew that when I was showing houses to a new client, it could take numerous visits until they found the right one."

"Mrs. Raines, did Mr. Raines ever tell you that he was not satisfied when the two of you had sex?"

"No, but he never wanted to stop with one time or two. He usually wanted to do it at least three times in one night. And even after three times, when I was exhausted and attempted to roll over to get some sleep, he'd sometimes want to make love again. At first, I thought he just couldn't get enough of me. He'd be gentle and loving the first time, but each time after that, he'd become rougher and rougher and much more aggressive. It was like I wasn't even there. He'd just pound me and make guttural sounds. His eyes would be open, but it was as if he wasn't seeing me. We'd be having sex, but it was almost like I wasn't there."

"It was often painful," she continued. "But when I told him he was hurting me, it was as if he didn't hear me. When he was done, he'd roll off me and get up without saying a word. I was so exhausted that I'd just immediately fall asleep. But once, I woke, and John wasn't in bed. So I went downstairs, thinking he was probably in another room watching TV, but he was gone. He had left the house," she said, sobbing again.

"Mr. Raines, where did you go?"

"I needed sex, so I went out," he said flatly.

With this response, Willa's sobs became even louder.

Shay noticed that John never once looked at his wife when discussing sex with other women. Even talking about sex seemed to make John's eyes glaze over.

Shay could not help but notice the bulge in his pants, indicating he was indeed aroused. His hand moved back and forth over his pants, stroking his erect penis. At one point, his breathing became heavy, apparently forcing him back to the conversation.

Finally, he removed his hand and looked up at Shay. He didn't appear to realize what he had been doing right there in the counseling office. As an experienced counselor, Shay could not help but diagnose that John Raines had the most serious sex addiction she'd ever seen in all her career.

Willa continued to sob. Shay moved the box of tissues to the table next to where Willa was seated. Willa pulled out a tissue and attempted to dry her eyes, but the tears continued to flow. Shay suggested Willa go to the restroom, pointing to the door slightly to the right of where she was seated. Willa obliged. She stood up and stumbled into the restroom.

Shay said, "Mr. Raines, it sounds as if you have a problem that perhaps would best be treated by you seeking the help of a sex addiction therapist. Will you make an appointment to see someone? I can refer you to an excellent clinic."

Willa stood frozen in the doorway of the restroom, looking from Shay to her husband, awaiting his response, still sobbing. John finally looked at his wife and walked over to her, attempting to comfort her.

He said, "Willa, please stop crying. I promise I'll go to see this therapist. Please stop crying."

Willa continued to sob. She now had her face covered and was weeping into a tissue.

"How can I believe you?" She wailed. "How can I ever trust you again?"

"Willa, look at me. I love you. I swear on my mother's grave that I will make an appointment and see this therapist."

With those words, Willa calmed a bit. The tears slacked off, and she moved toward her husband. Shay picked up her cell phone, and scrolled through her contacts until she found Dr. Anna Blake's phone number. Quickly writing it down, she handed it to John Raines.

"I've recommended this clinic to others with good results," she said, smiling kindly at John.

Chapter 4

Willa and John had left Shay's office holding hands that day. Shay lost track of time, as she sat in the lounge chair, thinking about her most recent session with the Raineses. Kimberly Alice huddled quietly in her lap while Pam sat near her chair. Every now and then, Pam laid her head on Shay's knee. Both animals seemed to sense how intense Shay's thoughts were. Thoughts that were now interrupted by the buzz of her cell phone.

"Hello," Shay said, looking quickly at the caller ID.

It was Willa. Shay wondered briefly if she was calling from jail.

"Dr. Jackson, this is Willa Raines."

"Yes, Willa. I saw the news report. Where are you?" Shay said without beating about the bush.

"They released me, Dr. Jackson. John told them it was an accident and that he did not want to press charges."

"I'm glad to hear that, Willa. Would you like to continue our session today?"

"I would very much. Can I come at eleven a.m., while my neighbor, Joyce, still has the kids?"

Shay glanced at her watch. It was nine-thirty. "Eleven a.m. will be fine. I'll see you then."

Shay quickly showered and dressed, arriving at her office thirty minutes before the appointment time.

"Good morning, Shay," Gwen said, giving Shay a surprised look. "I'm surprised to see you. I know you had only one appointment on your calendar today, and she's in jail. I wanted to phone you, but it was so early. I didn't want to interrupt you or Jeff. I saw it on the news this morning. He deserved all those stab wounds, plus some. He was a cheating, no good son of a—"

"Gwendolyn," Shay interrupted, drawing out Gwen's full name slowly. "That's kind of harsh, especially in light of the man's illness. His wife has been released."

Shay looked at her watch and added, "She'll be here in about twenty-five minutes."

"Okay, I'll stop, but I never told you that he tried to hit on me while his wife's back was turned. That was just after their last session ended. She had a coughing spell, and I directed her to the coffee room to get water. He then uses the time to hit on a gray-haired grandmother. Can you imagine that? I guess no woman is exempt from him. My sons, Steve and Erik, would be outraged at the thought. My granddaughter, Devenea, on the other hand, would probably roll on the floor laughing to think someone would actually hit on her old grandmother. I was so angry. I could have killed him myself. I actually slapped him. I was so furious."

Gwen added violently, "I hate cheaters! They came out of your office holding hands, but the minute I point to the coffee room where she ducks in to get water, he starts hitting on me."

"I'm sorry that happened," Shay spoke softly but firmly. "You should have reported it to me."

"I didn't need to tell you. I took care of him," Gwen said and pursed her lips. "She should have killed the no good…"

She paused, eyeing Shay. "Alright, alright," she said, throwing up both hands. "I should have just let you handle it."

Chapter 5

Shaking her head, Shay headed into her office. Gwen was very good at her job, but Shay understood how something like that could infuriate her. There were policies in place to handle sexual harassment Gwen was aware of them. Shay, however, couldn't help but think John got what he deserved. The moment the thought was complete, Shay felt guilty.

John really was sick! Who else would have sex with and recall the names of thirty women they'd slept with?

Then again, Shay had never seen Gwen that upset. She was usually calm and professional. Only the vilest thing—or person—could set Gwen's temper flaring. Shay made a mental note to take her friend to lunch one day this week to make sure there wasn't anything else going on in her life. She'd had enough sadness to last her a while. Usually Gwen's mantra was, "If they knew better, they'd do better."

I guess John Raines's behavior could try anyone's patience, Shay thought with a sigh.

At exactly eleven a.m., Gwen buzzed Shay. "Mrs. Raines is here."

"Show her in, please, Gwen." Shay answered.

She stood up when she saw Willa. She smiled when the woman appeared in her doorway and said, "Come in, Willa. I won't say good morning because I know it hasn't been good for you."

Shay watched as Willa fell into a chair. Her usually pretty face showed the remnants of the drama from this morning. Her thick auburn hair, typically worn in a neat ponytail, was a tad unkempt today.

"You look as if you could use some coffee," Shay said wisely, stepping to the sideboard where the coffee pot and a tray of cinnamon rolls sat. After pouring Willa's coffee, Shay let herself be tempted to take a cinnamon roll, which Willa declined.

"Thank you," Willa said gratefully, accepting the hot coffee. "It's the first cup I've had in the free world."

Then, her smile crumpled as she burst into tears. Shay let her cry for a while and then wordlessly handed her the box of tissues. Willa wiped her tears away and blew her nose. But she continued to sniff.

Shay watched the young woman with compassion. Willa was twenty-five years old and quite attractive. She watched as Willa dabbed at her long thick eyelashes that any woman would kill for. Her figure and legs were also great, and she was smart. And with the exception of today, Willa was usually articulate.

It was obvious that John didn't cheat because he was looking for a prettier or younger woman. Of course, this woman's husband actually had an illness. It didn't matter how his wife, or any woman for that matter, looked. The truth was John Raines could not be satiated – no woman could fulfill his need. He needed to be medicated. Shay was confident that if he'd followed through on her referral to the sexual addiction clinic, he could have been helped.

Willa again burst into tears. She now spoke through sobs, making it difficult for Shay to understand much of what she was saying.

Shay was accustomed to assuming her usual professional poise, but on a few occasions, she struggled to balance the required detachment with the compassion she truly felt. Unfortunately, this was one of those times. She could only imagine what Willa had been through today, and it wasn't even noon yet.

"Willa," Shay said softly. "Take a deep breath and tell me what happened this morning. I know it isn't easy, and I will help you get through this. But I can't understand what you're saying while you continue to sob. Getting what happened all out will be the start of your healing process. What do you think?"

"I think so. You're right, Dr. Jackson," she answered shakily.

Taking a deep breath, Willa began again, "I really didn't mean to hurt him, Dr. Jackson. I really didn't. But my spirits were uplifted after our last session, based on John's promise that he would seek help at the sex addiction clinic you suggested. He even swore that he would on his mother's grave. He loved his mom so much that I was sure if he swore on her grave, he'd have to follow through. He even held my hand as we left. Did you see that, Dr. Jackson?" Willa's eyes were pleading.

"Yes, I noticed he was holding your hand as the two of you left this office," Shay said, removing her glasses and looking directly into Willa's eyes to reassure her.

"He hasn't held my hand in years," she said with a sad smile.

"Anyway," she started again, "I tried not to bug him about making the appointment. But after about five days, I inquired about the date of his sex addiction clinic appointment. I tried to make it sound like I thought he had called and not that I was bugging him or accusing him of not calling. I just acted as if I assumed that he had made the call."

Shay nodded and replied softly, "I understand."

He told me he had an appointment for this morning. He even gave me the time. He said his appointment was eight-thirty a.m. He looked me right in my face and told me he'd called and that I could relax because the appointment was made and confirmed." Willa paused again as her eyes brimmed with more tears.

“Take your time,” Shay encouraged her.

Willa began, “That was about three days ago. I was pleased, thinking things were going to be better soon. I started dreaming, thinking that our broken relationship could somehow, through some magic, be fixed. But of course, it was all a delusion.”

She paused once again as it got hard for her to get the words out of her mouth. She tried speaking, but only sobs came out. She had to pinch the bridge of her nose to contain her emotions. Then, she said, “Last night, I set the alarm for six o’clock so that I could get up and fix John a nice breakfast before he left for his appointment. He likes bacon, eggs, hash browns, and toast, while I usually only fix cereal for the kids.”

Willa sniffed again but continued, “I went down to start his breakfast, but I kept listening for John to be moving about, and when I didn’t hear him, I went upstairs to check at about seven a.m. I found him still in bed. So I shook him gently awake and reminded him that he had an appointment this morning and that I had fixed him some breakfast.” She paused and took a deep breath.

“Well, that’s when he blew up, said he wasn’t going, and admitted he was now intimately involved with several women and liked it that way. He said he wasn’t keeping any more appointments with you or going to any sex addiction clinic. He confessed he had lied and never even made an appointment. He got out of bed and said he was going down to eat the breakfast I'd fixed.

"I sat down on the bed for a few moments and listened to his footsteps as he walked down the stairs. It was like the breath had been knocked out of me. My eyes started to blur. I could hardly see. I remember stumbling blindly down the steps to the kitchen." Willa paused and took another deep breath.

"Dr. Jackson," Willa said through tears. "I remember standing there in the doorway to the kitchen for I don't know how long, watching him wolf down the breakfast I'd prepared. He appeared to be enjoying it without a care in the world. I watched him feeling as if my world had collapsed around me. I felt deflated.

"I remember watching him rise from the table, taking his plate to the stove and loading up with more food. That's when I just exploded. All the rage I felt came roaring out of me. All my hopes of saving my marriage went completely down the drain. I walked, or I guess stumbled, toward him. I remember looking down at the knife on the kitchen counter. I had just used it to mince the onions John liked on top of his hash browns. I remember picking up the knife, but I don't remember stabbing him. But I know I must have done it because I had blood all over my hands and my blouse, and the police officer said I stabbed John three times, once in his shoulder, once in his lower arm, and again in his side." Willa paused as she twisted the tissue she was holding around and around her third finger.

"Go on," Shay said softly.

"After a while, I think I looked at him. The plate had fallen from his hands, but he never fell. He just stood there with the blood dripping from his wounds, looking at me, and I remember now that the look on his face was disbelief. It was almost as if he was thinking, how could you have done this to me? I could almost hear him saying, *'I've been so good to you. How could you have done this?'*

"Except he wasn't really saying anything. He just continued to stand there with the blood dripping. It was so red and so much of it. I just stood there looking at him. And Dr. Jackson, he wasn't good to me. You know he wasn't." Willa looked to Shay for confirmation.

She added, "He cheated and lied and even hit me a couple of times. But I still didn't really mean to hurt him. I remember the kids were awake and had come downstairs. They started screaming. That's when I came to myself. I called my neighbor, Joyce, to stay with the kids. Then I remember pushing him out to the garage and forcing him into the car. He didn't argue. He still didn't say anything. I guess he was in shock. I don't remember driving to the hospital, but I know I did. The car is now full of blood. I don't know why I drove him instead of calling an ambulance. I think, at the time, I just needed to take action. I don't know if I could have sat there calmly and waited for an ambulance to arrive."

Willa paused, and Shay gave her an encouraging smile, asking her to go on.

“I guess doctors are supposed to report stabbings or other crimes because the police arrived at the hospital, and then people with TV cameras showed up. I don’t remember much after that. I know they took me to the police headquarters. I think I answered their questions. I don’t remember the questions or answers I might have given. It all felt surreal, as though my life sort of came to an end. I was there – I was very much awake and there, but I can’t quite recall much. It’s as though I knew I was living a nightmare, so all sense just eluded me. But I was aware enough by then to know that it was real. I had stabbed my husband…my children’s father… The man I love…”

The last comment came out of her mouth and sounded more like a question than a statement.

“It was like that old TV show, The Twilight Zone. I actually never liked watching it. Those people were so lost and couldn’t seem to find their way or do a thing about it. That’s kind of the way I felt. Then the police said I could go. They said John would be okay and that he didn’t want to press charges. He told them it was an accident.”

Shay realized the effort and energy it took for Willa to replay all that she had just said. She allowed her to sit silently for a few moments, letting her collect her thoughts.

Then, Shay gently asked her, "And now what? Have you thought about what comes next?"

"Yes. I still love him. I know that sounds crazy, but I do," Willa said, lowering her eyes that were glistening with fresh, unshed tears.

Then, she lifted her head and shook it. Then, with a calm resolve, she said, "But I have to think about my kids. They cannot live like this. I know now that our marriage…"

She paused, trying to come up with the best phrase to describe it. She finally concluded, "Our marriage isn't going to work. So I'm taking the kids back to Chicago, where we'll live with my parents."

"Have you spoken with John?"

"No. I haven't. I did go to the hospital. I inquired about his room number at the hospital. It's 328! I got as far as his room, but I couldn't go in. I think that when someone drives you to the kind of violence I committed this morning, that relationship just cannot be a positive one. It cannot be saved, is what I have realized." Willa said with a sigh.

She looked bravely at Shay as she added, "Dr. Jackson, I am not a violent person. I am not someone who hurts people and takes pleasure from it. I am harmless; at least, that's what people thought about me. I don't hurt anyone; I've never even hurt flies in all my life. And never, in all the years of his cheating and our arguments, have I ever thought about hurting John. Even when he hit me, I never thought about hurting him. Even then, the only thought that came to my mind was that I needed to get away from him so he would never hurt me again. So – trust me when I say this – I honestly don't know what came over me. But one thing is for certain; I know that I must get away. I need to be away from John. I've suffered enough, and I've hurt John too, but I will not put my kids through anything like that again," Willa said sternly. Her voice had become stronger the longer she spoke.

She drew another tortured breath as she said, "I still hear their screams in my head, over and over."

"Willa, when John hit you before, did you ever report it to the police?" Shay asked even though she already knew the answer.

"No. I never even thought about it. I knew he didn't mean it. He was just angry because I couldn't please him. I knew it was my fault."

"Willa, a man should never hit a woman. It certainly was not your fault. John has an illness, and the fact that he is never satisfied is not your fault. So, please never think that."

Willa shook her head, "I guess I sort of felt as if I was failing him. I've never had sex with anyone else but John. I guess I didn't really know whether what John expected was normal or not." Willa again started to cry.

"Willa, I assure you what John expected was not normal," Shay said.

"Thank you, Dr. Jackson. You have always helped me. I don't know what I will do in Chicago without you. I don't have many people I can talk to. John didn't like it when I got close to anyone else, not even women. The only person he tolerated was my neighbor, Joyce. I guess that was because she would take the kids to her house whenever he wanted them out of our house so we could have sex."

"You know you can always call me from Chicago. Let me know if there is anything I can do to help with your transition. I can suggest someone in Chicago that you can also talk to."

"Thank you, Dr. Jackson. I'll call you when I'm settled. Thanks for all your help."

"How will you get to Chicago from Detroit?"

"I've made arrangements for the kids and me to take the train. I'm not taking anything but clothes. John can have the furniture and the car. I never talked about it, but I am a registered nurse, and I've kept my license. I worked part time between having the kids and before John and I married. I worked a year or so at a hospital in Chicago. I'm sure I can find a job. And until then, my parents will help. They are lovely and very supportive. Unfortunately, they saw the broadcast and were frightened. They begged me to come home so that they could care for the kids and me. I don't think they ever really liked John or wanted me to marry him. But they are not the kind of parents who would interfere. I know they just prayed. They wanted me to be happy, and if John made me happy, they were, too. And as far as they knew, I was happy with John. I would never have divulged all my problems to them."

She paused once again and added, "I have two sisters, they are both quite a bit older than I am. I told them a little but I couldn't bring myself to share everything with them. I swore them to secrecy where my parents were concerned. I'm the baby of the family. My parents had me late in life. My dad is now in his eighties. My mom is only in her sixties now but still too old to deal with my issues. There is no way I would have worried them about my problems." Willa took a breath and sighed. Then she smiled, "Things will be better now. I know they will."

Shay hugged Willa. She was truly fond of this young woman and certainly wished the best for her. It was unfortunate that it took this incidence of violence to open her eyes. Now, Shay thought, if John had just visited the sex addiction clinic, there might have been a different outcome. Shay shook her head sadly as Willa closed the office door quietly behind her.

Chapter 6

Once Willa was gone, Shay took a few moments to record notes into the Raineses' file. She felt sympathy for the young woman. Willa's decision to move to Chicago was probably for the best. But, as a marriage and relationship counselor, she sometimes simply had to acknowledge that ending a relationship might work better than staying.

After Shay completed her notes, she looked at her watch. She knew Jeff had probably not come in yet. After all, his first appointment was not until two p.m. Shay, toying with the idea of going to see John Raines, decided to see what Jeff thought about her decision. She dialed his cell phone number, but he did not pick up. She left him a message with the details, adding, "I even know his room number is 328. Willa wasn't able to go in, so I thought I might go to visit him. What do you think?"

Shay had never been involved in what might still be considered a criminal case. When he didn't answer, she decided she could always go tomorrow.

Shay rose from her seat and walked to the door. She had wanted to talk with Gwen about slapping John Raines, but she changed her mind upon seeing her partner, Dr. Sam Roberts, standing at Gwen's desk.

"Good afternoon, Sam," Shay said. "Are you coming or going?"

"Going, my dear, you know I come in early, so I'll have the rest of the day for golf." Sam smiled pleasantly at Shay. "I saw my first client at six a.m. this morning."

Even though Sam walked with a slight limp and occasionally carried a cane, he was an avid golfer and quite good at the game. Shay should know. He had beaten both her and Jeff on multiple occasions.

"I suppose you heard about the woman who stabbed her husband this morning?" Shay inquired as she and Sam stepped away from Gwen's desk.

"Yes, I heard about it but didn't get the entire story, as I was with my client when it aired live on TV. However, I heard a recap on a later broadcast. It is quite shocking, to say the least. Am I to understand that he was cheating on his wife?"

"Yes, on both counts. It is shocking, and yes, he was cheating. You know they were both my clients. I recommended seeing a sex addiction therapist at our last session, but he decided against it." Shay shrugged her shoulders and informed him.

"Well, as far as I'm concerned," Sam whispered out of the range of Gwen's hearing, "a cheating spouse is a no-good MF. He and all cheaters deserve to die. I was married to Edith for forty years before she died. I never once cheated or was ever tempted to cheat. On the contrary, I was grateful for the love of a good woman and the time we had together. Yet, these sons of bitches," Sam clicked his teeth, obviously deciding stronger words were necessary, "have what I no longer have." He paused and took a deep breath before continuing.

"They have love and companionship, and yet they cheat. Yes, they deserve to die." He uttered the last sentence passionately and through clenched teeth.

Shay blinked, taken aback. She had never heard Sam use profanity or harsh language in all the years they'd worked together. Shay looked at him sadly. He must be very lonely since his wife died, she thought. She made a mental note to invite him to dinner and maybe have lunch together more often. Shay admonished herself for not realizing sooner how lonely Sam was after losing Edith and that he needed more from her and Jeff.

Shay looked at Sam more closely now, as her eyebrows furrowed together in concern. His face was as red as his red hair. His breathing seemed labored.

"Come into my office," Shay said, guiding Sam through her open office door and pushing him into a chair. She opened the small office-sized refrigerator and handed Sam a bottle of water. He drank deeply. Once his color returned to normal, along with his breathing, Shay began to speak, her voice gentle and concerned.

"Sam, I'm concerned about you. Have you had a checkup lately?"

"Now, don't go sounding like Edith or Tessa on me. I'm fine. I've had a checkup recently, and I'm as fit as an old geezer like myself can be. I apologize for my outburst, Shay. It's just…."

He paused, not able to go on at the moment. Shay waited, noticing his eyes fill with tears.

"It's just that I miss her so much. I toss and turn all night without her beside me, and finally, I get out of bed at three a.m. It's unbearable at times. I come here before sunrise every morning to escape the empty house. There's nothing else to do that time of the morning. I play golf, not because I enjoy it so much, but because I can't bear to go home to those empty rooms. Everywhere I turn in that house, I see Edith's sweet face. Sometimes, even golf doesn't help because she used to play with me. I miss that." He paused and let out a sigh. "And yet that bastard John Raines has a sweet wife he doesn't deserve. I actually met her that first day they came to see you. She seemed nervous. I talked with her for a few moments while the bastard was in the restroom. From what I remember, she seemed nice."

"Yes, she is very nice. Don't worry too much about her, though. She'll be okay. She's taking the kids and moving to Chicago with her parents." Shay responded.

"That's good to hear. She doesn't need him. She deserves so much more— someone loyal who won't cheat on her," Sam scoffed.

"Sam, I understand your feelings, but please remember that the man has an illness. As a professional psychologist and marriage counselor, I know you understand that better than anyone. I was thinking that I might visit him sometime. I am, after all, his counselor, and Willa mentioned that he was in room 328. Even though Willa may be gone, he still needs treatment for his problem."

Sam shook his head. "I do understand, but the bastard could have sought help before this happened and decided not to do so. I have no sympathy for him. I remain lonely while he cavorts with every woman he comes across."

Shay knew that Sam's feelings stemmed from his loneliness, but the more he spoke, the more her concern for him increased.

"I've got an idea, Sam. Jeff and I are having dinner tonight at Como's in Ferndale. We always enjoy that restaurant, and I know you do as well. You're coming with us, and I won't take no for an answer. You've still got time to get in a game of golf and meet us there at eight p.m."

"I—" Shay cut him off.

"I simply will not take no for an answer," she said. "So don't argue." With that, Shay ushered Sam and his protests out of her office and closed the door behind him.

When Sam's wife became ill and died, Sam used his work to get through what he'd described many times as 'The Lonely Days and Nights.' Shay and Jeff both knew that Sam often spent the night sleeping on the sofa in his office when he couldn't face going home to an empty house.

Shay wondered if she should call Sam's daughter, Tessa. She knew how much Tessa worried about her dad. After the funeral, Tessa and Sam's two sons had tried to get Sam to give up the house and move in with them. Sam's son Jason practiced law in Memphis, and his eldest son, Terrence, and his wife and three children lived in Florida. Sam had turned each offer down. It appeared that even though he found it difficult to go into the empty house, he still couldn't bear to leave it forever.

Shay knew Sam would not have appreciated the interference, so she maintained a distance. But she knew that although he was spiraling into a deep depression, Sam constantly assured his family that he was fine. Thinking about this, Shay decided to postpone making any contact with his family. But she'd definitely see that she and Jeff spent more time with him. That was the least that they could do.

Chapter 7

The day was dark and dreary. Deep gray clouds hung suspended in the sky, threatening to send a barrage of water down. Yet, they did not. It was as if the threat was the whole point. Once the clouds burst, the threat would disappear. There would be nothing more to fear – nothing ominous to anticipate.

The elderly man gazed upward. The status of the clouds had not changed since his last glance toward the heavens some three minutes ago. They remained ominous.

He carried an umbrella, just in case they decided to burst after all. His gray cap was pulled down over the left side of his face. A red birthmark covered the right side. His gray coat appeared freshly pressed, but his gray shoes showed wear. Even though they were scuffed, with slightly turned-up toes, they seemed extremely comfortable. They were good walking shoes for the man who was now using the umbrella as a cane.

Shuffling slightly, he bent over only when others appeared to be watching. He was grateful that with the weather as it was, there were not many people moving about on the street—no one to encounter in the predominantly Polish American neighborhood of the Detroit suburb.

He strolled down Jos. Campeau, stopping every so often to glance behind him. The sidewalk of the Hamtramck, Michigan, street was uneven and difficult to navigate. He was careful not to fall. His vehicle had been left parked a block west of his current location. He now turned down a side street, keeping an eye out for the loft, which was his final destination.

Walking a few more steps, he stopped in front of a gray brick building. The dwelling stood out among the other multiple red brick veneers. The man climbed the five cement steps. Ringing the bell to the left of the door, he waited impatiently. Footsteps approached, and the door opened.

A short heavyset woman who appeared to be in her late sixties stood before him. Her curly hair, which had clearly once been red, was now mostly gray and bounced as she shook the man's hand with a smile.

"Come right in, Doctor," she said kindly, stepping aside to allow him to enter. Your space has been cleaned to perfection, I assure you" She smiled again.

The elderly gentleman gave a brief close-mouthed smile back but did not speak.

"Follow me," the woman said, walking briskly. Five feet down the wide hallway, she stopped at the door on the right. Turning slightly to look behind her, she waited as the doctor slowly arrived at the door. She fumbled in the pocket of her red-white-and blue-flowered smock for the key.

"Ahh, here it is." She unlocked the door and walked inside.

The man followed, remaining silent, looking around. The loft space was huge. The first floor was completely open, containing space for a large room with a fireplace. He glanced toward the kitchen and pantry, which were located at the end of the room. A laundry room and guest powder room flanked either side of the kitchen. Only one bedroom captured the entire second floor, and looked down onto the lower level.

She walked slowly up the steps, the doctor following. As he moved up the spiral wrought iron staircase, he could see that the bedroom was large and spacious. He could see the en suite bathroom, which, he noted, was also spacious and very clean. The large jetted tube gleamed. The double vanity sink provided counter space as well as six drawers underneath. The granite covering the counter was bright, and the pattern was not excessively busy. The doctor preferred clean lines and absolutely detested anything congested. The separate walk-in shower was encased in a sparkling glass enclosure. The doctor would discover later that the dark gray laminate floors in the bathroom were heated, as were the towel racks.

"As you can see, the steel window shutters have been installed as you specified. The fifty-inch television was delivered yesterday." Looking down into the great room, she pointed at the furnishings.

"The black recliner, lamps, table, and loveseat were delivered three days ago," she added.

She thought the all-black furniture made the room insanely dark, but she kept her opinion to herself. She also refrained from asking why the only seating included a loveseat and recliner but no sofa. There was no other furniture, not even a dining table, and chairs. Most peculiar was that there was no bed.

Then again, it wasn't her business. After all, he paid cash for everything, adding a handsome tip for her services. A thousand dollars just to let in a few deliverymen was certainly a bargain for her.

"Four additional boxes were delivered just fifteen minutes prior to your arrival. I had them stored in the pantry. I hope that's okay?" She said questioningly.

The man nodded but, this time, smiled widely. The woman seemed taken aback. She had rented the space two months ago. He had spoken very little in the rental office and had definitely not smiled. He had, she remembered, remained somber. Now, his smile appeared brilliant. He had beautiful teeth except for a small chip in his front tooth. So small that it would hardly be noticeable to anyone else. But she, Mrs. Edna Crombie, took pleasure in her ability to observe even the smallest nuances. Before retiring to care for her terminally ill husband, she had been a dental hygienist. Now, at sixty-eight years of age and newly widowed, she added to her income by renting out this property.

She was glad that he seemed pleased. His request for steel shutters, massive meat freezers, and what appeared to her to be an overabundance of rugs, yet a minimal number of other furnishings, seemed strange indeed. He had paid the entire year's lease in one cash payment, and he looked clean.

He had told her that he would be seeing clients here and that confidentiality was of the utmost importance. She had assured him when he inquired that the nearby neighbors on the street were all elderly and unable to get out much. They would definitely not be knocking on his door at all hours to borrow a cup of sugar. In fact, most were homebound and assisted by caregivers. He seemed satisfied with that. The spacing between the buildings on the street was also sufficient, the doctor had noted.

Now placing the keys in his hand, she turned to him. "Oh, one more thing Doctor, should you need anything else, my nephew, George Hayden, takes care of this building, along with three other buildings that I own on this street. He uses the garage attached to your loft to keep his vehicle and tools. We discussed that when you rented this space. You received a large discount because you cannot access the garage." She looked up at the doctor for confirmation.

"I remember." The doctor nodded.

“Should you have a leak or require any other repairs, George’s name and number are on a magnet on the side of the refrigerator. I assure you he is an excellent handyman, electrician, and carpenter by profession.”

He took the keys she offered as they walked toward the exit. He closed the door behind her.

“Oh, I know George better than you know. I have his number committed to memory. If only Mrs. Crombie knew her nephew’s real profession,” He laughed out loud.

Once he heard her footsteps echo down the hall and away from his door, he moved quickly toward the pantry and the delivered boxes. Pulling out a box cutter, he quickly sliced open the large containers. Pulling out the contents of one, he became mesmerized by the stainless steel tools. They simply gleamed. The other boxes contained, among other things, a commercial electric saw, three scalpels, and ten 25x25-inch tarps. He’d decided more could be purchased as needed. He carefully unloaded the items from each box. When satisfied that everything was as he ordered, he returned each to its proper box and sealed the boxes with tape. Returning them to the pantry, he rubbed his hands together, satisfied that everything was in order.

Yes, he and his office were ready for business. He already had three couples scheduled. They would be in next week.

The private investigator had found the perfect couples. The targets—two men and one woman. It was unfortunate, but yes, women cheated as well. This was a perfect arrangement.

The innocent parties hired the private investigator to follow their spouses. Once it was confirmed they were cheating, they would be referred to him for counseling. He would help them – well, he would certainly help the innocent partner out. They'd find his services very useful and satisfactory.

Once the investigator produced the pictures, the plan was set into motion. There were views of the targets making love from every conceivable angle. There could be no mistaking who or what the pictures represented.

Cheating, whether in a marriage or a relationship, would not be tolerated. It destroyed families and deeply hurt and humiliated those cheated upon.

"I must fix this. Cheaters cannot and will not get away with this. At least, not alive," he thought, smiling to himself.

Chapter 8

"Good afternoon, Dr. R.," the Bonner Memorial hospital nurse just returning from lunch said cheerily to the well-known figure as they met at the revolving doors.

Della smiled to herself as she struggled to recall why he was only known as Dr. R. She smiled widely, recalling her first encounter with the elderly man.

"Good morning, young lady," she now remembered the kindly older gentleman saying. "May I ask your name?" he'd asked.

"I'm Della Perry," she had said, awaiting his name.

"I'm just known as Dr. R."

He had seen the look of confusion on her face and replied, "No one can ever get my name right. So no one ever bothers pronouncing my full last name. Instead, they just prefer calling me Dr. R."

"Dr. R. is fine with me," she'd said all those years ago upon their first meeting. She remembered thinking that particular morning was not the day she wanted to grapple with pronouncing anyone's name. She'd had a hell of a headache. She had been rubbing her forehead vigorously as she talked with this stranger, attempting to get rid of the pain.

Dr. R. had given her a piercing look. "I can help you with that.

Where is the pain concentrated?" he'd asked.

"It's on both my right and left temples," she'd responded. She had continued to massage both temples with her fingertips.

"On a scale of one to ten, how would you rate the pain?"

She had quickly responded, "Right now, it is at least a nine, and I'm trying to be positive about it."

"What shape is the pain? Is it round, square, or triangular?"

Della had given the kind doctor a strange look but answered his question after pondering for a few moments. "It is round."

How big is this circle?" he'd asked.

"Not very big. Probably only the size of a dime at each temple," she remembered answering.

"Close your eyes and focus on the pain and keep focusing," he'd instructed her.

After a couple of minutes, Dr. R asked, "Now, how would you rate the pain?"

"It's gone," she had squealed, hugging the stranger.

Della still remembered being amazed. "You are a genius!" she'd told him.

The two had been friends ever since. Afterward, Della always went out of her way to speak with him when she passed him in the hospital halls. They would chat briefly about the weather or some hospital event. He always asked how she was feeling. Della was surprised that he seemed in a real hurry this afternoon. He was in such a hurry that he had not even responded to her greeting.

Dr. R., wearing his usual gray cap that always covered part of his face, walked as quickly through the doors of Bonner Memorial Hospital as one could walk in his condition. He was deep in thought and had neither noticed nor heard Della.

His usual gray suit had been freshly pressed. He was secretly known at the hospital as the gray man. He always carried a gray bag, and wore the same gray suit, and the gray cap pulled down over the left side of his face. On the right side of his face was what appeared to be a dark red birthmark. While his mustache was neatly shaped and cared for, his shoes were a darker gray than his suit, unkempt, and never polished. He walked with a limp. His frame looked sturdy, but he was bent over and used a cane.

It was common knowledge to all the nurses that Dr. R. had no medical privileges at Bonner Memorial. It didn't matter. All the nurses loved the kindly old gentleman. He often treated the nursing staff and anyone passing by to donuts, Godiva chocolates, and other sinful but delicious surprises.

Once, he even had lunch delivered from a restaurant for everyone. But the restaurant was not just any restaurant. It was Joe Muer's, located in the Renaissance Center in downtown Detroit. The food was delicious, but the prices weren't cheap. Joe Muer's was one of Detroit's upscale and expensive restaurants. The hospital staff adored the food and the man who was generous enough to treat them to it.

He was known for visiting various patients who always seemed happy to see him. Over the last few years, Dr. R. had become a permanent fixture at the hospital, visiting at least three or four times per week.

Today it was anyone's guess who he was there to see. Often, he stopped at the registration desk to find the room number of a particular patient. Today, he did not. He moved purposely down the hall and entered the elevator. Dr. R. got off on the third floor and entered room 328.

The man in the bed seemed surprised to see him.

"They call me Dr. R. I just wanted to look in on you. Your wounds are not life-threatening; I'm sure you will be fine. Is there anything I can get you?"

"No, I'm fine," the man said.

"That's good; nice to hear that. You'll be out of here soon, young man," Dr. R. told him with a smile. "I'll take my leave now, but I'll have a nurse sent up for your medications."

"Thank you," John said sleepily.

***

John awoke with a start to the sound of someone walking into his room with a cane. He looked up to see a man who seemed somewhat familiar, but he couldn't quite recall where he had seen him. Normally, John was excellent with faces and would recognize people easily. However, today, his brain was still fuzzy from the medication, so he couldn't quite recall where he'd seen the man before.

"Oh, it's good that you're awake. How are you doing?" The stranger asked John.

"I'm good; who are you?" John asked, wondering why this stranger was in his room. He wasn't dressed in the usual hospital garb. He wasn't a staff member – he appeared to have come from outside the building.

"I'm glad to hear you are feeling better, Mr. Raines. We've met before, but I don't think you recognize me, not with all the drugs and painkillers you are on," the man said.

John nodded and then winced with pain.

"Don't do that. Here, I got you some lemonade. You must taste it; it will make you feel better," the man said, taking the container out of the gray bag he carried.

John shot him a questioning look.

"Don't worry. I got the go-ahead from your doctor. You can try it. I'm sure your throat is parched, too. My wife freshly squeezed it. She likes to send lemonade to patients. It's refreshing and makes her feel like she is doing something useful. You see, she has Alzheimer's, and the only thing she can remember these days is how to make this lemonade. Won't you try it?" he said thrusting the container full of lemonade at John.

John took the container and drank. It really was good lemonade, and he told him as much.

The man watched him drink it with a satisfied look on his face, and once John was done, he carefully put the container back in his bag and left without so much as a word. Then, he returned to his Eastside office, as he'd decided to call the Hamtramck location. Now sitting quietly in his black leather recliner, he drank a cup of tea and sat awaiting the five o'clock newscast.

"There is a new development in the Willa and John Raines story we brought you earlier," the newscaster said. "We had been told this morning that John Raines, who was reportedly stabbed by his wife, Willa, had no life-threatening injuries; however, we have just received word that he has expired. His wife, Willa Raines, who was arrested and released, is once again in custody. Only this time, it is for murder."

He smiled as he rose from his chair, clicking the off button on the TV remote. He walked quickly across the room and exited the loft and the building, closing the door softly behind him.

The only problem to be solved now would be that of the wife. He certainly hadn't thought that the police would arrest her again.

Chapter 9

Shay smiled as she entered the restaurant that evening. Jeff held her hand as they followed the hostess, who showed them to their table. Shay was relieved to find Sam already seated. After leaving the office earlier, she feared he might not show up.

He stood as the couple approached the table. He shook Jeff's hand and hugged Shay. He looked much more at peace than he had this morning. He must have had a good golf game. He looked victorious, Shay thought.

He had ordered a martini and appeared relaxed. Shay did, however, notice that Sam had brought his cane, which was now standing near the table. It was the blue hurricane cane.

Shay had seen the cane advertised on TV and thought it would make life easier for Sam, so she had purchased it for him. He initially balked at using it. Shay understood that now that he was finally using it meant the pain had forced him to use it.

"Hello, partners." He smiled. "Thanks for allowing an old man to be the fifth wheel."

"You are never a fifth wheel with us," Shay said as she sat down and placed a hand over Sam's.

"Shay's right, Sam. You know better than that, buddy. We are always happy to have you join us," Jeff added.

"I have to admit," Sam said, looking around the spacious and festively decorated restaurant, "It's been far too long since I've had a night out on the town. Dinner is usually a boring TV dinner eaten in front of the TV. This is much better," he said, smiling and still looking around.

"Sam, we are going to see to it that you join us more often," Shay said as she noticed the waiter approach the table. "I guess we'd better look at the menu."

They gave the waiter their drink order. Shay had her usual chocolate martini. Sam continued to nurse his first martini, and Jeff passed on the alcohol, simply ordering water. Shay glanced at Jeff. He'd been quiet on the way to the restaurant. She thought she'd caught a troubled look on his face, but when she looked more closely now, he was smiling and joking with the waiter.

Sam attempted to apologize for his earlier outburst that morning over John Raines's behavior. Shay cut him off, letting him know she understood. She kept the rest of the conversation light, refusing to allow any talk of work to seep into their evening. Shay was satisfied when, as the evening continued, it was evident that Sam was enjoying himself.

Jeff once again held Shay's hand as they left the restaurant. "You've been a little quiet and maybe even a little distracted all evening," she said, looking up at him.

Pushing the door open as they exited, he placed his hand on the small of her back. He explained, "I guess I have had kind of a rough day."

"I'm sorry. You should have said something, and we could have done this another time," Shay said sincerely.

"Nonsense. Your day started far worse than mine could ever be. You needed this, and I'm glad we came. Sam needed it as well." Jeff smiled and hugged Shay.

Once seated in the car, Shay turned to Jeff. "Do you want to talk about your day?"

"Not really. It was just the difficult Jameson couple. They almost came to blows in my office."

"That's nothing new," Shay laughed. "They've been doing that each time they come."

"I know. Actually, believe it or not, they've gotten closer since they've been in counseling. I think they get off on screaming at each other. My sense is they couldn't wait to get home to make love. They probably stopped at a nearby motel, just as they've done before."

"So, if their behavior was the norm and expected today, what else is going on?" she inquired, her tone soft and kind.

Jeff hesitated before finally telling Shay what was bothering him, "I got a call from my sister. She wants to see me tomorrow."

"That's great. She is your sister, and I've never heard you say that the two of you have connected before. Would you like me to come with you? I can easily clear my schedule. After all, I'd really like to meet her and get to know your family."

"No, not necessary. It'll be fine," he said, leaning over to kiss her.

Leaning further over to Shay's side of the vehicle, he opened the glove compartment. Shay watched as he pulled a wrapped box out.

"For you," he said.

"For me? Why?" Shay asked with surprise.

"No reason other than I love you so very much," was his answer.

Shay's delight showed, but at the same time, she admonished him. "Jeff, I love you too, but how many times do I have to tell you that you don't need to keep buying me gifts? I know you love me, and I've got everything I need as long as I have you."

He grabbed her hand and kissed her palm. "I know, I know," he said. "But when I see something I want you to have, I'm almost helpless when it comes to ignoring the urge to get it for you. I know I don't have to, but you deserve it for making me so very happy. So please indulge me," he said softly. "Please let me do these things for you."

Shay knew he was sincere and desperately needed to make her happy. Knowing this, she gave in and excitedly opened the package. He looked like a schoolboy as he watched her unwrap the gift. It was important to him to know that she was pleased. And she was indeed pleased.

Taking the pearl necklace and earrings from the box, she recognized both: the effort Jeff took to please her and the box from the most expensive jeweler in Detroit. She placed them in her bag, deciding that she'd try them on when they exited the dark car.

Chapter 10

The doctor again parked his vehicle a distance away from his final destination. He carefully retraced his steps. Walking unsteadily on the uneven sidewalks using a cane was difficult. Arriving at the house, he fished his key out of his coat pocket and entered the building. He sat down heavily in the black recliner. Pushing his body into the back of the chair, he reclined back. He pulled out the throwaway phone he always used when dialing George's number. The phone could not be traced.

"I'm here," he said.

"I'll be there in five. I'll enter through the garage."

"As always," The doctor said, ending the call. He sat, waiting for his guest. He had something else on his mind today. Something he needed to take care of urgently. He'd first meet with George, he decided. Then he'd go to the hospital and make his rounds.

Soon he heard the noise of the garage door opening. George Hayden stepped into the loft.

"Are you sure no one else has access to the garage?" the doctor asked.

"I'm positive. Aunt Edna doesn't even have access. I changed the code and remote myself. You have nothing to be concerned about,"

George smiled as he walked around the loft.

“This open space is perfect for what we need to do. I’m not sure we’ll need the freezers for very long. I think we should be able to dispose of everything immediately. Everything is falling into place.”

“I was thinking the same thing.” The doctor smiled. “I don’t want to have any more contact with the investigator. We’ve spoken by phone, and that’s enough. You need to be the one who makes any further contact with him.”

“I have ways of getting in touch with him. He doesn’t have my real name, and he knows nothing about either of us,” George assured the doctor.

“What about the girl? Is she ready?”

“Yes, she is in a good place. You have nothing to worry about there either,” George assured the doctor. “I’ve also got the acetylene torch ready as well. It makes everything go poof and disappear easily,” he said, spreading his fingers to show how easily the disappearance could happen.

“Does the investigator have other cases lined up?” the doctor asked.

“Yes, he has three in Ohio and two in Wisconsin. Are you still available to travel?”

“Yes, traveling will be no problem,” said the doctor.

“I understand you’ve purchased a huge white truck, large enough for our needs, as well as the LED removable signage for the side of the truck, right?" the doctor asked.

"Yes, that's been taken care of as well. It was previously used as a FedEx truck, making the vehicle large enough to provide more room than we'll ever need. This isn't my first rodeo, you know," George said, amused that the Doc was so jittery.

"Just checking. I can't have anything go wrong. These things must be done properly, and they must be undetected."

"You worry too much, Doc." George patted the doctor on the back as he walked toward the garage exit.

"Now that we've taken care of that, would you like to continue with your counseling?" he asked George. It was the least he could do, the doctor thought. After all, George had helped him put his plans into action. But he knew he was still severely troubled over the breakup with his cheating wife. The doctor was unable to understand why George refused to have her taken care of. As long as she remained alive, George would need the doctor's counseling to continue functioning in the capacity the doctor required. He felt that only her death would release George. Nevertheless, he'd help him through this.

Chapter 11

George lit a cigarette as the flashbacks of the most painful time he'd ever experienced returned. As the doctor waited inside the loft for a response, George smiled and walked around the large white truck in the garage. He thought how easily his plans had fallen into place. Meeting the doctor was a miracle.

He'd simply looked in the yellow pages for someone who might help him get over his wife cheating on him. He still hoped for a reunion with Gracie, but she had clarified that she would stay with the other man.

"How dare she?" He had thought. And he still felt the same way.

Even now, he could not believe her arrogance. After all, she was the guilty party. But, despite everything, he loved her. He would continue to try to win her back. He remained confident that he could.

Looking around the garage, George decided to accept the doctor's offer. He reentered the loft and sat facing the Doc. The doctor waited patiently for George to speak.

"You know I pleaded with her. I lost all my dignity," he said brokenly. "My tears and offers of money, vacations, and anything else I thought she'd accept fell on deaf ears. She put me out of the house I'd built for her. She even resorted to trickery to get me out. She promised to think about our reunion."

"*I just need time to think* is what she had said." George now spoke through clenched teeth. "She said to me, '*please, just leave for an hour. Give me some time to think, and when you return, we can talk.*' She said that to me!"

Looking up at the doctor through tears, he said, "I believed her. Like the fool that I was, I believed her! I left and returned in an hour with flowers, only to find that my key no longer worked in the door lock. She had the locks changed." He sobbed.

The doctor handed George a tissue. "We can continue this at another time if you'd like," he said kindly.

"No, I've held this in too long. I need to get it out. I noticed a black Ford Explorer in the drive. I rang the bell and beat on the door furiously. I could hear a man's voice inside, demanding that I leave.

"I banged, cried, and pleaded. I refused to believe that this could be the end. Gracie and I had been married for twenty years. How could she allow some other man to force her to throw all those years away? He's the one who needs to die. He forced her. I'm sure of that."

"Anyway, I finally left the front door and ran around to the back. Again, my key didn't work. I felt lightheaded. I was sweating profusely. I could feel my heart pounding. I remember picking up a brick to throw through the window. As I lifted my arm, the pain in my chest was so intense I dropped the brick and fell to the ground. Writhing in pain, I wasn't afraid. I wanted to die. I guess I lost consciousness. I awoke in a hospital."

"You know what my first thought was? I thought that Gracie would surely be there for me. But she was not there. She never even came to visit, not once."

"The doctors had performed a triple bypass. I would live after all." He smirked. "Once released from the hospital, I tried returning to the house once more. I met my neighbor, Gregory Young, who told me he'd found me on the ground when I'd collapsed that day. I vaguely remember Gregory talking softly to me until the ambulance arrived."

"Anyways, he told me he was glad I was better. He'd tried visiting me in the hospital, but they said only family members were allowed in ICU. He said he'd then tried getting information about my condition from Gracie. But, the newspaper boy said she canceled the paper because she would be in Florida for the next few months. He wanted to know what the hell was going on with Gracie and me."

More sobs came following this revelation.

"Take your time. It will do you good to get it out," The doctor coaxed.

"Sh-she doesn't want to be with me any longer," George stuttered, breaking into sobs again. "This is all his doing. I know she would never have treated me this way without this man's influence.

"I remember Gregory leading me into his house. I knew he wanted to help, but I just couldn't speak any longer. I remember standing and blindly stumbling out of the house. I got into my car. I think I just drove around for hours. Finally, I ended up at Aunt Edna's house. It was the only place I had to go. She welcomed me with open arms. I lived with her for, I think, six months. For that entire period, I couldn't care for myself. Gracie divorced me and went off with her lover, leaving me severely depressed. I couldn't talk or walk. I stayed in bed. Aunt Edna cared for me and got me professional help who came to the house, but no one could get through to me. I couldn't talk to them. I wanted to speak. I knew Aunt Edna was worried sick about me, and I didn't want to do that to her, but I just couldn't speak. I'd open my mouth, but no words would come out."

He paused, and then he added, "But one day, I have no idea why. I just sat up and decided I needed to get help. I asked Aunt Edna for the yellow pages. I remember she tried to get me to just google what I wanted. But for some reason, I felt I needed to find what I was looking for in the yellow pages. That's where I found your number. Aunt Edna stood briefly beside me as I leafed through the phone book. Finally, she walked to the door and smiled. She told me that her prayers had been answered."

"The two of us are the only ones left of our immediate family. My mom was Aunt Edna's sister. I'm sure she felt really helpless and alone when she could not reach me mentally. There is no other family. I now know that Aunt Edna tried to talk with Gracie about our marriage and got nowhere. She had no luck convincing Gracie to even speak with me, let alone visit. She told me that she had tried twice. She gave up the third time when upon arriving at the house, she noticed the black Explorer in the drive and a man unfamiliar to her at the door. He advised her that Gracie was unavailable and asked that she not return.

"And since I could not answer any questions, she knows little about the situation. I regret that, but I can't tell her everything."

The doctor looked at his watch. "George, we'll have to end our session here. I see improvement and promise we will figure this out together."

Chapter 12

Jeff walked very slowly into the Union Street restaurant located on Woodward in Detroit. His shoulders felt tight. He moved his head from side to side, hoping to relax. It did not help. He looked around. The place was always busy and loud. He had no idea why she had selected it. It was the last place you needed to go if you were trying to have a quiet conversation. It was certainly the last place he would have selected if he didn't want to be seen with someone. He then chastised himself.

What a terrible thing to say. It wasn't that he didn't want to be seen with her; after all, she was his sister. But she was a part of his past that he would just as soon not think about or even have people know about. He did feel guilty, but even his wife was not totally privy to that part of his life. Yes, she knew he had a sister, but she was unaware that he ever spoke with her. It was also because he didn't talk to her very often. They'd probably connected in person only twice in the last twenty years.

She was a part of his life that he chose to forget. Of course, she wasn't the only one. There was something else too. It was a part of his life he shared with no one. Certainly, others knew, but no one would ever dare bring up the subject to him now after so many years. He looked up and saw her walk in. He stood.

The hug he gave her was stiff and cold. He didn't think she minded because that's how they were now. So much had happened, and neither wanted to remember.

"Hello, Dorothy," he tried to say warmly after the cold hug.

"Hello," she said. Her smile was strained at best. Jeff couldn't help but notice.

He wondered why she had called. They had long since stopped trying to see each other. They both sat. He looked across the table at her. She was just two years younger than he. At forty, she looked much older. Her hair was almost all gray. She was overweight, and her coat, while expensive, was ill-fitting. There was no sparkle in her eyes. They simply looked dead. She looked as if life had depleted all of her energy.

He still remembered her as a kid. He would only allow himself to remember her up until age eleven. At age twelve, terrible things that he did not want to remember had happened. It was a chapter of his life that he wished to close and never open again. So he simply promised himself he would not remember. He'd wipe them out. Only when he was forced to see her this way did the nightmarish memories return.

She probably needed money, which he had no problem shelling out. But why couldn't he just send it in the mail? All she needed to do was call, as she had in the past, and the money would be on its way immediately. She earned a decent living as a photographer, but some medical emergency, which he had not taken time to ask about, had made things tight. He'd always helped, as he would this time.

"I guess you're wondering why I wanted to see you," she said softly.

"Yes," was all he responded.

"Mona is twenty-eight years old now," she said, looking into his eyes.

Immediately lowering his eyes, he responded, "Okay." He waited for her to go on. Mona was her daughter and a grown woman now. Maybe she needed money for her.

"She's sick – it's an inoperable brain tumor. I thought you'd want to know."

"I'm sorry," he said, still not raising his eyes to hers.

"How can I help? Do you need money?"

She stopped him, "No, it's not that."

"Then what?" He knew he sounded cold, but he couldn't help it.

"I thought maybe because she's sick, you'd want to see her. Maybe even get to know her."

The breath went out of him. "So, you came here to ask me to

see the kid he spawned?"

"It wasn't her fault, and it certainly wasn't mine. You and I were both victims. Why can't you let it go?"

"I can only let it go if I don't have to think about or see the results of an evil crazy person." He softened. "It isn't that I don't love you. You're my sister. But every time I see you, I remember what happened so many years ago, and the pain is unbearable."

He stopped and wiped his hand across his moist eyes. "I'm sorry. That's just the way it is. Yet, when I don't see you, I can forget. I've been quite thorough in my quest to wipe out everything that happened all that time ago."

Dorothy couldn't help but notice the coldness that seemed to permeate his entire body. Nevertheless, she rushed on. "She doesn't have much time. She knows about you and has always wanted to know why she's never met her uncle."

"Dorothy, please don't ask this of me. Anything but this," he pleaded. "I don't want to be like this, but it's hard."

"It's probably harder on me," she said, a little angry. "In fact, I'm sure it's harder. He may have done something terrible to you, but I bore his child. She wouldn't be here if I had been older and understood what was going on. Had I been older, and hadn't felt so damned guilty about what he'd done to me, I would have spoken up.

No one even knew I was pregnant until it was too late to have an abortion. I was twelve years old. And then, because Aunt Ruth was such a religious fanatic, she wouldn't have allowed an abortion anyway, just as she wouldn't hear of my giving the baby up for adoption.

"I don't blame Aunt Ruth. She did the best she could and practically raised Mona. But when Aunt Ruth died, it was on me to do it. By then, I was twenty years old and had resigned myself to the hand I had been dealt. It wasn't all bad." She smiled.

"I love my daughter. And I've learned to forgive him. I had to for Mona's sake and my own. Holding on to that kind of anger and hatred can only cause pain. As a psychologist, you know that I'm sure."

She repeated all of this as if she were telling it for the first time—telling him for the first time. He already knew. He was there. He had tried to avoid this repeat of things in the past all these years. This was the reason he hadn't wanted to see her.

Now she repeated, "You do know that holding on to that kind of anger and hatred—"

He held up his hand to cut her off.

"Of course, I know," he said, almost smiling. "But I'm a damned good psychologist and believe it or not, I've counseled myself. My training taught me how to dismiss all those things that happened so long ago. I'm quite good at it until I see you or anyone related to the past. Then I'm reminded of everything that son of a bitch did."

His anger caused him to have to sit quietly without speaking. He meditated for the briefest moment. When he raised his head, he was calm.

Dorothy watched him carefully, wondering how long it would be before he broke down – before all that anger that he held so close to him finally errupted. She said nothing.

"How's Shay?" she said, changing the subject. Unfortunately, she'd never met her sister-in-law, but that was how her brother wanted it. She felt sad.

"Shay more than makes up for any darkness. She's wonderful." Just the thought of his wife lightened the dark moment.

He managed to touch his sister's arm. "I will think about what you've asked. In the meantime, I can refer you to and, of course, pay for the best doctors in Lansing. That is still where you're living, right?"

"Yes. We're still in Michigan's capital. There's no better place for a photographer to make a good living. Everything juicy that needs to be captured by a camera lens happens in the city where politicians work, love, and commit their crimes." She smiled, standing.

He stood as well, this time giving her a much warmer hug. Dorothy took a long look at her brother.

"Too bad he doesn't realize that a doctor cannot treat himself," She thought sadly as she hugged him.

Chapter 13

George climbed the stairs of the flat he had rented from his aunt once he could leave the safety of her home. Working with the doctor had been good for him. The work offered him the opportunity to take his anger out on others. All of them deserved to die anyway.

Assisting the doctor in creating ways to accomplish the deaths of those who had cheated was rewarding. It took his mind off his own troubles.

So far, they had killed people who deserved to die for various reasons. But the doctor always made the final decision about who would die. But this time, he was the one calling the shots. He got to choose who needed to die. He wanted his wife back. The person who took her from him had to— His thoughts were interrupted by a knock at the door.

He knew right away who his visitor was. He had no friends who would just pop in on him. Most of the people he knew were only acquaintances. They were either people for whom he made repairs or those who had helped him carry out the doc's orders. He opened the door quickly.

"Hello, Aunt Edna. Is there something you need me to do?" he said, stepping back so she could enter.

Looking around the room, she noticed clothes strewn everywhere; on the floor, chairs, and sofa. It appeared to Edna that everything her nephew had worn for the last month now adorned the furniture. To make matters worse, take-out cartons covered the tables and counter. At least the take-out meant he was eating regularly, which was some comfort to her.

But she didn't comment on this. Instead, she said, "I just dropped by to make sure you were okay. I do worry about you."

"I'm fine, Aunt Edna. I apologize that the place is such a mess." He knew she had noticed, even though she didn't say anything. "I've been working a lot lately and just haven't had time to clean."

She held up her hand to stop him. She smiled and said, "It's okay. I'm just glad you're okay. And, at least, I can tell you've been eating."

She was also relieved that he was changing clothes. She recalled that when he was with her, he was in such bad shape that he needed her to insist that he bathe, change clothes, and even eat.

"You've also been doing great work. Mrs. Stansky and her daughter raved about the new counter you put in."

"I appreciate you for trusting me to work for you. I try to do a good job," he said.

She stepped closer to him, examining his face. She still remembered his state when she first took him in. It was as though someone had ripped his heart out of his body – even his eyes looked dead. He looked pretty much like himself now, except for the obvious sadness.

"You know that you can talk to me any time. I'm here for you," she said, hugging him as she turned to leave.

"I know I can talk to you. You've been good to me," He kissed her on the cheek.

Once the door was shut, he proceeded with his earlier thoughts. He knew how and what had to be done.

Chapter 14

Sebastian Crawford, one of Detroit's finest police commanders, rubbed his forehead gently. The headache that had been attempting to take full effect since early this morning finally erupted. Stretching his long legs out under the desk, he leaned back in his chair, closing his eyes for only a moment.

Slowly opening his eyes, he stood and walked to the vending machine. He put in the required coins and pulled out a cold Dasani water bottle. Picking up a Tylenol bottle from the corner of his desk, he popped two pills into his mouth and washed them down with water.

He again closed his eyes; however, this time, he saw the face of the young woman the officers had brought in the morning after she had allegedly stabbed her husband. He was present the next day when they arrested her again, this time for murder. As she passed by his office, she had turned her head at just that moment. Sebastian had seen something in her eyes that told him she should not be here.

He disagreed with his subordinates, who believed it was premeditated. They felt she had planned for some time to retaliate for all the times her husband had cheated on her, which had been reported as much more than a single indiscretion on his part. Sebastian's instincts told him something different, and his instincts were usually not wrong. However, he was not prepared to interfere with his team's investigation. He believed they would investigate this case based on the facts, as they had been trained.

"You have a phone call, Commander," Crawford's assistant, Detective Rubye Weaver, yelled from across the room.

He so wished she would simply buzz him on the phone. He gave her the stop yelling across the room glare as he picked up the phone.

"It's your cousin Reggie," she yelled louder in her I-really-don't-care-what-you-wish-I-should-do voice. She knew how to push his buttons, but when it came to performing the rest of her job, nobody could do it better. They'd been together for twenty years. As he rose up the ladder, he took Rubye with him for one reason: she was the best. And she knew he couldn't do his job without her. That's why only she could get away with doing some things that irked him – only she would dare.

"Hello, Reggie. To what do I owe this call?" Sebastian said, knowing Reggie wanted something.

The last time he needed a parking ticket fixed—the time before that, he needed tickets to some event that the police department usually got discounted. And the time before that, he and his wife, Joyce, desperately needed a babysitter for their two kids after their regular sitter had cancelled. According to Reggie, who was an executive for Ford Motor Company, this was an event they could not miss.

Sebastian liked his cousin's wife and loved the kids, so he'd said yes. He wondered what it would be this time. Reggie was his first cousin, but Sebastian wished he would just, for once, turn to other family members when he needed something.

"Don't sound like that, cousin," Reggie said, recognizing the voice Sebastian always used with him.

"What can I do for you, Reggie?" Sebastian asked, impatiently waiting.

"We kind of have a distant relative who needs help."

"How distant would that be?"

"Well, she is a cousin of a third or fourth cousin by marriage," Reggie said quickly.

"So, does that make her my relative or yours by marriage to Joyce?"

"The truth?"

"Yes, the truth, Reggie, because I really don't have time to sit here and lay out our family tree with you today," Sebastian said tiredly.

"Okay. She is really a very close friend of Joyce's, almost like family. She really needs your help. She's our neighbor and a good kid."

"Who is she, Reggie, and what has she done?"

"Her name is Willa Raines, and she stabbed her no-good husband."

Sebastian sat up a little straighter. "Reggie, what is it you think I can do? I've assigned detectives to the case, and I usually don't butt in."

"Just talk with her. This isn't buttering you up, but you are good at what you do, and I know your instincts are good. Once you talk with her, you'll know she would never have intentionally killed anyone. Please, she is like family. You actually would have met her at parties at our house if he hadn't disappeared each time she and her husband were invited. Out screwing some other woman, no doubt. While she ended up staying home. One time, he just flat-out refused to allow her to come. He seemed uncomfortable around people and even more uncomfortable about allowing Willa around others. Joyce knew Willa's situation well and understood why she could never attend our parties. They are very close. Joyce seemed to be the only person John trusted to befriend Willa. And even that took some doing."

Reggie paused and added, "Things got so bad between Willa and John that Joyce encouraged them to see a counselor at that Relationship Fix Group place in the Renaissance Center on Jefferson. He didn't want to go, but he and Joyce are sort of cool, and he seemed to respect her, so she talked him into at least trying it. And, they did.

"They only live a few houses down from us. Joyce is who Willa called to come and get the kids after it happened that morning. We still have her kids after they came and picked Willa up again after John died. That was suspicious. I don't understand how he died when they'd initially said there were no life-threatening injuries. Please do this for me, actually, more for Joyce. She's worried to death about her friend. If you say no, the next voice you hear in your ear will be Joyce's. I promise, if you do this, I will never ask anything else."

"I doubt that, but alright, I'll see what I can do, but no promises."

"Thanks, cousin. Are we still on for Sunday dinner with the rest of the family?"

"Wouldn't miss it," Sebastian said, ending the call. He looked forward to his big, loud, affectionate family every Sunday.

Sebastian picked up his phone and dialed extension 58. "Rubye, where are they holding Willa Raines?"

"She's on eight, Commander," Rubye said, indicating the eighth floor of police headquarters. "What's your interest in this case, if I might ask?" Rubye knew this was not something that would pique a commander's interest.

"Even if you say you might not, we both know you will ask anyway," Sebastian responded. "If you must know, I'm doing this as a favor to my cousin Reggie. I don't know why you asked when I know very well that you heard the entire exchange between Reggie and me."

Rubye simply smiled knowingly. After all, she thought, it made sense that Mrs. Raines would have gotten tired of her husband's cheating and waited for just the right moment to get him. There were no police reports of prior assaults or any kind of family trouble from that address. There was also no claim of self-defense. She knew all this because she had overheard the other investigators talking. So it just might be that she got tired of him running around on her. You couldn't blame her, but then again, you can't kill every cheating partner.

In actuality, it wouldn't hurt if the Commander got involved. He'd dig around until he got all sides of the story, Rubye thought. She'd also glanced at the Raines woman's face and wasn't so sure that the assumptions about the case were correct.

Sebastian pushed back his chair and headed for the elevator. Rubye watched him as he went. She had heard the entire conversation he'd had with his cousin. He was such a softy. She knew he'd give in and look into the case.

Rubye was extremely happy working for the Commander. He was fair but, most importantly, an excellent cop. He never asked his detectives to do anything he wasn't willing to do. And above all, he listened to them. Even the union representatives liked him. If they laid out a case that showed clearly that discipline should be overturned, then that's what he'd do. He was also willing to give the benefit of the doubt at least the first time. He never harassed anyone as long as they did their job. But if they screwed up, he'd come down hard and heavy. Everyone knew that about him. The union respected him and knew they'd better have a darned good defense if they were going to go up against Commander Sebastian E. Crawford.

Sebastian rode up to the eighth floor; however, his conversation with Willa Raines netted nothing that would help the young woman. It only made things worse.

Upon questioning her relationship with her husband, she mentioned that he had hit her a few times. And no, according to Raines, she had not made a police report about the assaults. So, in addition to infidelity, physical abuse was now added as a motive for murder.

Yet, when he looked into her eyes and listened to her soft, tearful voice, Sebastian still had that strong, nagging feeling that she should not be there.

She confirmed that she and her husband had gone to a counselor to work on their marriage. All in all, Sebastian understood why his detectives believed she had planned the murder and waited for the right time. Who would endure what she had without at least thinking about killing the sick son of a bitch?

Chapter 15

He took the elevator back downstairs to the second floor. As he strode through the door, he waved Rubye over to his desk.

"Get me a phone number for the Relationship Fix Group, Inc, in the Renaissance Center," he said softly. "Oh, and tell me who runs that place."

Two minutes later, Rubye buzzed Sebastian. "The Relationship Fix Group, Inc, is run by three people. Dr. Jeff Jackson, his wife, Dr. Shay Jackson, and Dr. Samuel Roberts."

"I thought only psychiatrists were considered doctors. Why, as psychologists, are these three considered doctors?" he asked.

Rubye smiled, glad to know something her boss didn't. "It's all about their education," she answered. "They aren't medical doctors, but all of them have PhDs that entitle them to be called a doctor. That's a lot of schooling and money. I think if I had more than a master's degree, I'd damn sure demand that everyone call me doctor, even you." She smiled. "The Relationship Fix Group, Inc, is waiting on line two."

Sebastian pushed line two. "Good afternoon, this is Commander Sebastian Crawford from the Detroit Police Department. I'd like to speak with Dr. Jackson, please."

“Which one?” Gwen asked. “There are two, Dr. Jeffrey R. Jackson and Dr. Shay M. Jackson.” Gwen waited while the Commander decided which Dr. Jackson he needed to speak with.

“I’d like the one who counseled Mr. and Mrs. John Raines. I believe that’s going to be Dr. Shay Jackson.”

“One moment, please, sir,” Gwen said politely, as she buzzed Shay.

To Shay, Gwen smiled and said, “There is a Commander Crawford from the Detroit Police Department on line one. His deep voice is certainly dreamy. I’d take this call if I were you.”

“Put him on, Gwen. And by the way, I have my dreamy-voiced husband.” Shay smiled into the phone at Gwen’s comment.

“This is Dr. Jackson,” Shay said into the phone.

“Dr. Jackson, this is Commander Sebastian Crawford of the Detroit Police Department. I wonder if I could have a word with you at some time today about Mrs. Raines’s arrest.”

“Certainly, Commander, but two things. First, I thought she had been released with no charges filed. Second, you know that whatever Mr. and Mrs. Raines said to me is confidential and protected by the client-therapist privilege.”

“I understand, Dr. Jackson, but I really am trying to help Mrs. Raines. I guess you haven’t heard. Her husband died and she was picked up and placed back into police custody. There just might be something you can share that does not come under the heading of confidential that might help her. I promise not to take much of your time."

"Oh my God! No, I had not heard. I am so sorry to hear this. I thought his wounds were non-life-threatening, so I'm really shocked. But yes, of course, I will see you, Commander. Is it possible for you to be here within the hour?"

"I'll be there." Might as well get this over now, he thought, as he pulled on his jacket and headed toward the door.

Shay looked at her watch. It was one o'clock. She had arrived at eight thirty this morning for her first session. She'd skipped breakfast with Jeff in favor of sleeping a little longer.

She'd felt drained after yesterday's session with Willa and her conversation with Sam and Jeff at the restaurant last night. The two men had difficulty forcing themselves to talk about anything other than work. However, Shay took command of the conversation and continued bringing it back to lighter issues. Even doing that was a tad bit exhausting. After all, she had wanted Sam to get out and enjoy himself, not discuss work. Ultimately, they'd all had good meals, drinks, and conversation. Sam seemed to loosen up considerably.

Afterwards, Shay and Jeff went straight home and went to bed without watching the news. She understood how she'd missed that

John Raines had died.

She felt so sorry for Willa. Of course, she'd do whatever she could to help her.

Returning to the present, Shay couldn't help thinking that the rich, baritone voice of the caller had not escaped her. She smiled. Gwen was right. His voice was kind of dreamy. Even though Shay couldn't help wondering why this was necessary, she was sure that once this interview was done, the Commander would see that this was a waste of his time. Shay was positive there was nothing she could divulge to help the Commander or Willa.

At exactly one-thirty, Gwen buzzed Shay. "The Commander is here."

"Show him in, please," Shay said distractedly, still wondering why a high-ranking member of the police department would seek her out.

Sebastian knocked and then entered Shay's office. He looked at the lovely woman before him and immediately caught his breath. He didn't know why. He'd seen many beautiful and sexy women before. And while she appeared to be both, something else was causing the sharp intake of breath. She could be described as attractive but not gorgeous. She was certainly sexy, but not overly. She was dressed tastefully but not provocatively.

Upon seeing her, he couldn't help but wonder why he felt the way he did. And even more frustrating was that he didn't know how he was feeling. He would not have been able to describe it to anyone. His stomach was doing flip-flops. Sebastian silently ordered himself to focus on the task he was there to complete.

Looking up from her computer, Shay felt a warm flush start at her head and continue down to her extremities. She found the feeling most uncomfortable.

Greetings between the two were slow to come.

"Good afternoon, Dr. Jackson," Sebastian finally said, finding his voice first. I'm Commander Sebastian Crawford from the Detroit Police Department." He handed her his card.

"Good afternoon, Commander. How can I assist you?" I need to get this over quickly, she thought.

Sebastian continued to stand and stare. The room felt warm, and he continued to find it difficult to focus—on why he was there. He was focusing on the doctor quite well.

"Please have a seat," Shay said, directing him to the chair to the right of her desk, which felt much too close at the moment. She found herself wishing she had motioned him to a chair further away from her desk and across the room.

Sebastian, however, was grateful that the chair she had pointed him to was relatively close, as his legs didn't seem to want to work correctly. Only needing to take two steps to seat himself worked well for him.

Shay, now having gained her composure, smiled at the Commander. "How can I assist you, Commander?" she asked once again.

Her smile made Sebastian's stomach do another flip-flop.

"I, uh, don't usually conduct these kinds of investigations, but I'm actually here at the request of a relative. I ac-actually want to see if I ca-can help, Mrs. Raines. As I mentioned on the phone, Mrs. Raines has been detained once again." Sebastian hadn't stuttered since receiving therapy as a small boy.

"That poor woman," Shay said. "What's to become of her kids?"

"Her children are safe for the time being with a neighbor," Sebastian said, in a voice that still did not seem normal to his ears, but he now focused on speaking without stuttering. "I'm afraid the charge is now murder. In fact, some believe it was premeditated and that Mrs. Raines followed her husband down the stairs to the kitchen, where she intended to kill him. And possibly, in light of what she told us about their relationship and his cheating, she had been planning this all along."

Shay shook her head. "That's ridiculous, Commander. But I don't know how I would be able to help you. As I told you on the phone, I won't be able to divulge the conversations I had professionally with Mrs. or Mr. Raines."

"You might not legally be able to tell me what Mrs. Raines discussed with you, but maybe you can tell me what she did not discuss?" Sebastian said, deciding on another path.

"I don't know what you mean, Commander. You want me to tell you what she did not say? How would I do that?" Shay wrinkled her forehead.

"Well, in a way, yes." He smiled.

What a beautiful smile, Shay thought automatically. Her stomach did a flip-flop before she was able to actually focus on his words.

"I guess I'm trying to get in through the back door, here. If I asked you if Mrs. Raines ever said she wanted to kill her husband, if she did, I'm sure you would not legally be able to tell me what she said. But if she did not say that, then you could probably tell me that she did not, or there was no discussion like that." In his current state, Sebastian wasn't sure if what he'd just said made sense, but was relieved when Shay quickly responded.

"No, Commander, Mrs. Raines never told me she wanted to kill her husband. I can tell you that they left my office holding hands and that she was optimistic."

"So something must have happened to douse that optimism. Just thinking out loud," he said quickly. "I don't really expect you to respond to that."

"I now need you to tell me something, Commander. If the broadcast I heard was correct and Mr. Raines's injuries were not life-threatening, what happened?"

"He died of some infection. I don't have a medical degree, but I'm told it was some infection that commonly occurs in hospitals."

"But that wasn't Willa's fault," Shay said sternly

"Well, in part, it was. He wouldn't have been in the hospital if she had not stabbed him. In addition, it's also about her intentions before she stabbed him. It's about whether or not it was premeditated."

"I can't share any more than I have already," Shay said. "However, I'm convinced Willa Raines would not have planned such a thing if for no other reason than for her kids' sake. I can't imagine that she would have planned to murder the father of her children despite his infidelities. And," Shay added, "despite his infidelities, I believe she still loved him."

"Should I have more questions, may I call you?" Sebastian said softly. Realizing he sounded as if he were asking for a date, he quickly attempted to sound more professional. "I am trying to help Mrs. Raines, so I will continue my investigation." He stood, not wanting to leave, but his brain would not allow him to think of any more questions that would prolong the visit. He continued to stare at Shay. Giving a shake of his head, he refocused and looked instead at a painting on the wall.

"Certainly," Shay said, handing him her card. "Call any time you'd like." She wondered why she'd felt the need to add the last comment. Becoming aware that she had been staring at the Commander, she now focused on the painting on the wall. Her husband, she reminded herself, had given her that painting.

Sebastian attempted to only shake Shay's hand, but once her soft, smooth hand was in his, he found himself holding it for just a scant second longer than necessary. Embarrassed, he quickly let go and turned to leave.

"Goodbye, Dr. Jackson," he managed to say as he opened the door.

On the other side of the door, only Gwen noticed the breath he exhaled as he nodded at her and moved past her desk.

Chapter 16

Sebastian stepped into the elevator and rode down to the lobby in a daze. He had not noticed the two women who had entered the elevator one floor down. Nor had he noticed the morbidly obese man who entered on the third floor and who looked enviously at Sebastian. The newcomer to the elevator watched as the women, unbeknownst to Sebastian, stared at him adoringly. He made a striking figure in his crisp navy-blue uniform, broad shoulders, and mixed gray hair.

Exiting the elevator, he shook his head as if to clear whatever it was that was upsetting his equilibrium. He might be mistaken, but he could swear that Dr. Shay Jackson felt it as well. The electricity passed between them when their hands touched, and he believed it to be obvious to them both. The attraction left him feeling like a silly school boy. "Get a grip," he said out loud, as he strode toward the building exit.

As he walked across the street to the parking lot, he realized that he had not been aware of his surroundings. He had observed nothing while in the elevator, and until he'd given himself a good talking to, he was totally oblivious to everything around him. That scenario did not play well for anyone who was out and about, but it could certainly be detrimental to a law enforcement officer who had been trained to be aware and observant at all times. What happened to all that training? he asked himself.

Back in his office, Sebastian slowly went over his contact with Dr. Jackson. Just thinking about her made his heart beat a little faster. This was all new to Sebastian, who had not even noticed another woman since his wife had died in a car accident some five years ago. The details surrounding her death were normally kept locked deep inside him. It was not something he cared to discuss or even think about, even though he certainly thought about her every day. She was the first thing on his mind in the morning and the last at night. How, he thought, could he dismiss her so easily in favor of someone he'd only seen once? Someone he'd spent less than thirty minutes with? Even worse, someone who was married?

For thirteen months after his wife's death, he threw himself into his work. Finally, Rubye put an end to his moping and feeling sorry for himself. He vividly remembered her words.

"You are going to kill yourself working like this. You look as if you haven't had a good night's sleep since she—since forever. You've lost weight, and you aren't taking care of yourself. I'm not going to have it. You are cramping my style. I can't watch this any longer. You're actually making me depressed. Everyone knows you may be the boss, but I’m responsible for you. I take care of you. The fact that I’m failing miserably at that job doesn’t bode well with me." She had paused when Sebastian made a gruff sound.

"A bunch of us are going bowling tonight," she’d told him. "And you are coming with us. We hang out at the bar across the street on Friday nights, which you know very well because you used to join us at least once in a while, even if you only stayed a half hour. You will be joining us again this Friday, and any other time we hang out, you will come with us and you will enjoy it. I will drag you there if need be. And if that doesn’t work, I will call your mom," Her voice was elevated; the finger from her right hand pointed a few inches from his face, and her left hand was placed firmly on her hip. Sebastian knew she meant business. He’d turned around, and others were watching the scene. No one seemed surprised. He figured they were all in on it.

"Okay, okay, I’ll come with you tonight," he’d said reluctantly.

"Tonight, and every night," Rubye said under her breath.

After that, everyone in the office who knew of a planned event or a get-together of any sort forced Sebastian to come along. After a while, he discovered that, once forced out of the office, he was enjoying himself. He still didn’t date and drew the line at letting anyone set him up on blind dates, but he had indeed started enjoying life. He knew Sara would not have wanted him to mope around as he'd been doing. He couldn't help but wonder if she was still as angry with him as she had been before the crash.

Once again, Sebastian shook his head to clear his thoughts. Yet, he wasn't absolutely certain which thoughts he was attempting to clear—those of his deceased wife, or those of Dr. Shay Jackson?

Chapter 17

Shay sat motionless. She continued to stare at the door that Commander Crawford had closed behind him. The clock chimed, signaling that she had been sitting there for the last ten minutes.

I don't have any idea why this man affected me the way he did; she thought, but I need to dismiss him and whatever this feeling is.

Meditation! she thought.

Meditating always cleared her head and allowed her to move forward. Pushing her chair away from the desk, Shay sat, knees pressed together, hands palms up, and lying gently on her thighs, head up, eyes closed.

She gave it her best shot. Another twenty minutes passed, and she just could not shake the visual. The tall, bronze-skinned, distinguished man with graying temples, exquisite in his uniform and possessing one of the most beautiful smiles she'd ever seen, continued to come into focus. Obviously, the meditation had not worked. For twenty minutes, she pushed Commander Sebastian Crawford's face out of her head, and seconds later it returned.

"It's no use," she said aloud, rising from her seated position. Shay walked into the smartly decorated bathroom attached to her office. She closed the door and leaned against it before walking to the basin and looking into the mirror. I look the same, she thought; so why am I acting so differently? What is it about this man that has me acting as if I haven't a clue about what to do next? I do know what to do, Shay argued with herself. You get yourself together, return to your desk, and wait for your next client to come in. She managed a smile.

Understanding that this was the cue to splash water on her face as they usually did in the movies, she smiled. Obviously, that was not her next move considering she had carefully applied makeup this morning, so splashing water on her face was not an option. But oh, how she wished it were. She felt sure that cool water would have taken care of everything—erased everything. It might even have cooled the fire that was raging inside her.

These feelings were just temporary. Actually, they were probably quite normal. After all, Shay reasoned, he was quite striking in his uniform. She never had, but many women drooled over a man in uniform. This was no big deal. All she really did was notice a good-looking man. "You've never done that before since you married Jeff," a little voice in the back of her mind said. Shay ignored the voice. Men looked all the time. She'd bet Jeff had looked at some attractive woman before. There was nothing wrong with her noticing that a man was good-looking. "He smelled good too," the little voice said. The little voice became a louder one, saying, "Stop rationalizing and do not, and I repeat, let this go any further." There was no this, Shay thought, feeling even more guilty when she thought about Jeff. She was pretty sure that even if he noticed a pretty woman, she probably would not have solicited for him what Shay was feeling. Stop being silly, she told herself silently. I'm not really feeling anything.

Shay buzzed Gwen. "Please bring me the Palmer file. They're my next clients. I'll also need the Bradford file as well. I'll be seeing them in the morning. I just need to refresh my memory on the facts of their cases."

Gwen gave Shay an odd look as she left the room to fetch the requested files. She'd never known her boss to forget the facts of any of her cases. She had a memory that was almost photographic when it came to her clients. Even if she had not seen someone in months, Dr. Shay Marie Jackson could immediately recall the facts of the case. So, her asking to go over the files was indeed odd given that Shay could have easily pulled the information up on the computer that sat just to the right of her desk. Gwen shrugged and did as she was told, retrieving the paper files, which were only kept as hard copies for thirty days.

Gwen entered Shay's office and placed the files in front of her boss. Shay, now perfectly composed, thanked Gwen. It was so silly, she decided, to think that someone as dedicated and devoted to her husband as she would be moved by another man. She and Jeff had their own marital issues, actually only one issue, but Shay knew that they loved each other and would be together a lifetime. Not only was there love, but also respect, trust, and admiration.

Jeff was affectionate to a fault and constantly showered Shay with gifts. Shay, on the other hand, made life comfortable for Jeff. They were both relaxed with each other and perfectly matched when it came to the things they loved to do together. They loved snorkeling, diving, golfing, having meals out, reading, and traveling. The list went on and on, Shay thought, now smiling as she remembered their upcoming vacation. Their Hawaiian trip with their close friends James and Saundra Hunter was going to be wonderful. They had planned the vacation one evening when they'd had dinner with the Hunters, as they often did. The camaraderie between the two couples was every bit as perfect as that between Jeff and Shay.

Shay and Jeff shared everything, and even though they had been married for fifteen years, they never grew bored with each other or were at a loss for conversation between them. They laughed often and sincerely enjoyed one another's company. There was only one issue that they could not discuss. Well, Shay thought, they had discussed it once, and Jeff had asked her never to bring it up again. And she had not done so.

Chapter 18

Gwen buzzed, interrupting her thoughts. "The Palmers are here."

"Show them in, please," Shay said, smoothing her black pencil skirt down as she rose to greet them. She shook hands with Mrs. Marilyn Palmer, a slightly overweight woman about five feet tall. Mrs. Palmer was tastefully dressed in a conservative black suit, adorned with a pearl brooch, and wearing a pearl necklace. Her dyed blond hair was neat and swept up. Shay now extended her hand to Mr. George Palmer, who was only slightly taller than his wife. He wore dark-rimmed glasses and was also dressed conservatively in a blue pin-striped suit and a white shirt with French cuffs.

The couple seemed a little stiff and far too formal with each other. After fifty years of marriage, they appeared to have become jaded. There seemed to be no joy or laughter in their relationship. Shay had to admit that she rarely saw couples who had been married as long as the Palmers. Usually, after being married for that long, couples just seem to accept that they will grow apart. Most felt it was a natural occurrence and that there was nothing that could be done to change it. Older couples often accepted and tolerated whatever their marriage had morphed into, whether good or bad.

Shay now watched the Palmers as they seated themselves. Mrs. Palmer settled on the love seat, while Mr. Palmer sat in an armless chair placed on the opposite side of the room.

"I'm going to ask that you both sit on the love seat," Shay said, smiling, as she walked over to Mr. Palmer, placing her hand lightly on his shoulder to gently guide him across the room to where his wife was seated. Mrs. Palmer had sat down first on the love seat, so Shay now turned to Mr. Palmer.

"Mr. Palmer, why did you select the chair far across the room when your wife was already seated on the love seat?" she asked.

"Uh, I don't really know." He seemed both baffled and uncomfortable by the question. He appeared, however, to answer honestly. "I really don't know. I remember when we first met, long before there were separate seats in cars. There was no console between the two seats, just a long seat. Marilyn used to sit next to me as I drove. She would sit so close that she was almost in my lap." He smiled, as if remembering fond memories. "All the young couples did that back then. The girl would snuggle up next to the boy." He looked over at his wife, who was now giggling.

"Do you remember that as well, Mrs. Palmer?" Shay asked.

"I sure do." She smiled. "In those days, we didn't have a lot of money or a lot of places to go. We kind of just rode around. Of course, gas was much cheaper then. He drove while I snuggled up to him as close as I could. It was wonderful. Then we'd ride out to the park and neck. That's what making out was called back then," she explained with another giggle.

"So, what happened?" Shay asked.

They were both quiet for a moment. Then both started to speak at once.

"I guess life happened," Mrs. Palmer said.

"Children," Mr. Palmer chimed in. "We have eight, you know. Three boys and five girls—I guess that many kids, all born during the first eight years of our marriage, can take the romance out of anything. Not that we don't love them dearly," he added quickly.

"Yes, I guess that's how we started to lose what we had in our younger days." Mrs. Palmer said.

"I got pregnant only three months after we got married. Then I got pregnant every year after that for the next seven years. We're Catholic, you know," she explained. "The Catholic Church forbade us to use birth control back then." She smiled. "I guess we might have had—Lord knows how many more—had I not gotten sick and had to have a hysterectomy."

"Then I took a job where I was working all the time when I was here in Michigan and pretty much spent the remainder traveling to other cities for work. By the time the kids were grown and I retired, I don't think we even knew each other anymore," said Mr. Palmer.

"We didn't know what to do together because we hadn't done

anything together in so many years," Mrs. Palmer stated.

"I know that you'd like to get back what you lost so many years ago, and I can help you. But you have to promise me that you'll continue to renew your friendship and your love. Get to know each other again. Spend the same amount of time together talking about yourselves, your hopes, and your dreams as you did when you first met. Years have passed, and your original conversation detailing your dreams, hopes, and aspirations has probably changed. So share those changes now. You can't just let your relationship go along on its own. You must be the catalyst to make it happen. Do you think you can do that?"

The couple smiled at each other. "Yes," they said in unison.

Try going for rides as you did when you first met. Of course, you won't be able to sit side by side." Shay smiled. "But just ride. I think you can probably afford the higher price of gas now." Shay paused. "Actually, why not try Lyft or Uber? Call one of them and let them drive you around so that you can sit close together in the back seat. Intentionally explore things that you can do together, like concerts, picnics, and travel. Try doing some of the same things you did before the kids were born. And most of all, laugh together." She paused again, now smiling at the couple.

They both looked at each other and appeared a bit embarrassed that the answer to their issue could be so simple. Shay knew they, as many others did, were wondering why they hadn't thought of just what she had told them.

"I think that concludes our session," Shay said. "You can make a follow-up appointment with Gwen for three weeks. However, my guess is that once you make an effort to come together, your next appointment will be your last. I will look forward in three weeks to hearing about your renewed relationship."

The Palmers stood up. Mr. Palmer took Mrs. Palmer's hand. "We used to always hold hands," he said, smiling.

Shay smiled as well, as they left her office. It was a joy to counsel someone like the Palmers, who simply needed a little prodding to put the life back into their marriage.

Chapter 19

Shay felt lighter than she had felt earlier. Maybe she'd go home and prepare a good dinner for Jeff. She'd stop at the Whole Foods on Woodward Avenue and pick up his favorite roast chicken, since she hadn't taken anything out of the freezer before leaving this morning. She also picked up fresh green beans to sauté and frozen rolls to pop into the oven. She'd add salad, some quinoa, and his favorite wine, of course. She even picked up his favorite snack, ginger snaps, which she herself disliked. But this was about pleasing Jeff, not herself. She thought once again that he was a good husband.

The small voice in the back of her head returned and said, "Then why are you so attracted to another man?"

"He is a good husband," she retorted out loud. "Sex isn't everything. And I am not attracted to another man," she said emphatically.

Jeff was sweet and kind. There wasn't anything he wouldn't do for Shay. For Jeff, providing sex was just not one of those things. Shay knew he would if only he could. That, she thought, was another story, one she tried not to think about or care about, considering how well her husband treated her in every other way.

Chapter 20

Once home, Shay started the food preparation and looked down at the dog. They'd gotten Pam when they both realized there would be no children. They had added Kimberly Alice, the cat, when she somehow got into the house while the carpets were being cleaned and the door was open. Once inside, she refused to leave. Shay remembered Jeff gently picking her up and placing her on the front porch. But before he could get back into the house and close the door, the tiny kitten had run back in.

The commotion had roused Pam, the black Cocker Spaniel puppy at the time, who cautiously and slowly walked toward the small white kitten. Shay and Jeff watched in amazement as both animals rubbed noses, sniffing each other. To this day, the odd couple animals are the best of friends. These two became Shay and Jeff's children.

Shay looked down as Pam held her leash in her mouth. Shay laughed. "There's nothing subtle about that, is there?" She asked the dog with the big, gentle eyes and the silky black coat. Shay shook her head with a smile as she bent to take the leash from Pam and secure it to the collar around her neck. Yes, Pam and Kimberly Alice were Shay and Jeff's babies. She bent down to pat Kimberly Alice's head before checking on her meal and opening the garage door for an excited Pam.

Even though Shay had no children, she had numerous friends whose kids fondly referred to her as Aunt Shay. Even her best friend, Saundra's grandchildren, called her Aunt Shay. So Shay made herself content with the children of her friends. And of course, Gwen's daughter, Lisa, had also referred to her as Aunt Shay. What she often forced herself to be content with was the lack of lovemaking between her and Jeff. Lack was an understatement, Shay thought, as she and Pam crossed the street to get to the dog park. If Shay was to complete dinner before Jeff arrived, she really didn't have time to let her thoughts take her down that road.

Once Pam had played with her usual buddies, who frequent the dog park, sniffed every bush and blade of grass, and taken care of her toilet needs, the pair headed back home.

Shay finished her dinner preparation with love. Somehow, she felt she owed Jeff his favorite meal, which she hoped would erase her guilt regarding that darn police officer, as she now decided she'd brand him. Refraining from using his name seemed to make today's events less formidable.

Shay was just popping the rolls into the oven when she heard Jeff's black Navigator pull into the garage. As Shay stood at the sink, Jeff entered the room, grabbing her around the waist and hugging her tightly. There was a sadness in his eyes that only Shay could detect. The sadness seemed to appear any time he touched her, knowing he could do no more. Shay understood. “Or at least you pretend you do,” said the small voice. Shay closed her eyes. How she wished that voice would stop taunting her. Of course, she understood Jeff’s problem.

Turning in his arms, she gave him a brilliant smile, naming all of his favorites on tonight’s menu. "If you’ll open the wine, I’ll get dinner on the table," she said brightly.

"Wine, too. Wow, that’s great. I get my favorite meal plus wine, and you haven’t even seen what I brought you yet," he said as he walked into the powder room to wash his hands.

"Jeff, you know I love gifts, but I have everything I need, plus you," Shay said, and she sincerely meant it. Whenever Jeff spoiled her, she realized how, in spite of everything, she was a very blessed woman.

Jeff opened the wine while Shay put the finishing touches on the exquisite table she had set. She was lighting the candles when Jeff came up behind her carrying the wine.

Shay and Jeff enjoyed the meal and each other’s company. As usual, they both talked about how their day had gone. Shay and Jeff often intentionally stayed away from each other at work. They preferred to share over dinner instead of in the office. Once in a while, they had lunch together during a slow afternoon at the office. This practice and their marriage had worked for them over the years. The fact that Shay had not brought up Sebast—that darned police officer—during this evening's catch-up conversation mildly disturbed her.

Tonight, in addition to catching up on things that happened during the day, they joyfully discussed their upcoming trip to Hawaii. They both imagined how great it would be to enjoy the beautiful island state. This month would go fast, and by April, they would be enjoying the sun instead of the cold and snow they faced today.

February is often the coldest month in Michigan, but neither Shay nor Jeff minded this year as they got closer and closer to the deadline for their much-deserved vacation. It would have been nice if they could have gotten away even earlier. But it wasn't to be. It was just too busy at the office, and besides, they had to allow for Saundra's and James's schedules as well. Shay had spoken to Saundra by phone, so she knew that Saundra and James were looking forward to getting away from the cold as much as she and Jeff were. The two couples often traveled together.

Once dinner was over and the dirty dishes were disposed of by both Jeff and Shay, Jeff led Shay into the great room, where he unearthed a box from its hiding place behind a set of books on the bookshelf next to the fireplace. He handed the red box to Shay. The box contained the most beautiful gold rose she'd ever seen.

"It's a genuine rose preserved and then dipped in eighteen-karat gold." Jeff said, proud of his find. The vase that held the rose was also exquisite.

"I thought of you the minute our jeweler mentioned it. I know how you love flowers, and I never tire of sending you flowers, but I thought this would be a little more special. It will last forever." Jeff smiled. "You deserve this. I love you."

"I love you too," Shay said quietly. "You are always so kind and thoughtful. And it isn't even my birthday, Valentine's Day, Christmas, or our anniversary. What on earth did I do to deserve you?" Shay said, shedding tears of joy mingled with a smidgen of lingering guilt.

Sleep eluded Shay that night. Each time she closed her eyes, the face that appeared belonged to a tall, distinguished man in a uniform. Once fully awake, Shay realized the face belonged to Commander Sebastian Crawford. He had come in and out of her dreams. No matter the theme of the dream, he was always there, just lurking, Shay thought. She dreamed of already being in Hawaii. He was there. She dreamed of walking in the snow in Michigan. Commander Crawford was there, throwing snowballs at her and helping to make the snowman.

After continuing to dismiss his face, Shay finally quietly pulled the covers back and slipped out of bed so as not to disturb Jeff. Looking at the clock, she noted that it was barely four in the morning.

Convinced it was no use returning to bed, she showered and dressed. Her first clients weren't due until eight this morning, yet Shay was dressed and ready to leave the house by five thirty.

She sent Jeff a text, letting him know she was going into the office early to review some notes, and quietly let herself out of the house. Even though she had arrived by six o'clock, she saw the light under Sam Roberts' door. It was not surprising. He was always in early. As he'd said before, he had nothing better to do. She did not disturb him.

It was so cold that poor Sam was forced to hit golf balls in a dome instead of on the golf course.

Chapter 21

The Bradfords were due at eight a.m. Shay kept track of the time on her gold Samsung phone watch – also a gift from her loving husband. None of the office staff were due until eight-thirty which meant that Gwen wouldn't be there to greet them.

At exactly seven-fifty-five a.m., Shay heard the door to the outer office suite open. Shay exited her office to go out to greet Mr. and Mrs. Bradford.

Julie and Grayson Bradford had been married for almost thirty years. Grayson had been involved in affairs on and off as many as five or more times that his wife could confirm during their marriage. Julie had become tired of her cheating husband and had finally found the courage to inform him that she wanted a divorce. However, she had insisted that Grayson come with her to counseling before completely ending their marriage. Julie secretly hoped against hope that counseling would knock some sense into Grayson.

Shay took a moment to look at the couple before her. It seemed as though they were both angry. But it was obvious that Mrs. Bradford still wanted to save the marriage.

Mrs. Bradford spoke first. "Dr. Jackson, I don't exactly know what I hoped to accomplish when I insisted that Grayson come here. I believe that he has been involved with this latest woman longer than any other. And even though he won't admit it, I think he is in love with this one. I'm pretty sure he was thinking about leaving me for her, even before I just recently told him I wanted a divorce," she concluded, taking a deep breath.

"Is that true?" Shay said, turning to face Mr. Bradford.

"No, it is not true. If I were planning on leaving my wife, I would not be here humiliating myself and allowing my personal business to be discussed in front of a total stranger."

He now turned to glare at his wife, "When you asked for the divorce, I would simply have found that to be an easy way out if what you believe were true. My affairs are simply distractions," he said, now turning to Shay. "But I have never had any intention of leaving my wife. I will call it off immediately, without a problem," he said, still facing Shay. "It is not, as my wife prefers to believe, that serious."

Mrs. Bradford listened as her husband spoke. Her face displayed doubt after numerous years of enduring her husband's cheating and lies.

"Are you willing to do whatever it takes to save your marriage, Mr. Bradford?" Shay asked.

"Yes, of course, I am," Mr. Bradford answered a little too quickly.

"Mrs. Bradford, do you really want a divorce, or would you rather try to save your marriage?" Shay asked.

"I want to save my marriage, but this time, he is involved with Jennifer Bloom! She's a beautiful young model – extremely famous too. She happens to be younger than our youngest daughter. I know where she lives and that they've been spending a lot of time there. I also know that she also has a husband, even though he does not live in the home that Grayson visits."

"How do you know these things?" shouted Mr. Bradford. "Have you hired someone to spy on me?"

Realization hit him. His voice faltered as he said, "You've hired a private detective, haven't you?"

Mrs. Bradford did not reply to her husband's question but turned to Shay, "Dr. Jackson, what my husband won't tell you is that he is simply trying to hold on to our marriage for another two months. You see, we have a prenuptial agreement. Grayson gets to walk away with a large portion of my money if we stay married for thirty years. Our thirtieth anniversary is May seventh. So, I see nothing further to discuss. I made a dreadful mistake coming here. Dr. Jackson, I am so sorry to have taken up your time. I will of course see that you are adequately compensated at double your usual rate."

"That will not be necessary, Mrs. Bradford. I do agree that this session is over. However, should either of you change your mind and require my assistance, I will be more than happy to help you. It is certainly never too late to save a marriage. Why not go home and at least consider it? Talk things over and I will be here if you need me."

Chapter 22

Shay watched sadly, as the couple left her office. A marriage that could not be saved always brought sadness to Shay. Shay made a mental note that Mr. Bradford had not even bothered to deny his wife's accusation that he simply wanted to stay married to satisfy the prenuptial agreement. Shay made some notes on the recorder to the Bradford file and went out to the sitting room where the coffee room was located in an alcove. Shay was pouring herself a cup of tea when Sam Roberts walked up behind her.

"Tea, not coffee?" he asked.

Shay turned around, now smiling, "Good morning, Sam. I thought I'd change it up this time. I hope the tea will warm me a little. I always feel cold when I can't save a marriage."

"If that's what you have before you, we should talk. Would you like to tell me about it?" the older man asked.

Shay hesitated only a moment. It always helped to talk some cases over with both Jeff and Sam. "Are you sure you want to hear about it? It is another case of a cheating spouse."

"I actually do want to hear. I apologize again for my outburst about how I feel about cheating partners. I realize that I was truly ranting and I am sorry about that. Please accept my apology."

"No apology necessary, Sam. I understood your feelings perfectly. I told you that when you tried to apologize before."

"Well, let's have it. Even though I deplore cheating, I can still give sound advice. It is my job, you know." Sam smiled. "Come into my office, young lady."

Shay followed Sam into his office and relayed the sordid details.

When she was done, Sam spoke, "That's ironic. I actually know Jennifer Bloom and her family personally. She is indeed beautiful, but very spoiled. She would never let Grayson Bradford dump her even if he wanted to, and I'm pretty sure he does not. Besides, she already has a husband. I also know Julie Bradford. I helped her with a problem recently, I just was not aware that Jennifer was involved at the time."

Sam did not elaborate on whatever problem he had helped Mrs. Bradford with and Shay did not pry. She returned to her office after thanking Sam for listening.

Later that morning, Shay cornered Sam and urged him to have lunch with her. The two decided to eat at Fishbone's Rhythm Kitchen in an area of downtown Detroit called Greektown. Fishbones provided a Louisiana flair. Dishes on the menu included crawfish and gumbo. The restaurant location was bustling and Greektown was one of Shay and Jeff's favorites.

When they arrived at one o'clock, the noon lunch crowd was leaving and allowed Shay and Sam to enjoy a quiet lunch together. They briefly continued their conversation about Bradford and Jennifer Bloom.

Shay had created a new policy regarding discussing work during meals with Sam. Especially since she was trying to get him away from work and provide some fun and relaxation—both of which he had been lacking since his wife's death. Her new policy was that any discussion of work or work-related conversation was to be done only at the beginning of the meal, prior to the food being served, and could only last for fifteen minutes, no more. After the expressed time, all work conversation was to immediately cease. With a slight bit of nudging, Sam adhered to the policy and enjoyed a nice lunch.

They could both, she decided, use the time away from the office and from work discussions. She hoped that the older man would start to leave work at the office and enjoy life more. She and Jeff had both agreed that they would spend more time with Sam. Shay convinced Sam to meet for lunch again next week. They even selected Pegasus, another restaurant in Greektown, for their next lunch meeting. And possibly the Rattlesnake Club for an evening outing. After all, the Detroit area had no shortage of fine dining.

With plans made for the future, Shay and Sam return to the office. Sam was done seeing clients for the day and was off to do whatever it was he did after leaving the office. Shay had two more clients but was done with her day by five-thirty when she started home to see what Jeff was up to. She had actually only seen him briefly. Shay had taken just long enough to tell Jeff about her session with the Bradfords. "Another cheater," was his only response. He had seemed a little flushed but was on his way into a session. His door was closed when she and Sam left for lunch and the "In Session" sign was showing. Consequently, Shay and Sam had not disturbed him.

On the way home, Shay received a text from Jeff letting her know that he was having dinner out with some other colleagues and not to expect him for dinner.

Chapter 23

The dark vehicle pulled up in front of a house located on the northwest Detroit Street. Palmer Woods was a prominent Detroit neighborhood offering mansion-like housing to attorneys, judges, doctors, and the like.

He'd followed the man here. He'd watched the man and woman kiss when he arrived. Only five minutes later, they'd come out of the house holding hands and got into his silver Bentley parked in the drive. Once again, they kissed. This was certainly no indication that would signal the end of an affair. No, it was quite clear that this was not a farewell meeting.

He pulled his car around to the rear of the house. His eyes glowed as he noticed the partially opened window. God wants me to do this, he decided. Why else would He make it so easy? The window was open just enough so that the tools he had brought to pry open a window or door were unnecessary.

Once inside, he took out the jar of lemonade. He had already laced it with the deadly ingredient. He then set the empty pill container on the table. The pill bottle was void of a label but the remnants of the pills inside remained. He looked around. He'd worn gloves so he wouldn't leave prints.

He touched the gun where it rested in his jacket pocket. Just a little friendly persuasion, he thought. There was nothing more to do but wait for them to return. He pulled the gray hat down more securely on his head. He'd touched up the scar on the side of his face with makeup to make it even more prominent. He was pleased that between the pulled-down hat and the scar his face was quite distorted. No one would recognize him. The vehicle he used contained no license plate. He'd removed it before pulling up to the house. When he'd exited the vehicle, he'd made sure to walk even more bent over than usual.

The sound of the key being inserted into the lock alerted him that they had returned. He quickly slid into the closet near the door. He looked down, noticing there was luggage in the closet. Moving it quickly out of his way, he realized that the bags were packed. He left the closet door ajar just enough for him to see them as they entered the room. As they stood by the door, locked in an embrace, he came out of his hiding place. It was better to surprise them as they stood at the front door. They both looked up, startled by his appearance.

She opened her mouth to speak, but no words came out.

"What is this?" the startled man said. "If you want money, please take it and go."

The intruder smiled but said nothing. He kept the gun pointed at them.

“Sit down there on the sofa.” He pointed with the gun. They did as they were told. They were of course, frightened. They should be frightened, thought the intruder. They are nasty and pathetic cheaters. They are scum. “You would not be in this situation had you both honored your marriage vows and refrained from acting on your despicable impulses. You do not deserve to live.” His detective had found them so that they could be punished.

The man and woman were really frightened now. “Please don’t hurt me,” cried the woman. “This wasn’t my fault. He forced me. I didn’t know he was married.”

The intruder smiled again. Lies, all lies, he thought. If she didn’t know he was married, she certainly knew she was. Both his wife and her husband would be much better off without the two of them. The fact that with their deaths he would actually be helping two people made him gleeful.

She continued to beg. “Shut up,” the intruder finally said, silencing her by taking a step toward her and pushing the gun into her face. “Don’t either of you cheaters say a word.” Then he smiled. “You do deserve some nice refreshing lemonade.” There were already two empty glasses on the table. How convenient, he thought. It has to be God making it easy again. He motioned with his gun to the man, to fill both glasses with lemonade from the jar. The man’s hands shook, but he did as he was instructed, spilling just a little on the table.

"Now drink the liquid down quickly," he demanded.

"What's in here?" the man inquired.

The intruder watched without responding as they both consumed the entire contents of the glasses as he had demanded they do.

"I think you should have more," the intruder said, pointing to the remaining contents in the jar. "Pour the rest into the glasses."

Again, the man poured, hands shaking. "Please don't do this," he begged.

"You are both nasty, filthy, vile scum of the earth cheaters." The intruder's voice showed his disdain as he shouted at the two confused and terrified individuals. "Drink it," he yelled. The woman jumped at his loud voice. Both did as they were told.

Looking at the man, he shouted, "Where's your cell phone?" The man pointed to the pocket of his jacket. "Take it out," the intruder shouted again. The man quickly took his phone out.

"Now go to a previous text to your wife. I know her name is Julie, so don't try to fool me."

The man once again did as he was told.

The intruder, still holding the gun, stepped behind the sofa on which the two were seated. He stood behind the man. "Hold the phone up so that I can see it." Satisfied that the contents of the previous texts were truly to his wife, Julie, he smiled. There had been a text message from earlier that day telling her that he would put an end to the affair tonight. He ended the text by saying he loved her.

How sincere, the intruder thought. But Julie believed him. Her text responding to his had read: “You won’t regret this darling. I love you and will do anything to make our marriage work. Please hurry home.”

Unfortunately, the intruder thought with another smile, he will regret it and in just another fifteen minutes, he won’t be able to hurry home.

“Now type exactly what I tell you.” Under the intruder’s watchful eye, the man typed as the intruder dictated.

“Jennifer and I truly love each other. We cannot part. We’d rather die together than be apart. I’m sorry I hurt you. Please forgive me.”

The man’s face showed terror, as the intruder yelled, “Send it now.” The man pushed the send button. The intruder watched as both his victims clung to each other, quickly becoming drowsy. When he was satisfied that they were both unconscious, the intruder picked up the lemonade jar, rinsed out the glasses, and returned them to the table next to the empty pill container.

Taking one last look at the two bodies, he smiled, made sure the top was secure on the lemonade jar that he now stuffed back into his gray bag, and quietly let himself out through the rear door.

Chapter 24

Julie and Grayson Bradford had shared dinner, just as they had when they were first married. The conversation had not flowed as Julie would have wanted, but Grayson did continue to remind her that he would end his relationship with Jennifer tonight. Those were his exact words, repeated to Julie at least twice during dinner and in a text message Grayson had sent her earlier.

Now Julie continued to pace as she had for the last thirty minutes. Grayson had left home over two hours ago to end things with Jennifer Bloom. Julie was not confident enough to believe this would happen. In both his text to her and over their earlier dinner, Grayson finally convinced her that he was sincere about wanting to end the relationship. He admitted that he had actually thought he was in love with Jennifer for a while. But he assured Julie he had come to his senses. He loved only Julie and now wanted to get out of the relationship with the younger woman. He realized – he had confessed to Julie – that the woman was much too young for him.

"Why, she's younger than our Katarina," he'd said.

Julie now smiled sadly, thinking, "As if I didn't already know that his latest sex partner was two years younger than our youngest daughter, who is twenty-six years old."

The detective she'd hired had done an excellent and thorough job.

The detective agency had been suggested by Julie's friend, Sam Roberts.

Julie knew Sam counseled couples professionally; however, she had not gone to his office but simply met with him as a friend and sought his advice. Sam was both appalled and disappointed that Grayson could be cheating. His advice about hiring the detective was sound. She needed to know exactly what Grayson was up to. Now, because of the detective's work, there was nothing she didn't know about when Grayson and Jennifer were together, where they went, what they did, and how much time they had spent together. She even knew what they'd eaten at restaurants. The detective had shown her pictures that she was unable to do more than glance at through her tears. But now she realized that she must hang on to hope – the hope that Grayson was telling the truth this time.

Julie had suffered through all his other indiscretions, knowing they were just that. But now she was unsure because this one seemed different. Where Grayson had been cautious before, still arriving home at a decent hour after his rendezvous and being careful about meeting in discreet places, he didn't seem to care this time. Unfortunately, because of his feelings for Jennifer, he had often not arrived home until the early hours of the morning. With this one, he seemed to have thrown all caution to the wind.

According to the detective, they had been seen at places like Joe

Muer's, Fishbones in Greektown, Andiamo's in the suburb of Dearborn, Nickola's in Southfield, another suburb of Detroit, and a Thai restaurant in Dearborn. These were all popular spots in the Detroit area, none of which were discreet.

Another telltale sign was the scent of soap, a different soap than was used in the Bradford household. On several occasions, Julie noticed the smell, even though she'd said nothing at the time. He had gotten careless, and the thought alarmed her.

Love will do that to you, she thought.

She shook her doubts and troubling thoughts away, telling her to calm down. She thought, "*He said he would end it, and he will. He ended others and will do the same with this one.*"

She continued pacing, only interrupted by the phone ringing.

"Hello," she said, rushing to the phone, hoping it was Grayson. Instead, she was greeted by an unknown woman's voice.

"I'm so sorry to call so late, Mrs. Bradford. My name is Sylvia from the travel agency. I spoke with your husband at about three p.m. today. I'm calling because I know how excited you and Mr. Bradford are about leaving on the chartered red-eye flight scheduled for ten p.m. tonight to Cancun, but the plane had some issues, and that flight has been canceled. Knowing, however, that your husband expressed how important it was to leave this evening, I have booked you a first-class flight on a Delta flight that leaves…"

Julie had stopped listening. She didn't need to hear more. She simply replaced the receiver on the phone without hearing the remainder of the travel agent's conversation. The landline phone rang again. She did not answer. For some strange reason, she remembered the agent's words. She'd said it was a chartered flight. She laughed, making a ragged sound. They owned a private plane, but of course, he wouldn't take it. He knew the pilot would have immediately informed her, as she had the last time he dared to woo one of his conquests by showing off the private jet.

Sitting on the sofa near the phone, she wiped her tears away. *Well, there's your answer,* she thought sadly.

That's when the realization finally settled: he never intended to end the affair. Over a mouth full of pot roast during their earlier dinner, he had lied. He knew then that they planned to leave the country tonight. She should have asked the travel agent if the tickets were round trip, as she now wondered if they had been planning on returning. For this one, it seemed he'd even risk abandoning the prenuptial.

Out of the corner of her eye, Julie saw her cell phone. It was lying on the sofa cushion next to where she was now seated. She noticed the icon signaling that a text had come in. Slowly, she picked up the phone and read the text.

"Oh my God," she screamed, grabbing her purse and running to her car. She jumped in and shakily backed out of the garage. As she did so, she dialed 911.

"This is Julie Bradford. I received a text from my husband that he is about to commit suicide." Julie gave the 911 operator the address she had been given by the detective of Jennifer Bloom's residence. She had committed it to memory. In fact, she knew exactly where the home was located, as she had driven by only two weeks ago and spotted Grayson's silver Bentley in the drive.

"Please send an ambulance as quickly as possible," she told the operator.

Julie arrived at the house in Detroit just as the ambulance drivers took the second stretcher out of the door. Jumping from the car, she ran to the stretcher. It was Grayson.

"Is he…?" She couldn't bring herself to say the word.

"No, he's still alive, but just barely," The EMT answered. "He's unconscious."

"I'm his wife. I'm riding in the ambulance with him."

The driver looked skeptical but made no move to stop Julie as she climbed into the back of the ambulance. She sat beside her husband and started praying for his life.

It's okay if he doesn't want to stay married to me, but I don't want him dead, she thought. *He's the father of our children, and even though it hasn't been all happiness, we've been together for a long time.*

"God, please don't let him die. Don't take him from me," she said aloud, pushing the thought back that Jennifer had already taken him from her.

It was only a short ride to Bonner Memorial Hospital. TV cameras, always lurking in the area looking for news, were anxious to report on anything significant that they could get their hands on. And the love triangle between a well-known fashion model, a prominent attorney, and his socialite wife was certainly significant and most newsworthy.

At ten o'clock that evening, the report was released.

"This is Greg Bowens, live here at Bonner Memorial Hospital. A short while ago, the well-known supermodel Jennifer Bloom was brought into the emergency room by ambulance. Grayson Bradford, a member of a prestigious law firm in Detroit, along with his wife, socialite Julie Bradford, just arrived in a separate ambulance. The Detroit police are also on the scene. Mr. and Mrs. Walter Bloom, Jennifer's parents, have also arrived and entered the hospital.

"There is no word yet as to what happened here. What we do know is that attorney Grayson Bradford and supermodel Jennifer Bloom were both brought into Bonner Memorial Hospital unconscious via two separate ambulances that arrived at approximately the same time. We will update you as more information is released. Greg Bowens, Channel 4 News, reporting live from Bonner Memorial Hospital." The reporter turned to accept a message from a colleague and turned back to the camera.

"I have just received word that supermodel Jennifer Bloom was pronounced dead five minutes ago. We will continue to keep our viewers abreast of any further developments."

Chapter 25

When Shay arrived home that evening, Jeff was not home yet. She was still tired from her restless night and hoped to sleep without interruption. She sent Jeff a text advising him that she would turn in early.

Shay prepared herself a small salad for dinner. Afraid she would again not be able to sleep, she took a sleeping pill and climbed into bed. She saw that darned police officer in her dream but did not wake up. In fact, it wasn't until morning that she again realized who the handsome man was.

Shay didn't know when Jeff had come to bed last night; it appeared he was already gone this morning. She looked at her phone. Jeff had texted her to say that he had an early morning counseling session and would see her tonight. Shay turned over in bed, stretching out across Jeff's side. She was grateful for sleep, even if she couldn't escape the police officer in her dreams.

Her first appointment was later that afternoon. Shay used the time to throw on some running clothes and take Pam with her for a jog. Looking at her bowl and the cat's, it appeared Jeff had already fed them. Shay's jog turned into a run. Getting rid of nervous energy was always good, she thought. She looked down and saw that Pam was looking a little tired. She was no longer a young puppy. Shay slowed her pace as they reached the dog park.

Returning home, Shay showered, prepared, and ate a light breakfast before heading out to the office.

Chapter 26

The doctor sat watching the newscast. "That should not be," he shouted. They should both be dead, he thought. I must finish the job. He cheated. He does not deserve to live.

He needed to take action. He could not afford to take the chance on Bradford coming out of his unconscious state. According to the newscast, he'd monitored every chance he got, they did not expect him to live. But it was now time to take action to ensure he didn't. It had been four days since Bradford was brought into the hospital. He'd allowed the police and media to move on to something new. It would be easier for the doctor to get to him without interference now.

Rising from his comfortable recliner, he grabbed a bottle of lemonade from where it was always stored on the top shelf in the refrigerator. Opening the loft door and locking it behind him, he quickly walked down the hall of the neat brick building. He'd take care of Bradford first thing tomorrow morning, he decided. It was time.

The next morning, he drove toward the hospital, carefully following all the traffic rules. He certainly did not need to be stopped by any overzealous police officer.

Once inside the hospital, he talked with the nurses who knew and loved him. They seemed to want to talk about their latest patient, who had created quite a stir around the halls of the north wing.

"Good morning, Della," Dr. R. pulled his gray cap further down on his head as he greeted his favorite nurse.

"Good morning, Dr. R. I guess you heard about Jennifer Bloom and her lover being admitted here. It's really too bad that Jennifer died. She was such a beautiful young woman," Della said sadly. "Her parents were as broken up as I'd ever seen anyone. I had worked an extra shift that night, so I was here when they arrived. I hear they had no idea their daughter was carrying on with Mr. Bradford.

"Mrs. Bradford was pretty torn up as well. To find out her husband was having an affair and that he was near death seemed to have really taken a toll on her. I saw her when she entered the hospital and then again as she was leaving with her daughters. She seemed to have aged just in the few hours since she'd come in. It's really too bad," she repeated once again.

"Yes, I agree. It is a shame," Dr. R stated, using the right amount of compassion, he thought. Of course, he did have compassion for Mrs. Bradford, but none for the husband or his mistress.

"Mr. Bradford is still in 430 North, you know. It's one of the few rooms with an exit door from the bathroom leading out to the hall. It's too bad he won't be using it. He may live, but I don't know if his brain will work again. He's been in that coma for a while now.

The drug he took did a lot of damage to his brain and his already weakened heart and liver as well," Della divulged to the doctor.

Dr. R. smiled to himself. He never had to ask for information. The nurses here loved him and assumed sharing medical information with another practicing doctor was fine.

"That is not good news," he said sympathetically. "Keep me updated about his condition, please. I hope he recovers. But in the meantime, I must look in on a few patients," He waved as he moved slowly down the hall.

Della watched him walk away for a moment. She noticed that he seemed to be more bent over than usual today.

Dr. R. headed to the elevator. He got off on the fourth floor and headed in the opposite direction of room 430 North. He stopped to say hello to a couple of nurses standing in the hall and moved slowly until he was out of the nurses' sight. Once he knew he could not be observed, he quickly doubled back down a back hall leading to the rear of room 430 North. Once he got there, he looked around before entering the bathroom that Della had told him about.

Through the bathroom, he quietly entered the room. He disconnected the IV, quickly filling the IV bag with the deadly lemonade. This time, he decided, he'd stay until he knew his victim was dead. He'd hide in the bathroom near the door leading to the hall. Should someone enter the room, he knew he could quickly let himself out.

It took only a matter of minutes for the deadly lemonade to work. Dr. R. quickly checked for a pulse. There was none. He slipped out the back door as the beeping sound blared, alerting the nursing staff that attorney Grayson Bradford was now dead.

By the time the medical staff arrived at Grayson Bradford's room, Dr. R. had already ducked into another patient's room. He had previously checked the patients surrounding Bradford, finding one nearby whom he knew to be in an unconscious state. He ducked in, closing the door behind him. He certainly did not need to explain to any wide-awake client why he was entering their room. He had taken every precaution to ensure he would not be spotted going in or coming out of Bradford's room. Having made it unseen to the nearby room, he knew no one would be coming in. The medical staff were busy in Bradford's room, trying to save his miserable life. Only this time, he had ensured he could not be saved.

Chapter 27

"Good morning, Gwen," Shay said cheerfully. She had finally gotten a good night's sleep without the troubling dreams and that darned police officer's face interrupting them. It had been four nights since she'd slept well. Well, maybe three nights, she corrected herself. She'd gotten home late that night, and Jeff wasn't home. He'd texted her to remind her that he would be volunteering and would probably be later than usual.

Knowing Jeff would not be home, Shay had used that time to see Willa in the county jail. Shay had no difficulty getting in to see the woman, as she had often been asked by the Wayne County Sheriff to look in on some prisoners. Willa had shed tears when finding out her visitor was Shay. Willa obviously had not looked well. Who would, in prison? Shay thought. Even as a practicing psychologist, Shay found no words that could comfort the young woman.

Her situation was bleak. The one ray of comfort for Willa was that her children were being taken care of by her parents. She owed that, she said, to the friendly Commander Crawford, who had seen to it that the kids did not have to be placed in foster care. He had pulled some strings to get them to her parents in Chicago. He'd even paid for their transportation and sent a female police officer with them. Shay flinched at the mention of the police commander's name.

Willa had tried to make light conversation with Shay, mostly about her kids. She was hearing from her mother regularly that the kids were doing fine. They thought their mom was just away for a while. Shay hoped and prayed that would be the case. She said goodbye to Willa, promising to return soon.

That night, Shay had arrived home, finding that even though it was almost eight o'clock, Jeff was still not home. He said he'd phone if he were going to be really late. Shay knew about the difficult suicidal client to whom Jeff was forced to provide additional counseling. Shay had stayed late at the office with Jeff just a night or two ago in case he needed her.

Shay had opened the refrigerator and closed it back. She had not eaten but wasn't hungry. She fed Kimberly Alice, and Pam their dinner. After they'd eaten, Shay walked Pam around the cul-de-sac.

Once that was taken care of, she went straight up to bed. Going to her medicine supply drawer, she looked for some sleeping pills Jeff had brought home a while ago when he was having trouble sleeping. She hoped they weren't expired. She dug around in the drawer where they kept the medications and finally came up with the pills. She checked the expiration date and was glad to find the pills had another several months before they would expire. She popped one into her mouth with some water, undressed, and got into bed, rubbing Pam's and Kimberly Alice's heads before falling off to sleep. She remembered thinking how lucky she was to have Allison, the teenager who lived a couple of doors down, who automatically entered with her key to look in on Kimberly Alice and walk Pam when Shay and Jeff were not home.

The police officer's face still forced his way into her dreams, but surprisingly, when she awoke that morning, she at least felt rested. She didn't even know what time Jeff arrived home.

Chapter 28

This was a good morning. While the police officer's face appeared during the night, Shay did not recall any dreams. And hoped that the darned police officer would soon be out of her system and her dreams for good. She now sat at her desk thinking about her next client.

Immediately after that thought, Shay's private line rang.

"Hello, this is Dr. Jackson," she answered.

"Dr. Jackson, this is Commander Crawford."

Shay froze. She had, of course, recognized the voice.

"We spoke a couple of weeks ago about the Willa and John Raines case," he said in an effort to remind her of who he was.

As if she needed any reminder, she thought. "Yes, Commander. What can I do for you?" Shay asked, hoping her voice sounded normal as well as professional. For a moment, she wondered why her private line and then remembered she had given him her personal card, which had displayed her private number.

"I'd like to connect with you again on a case."

Connect, Sebastian thought, is an understatement. After several sleepless nights, he had come to the scary conclusion that this woman was certainly someone with whom he wanted to connect.

He'd fought the urge as long as he could. He kept repeating over and over that she was married. He had no reason to believe that her marriage was anything but good. And even if it wasn't good, she was still married. But somehow, he sensed her marriage might not be as happy as it could be. He had no facts on which to make that assessment. Just a hunch and, of course, wishful thinking. He now shook his head to clear it. The bottom line was that he reminded himself once again that she was married. That in itself made her off-limits. Her voice pulled him back to the present.

"What case is this, Commander? I can't tell you more about Mrs. Raines than I relayed last time we spoke."

"I understand, Dr. Jackson. This is about another case. Is there someplace we can talk away from your office?" He knew he was treading dangerous waters here, but he couldn't seem to help himself. He held his breath, awaiting her answer.

"Yes," she answered slowly. "If you feel it is absolutely necessary." She knew she was treading dangerous waters but could not seem to help herself.

"Can we meet for lunch at the Whitney?" The Whitney was a popular and elegant restaurant in Detroit located in a beautifully decorated mansion. It was Sebastian's favorite. "We could meet at two o'clock," he suggested, aware that the regular lunch crowd would have cleared out by then. The place would be practically deserted at that hour.

Shay hesitated. "Commander, my last session ends about one-thirty, and I had just planned on picking up a sandwich and then maybe doing some shopping, something I seldom get an opportunity to do."

"If you could meet me there, I promise not to take up too much of your time, and you could have that sandwich there. I could even come along to carry your shopping bags afterward if you'd like." That, he realized, somewhat mortified, had just popped out. He hoped he hadn't offended her with that comment. He would have to get better control of himself when around her. He needed to install some kind of filter so that he would not just blurt out everything he was thinking. He again held his breath as he awaited her answer, scared to death that he had blown it with that comment.

"I will take you up on the sandwich," she simply said without responding further.

At two o'clock on the dot, Sebastian sat at a table in the fine old restaurant feeling as nervous as if he were awaiting a blind date. He hoped he had toned down the brilliant smile that crossed his face when he looked up and saw her walking toward his table. She was dressed smartly in a crisp white cotton shirt, a patent leather belt around her waist, a black wool pencil skirt, a black blazer also made of wool, with the sleeves smartly pushed up, a black patent leather purse, black patent leather high-heeled pumps, and carrying a black and white houndstooth cape. Her dark thick hair was pulled back and cinched at her nape with a large black bow. Yesterday it had barely reached forty degrees; however, today, the sporadic temperature, typical of Michigan weather, had actually jumped to almost sixty-five degrees. Her outfit was perfect both for the weather and for him, he thought. And evidently for others as well. There were only a few lingering from the earlier lunch crowd. Two of the men seemed to have their eyes on Shay as she walked. Sebastian was aware that she struck a tall impressive pose as she moved.

He stood as she approached the table. Pulling out a chair for her, he could almost feel the goofy grin he now had on his face. He, however, need not have worried, as Shay avoided looking at his face as she took her seat.

Her voice when she spoke was professional. "Commander," she said, "How can I possibly help you this time?" Her tone was impatient.

Sebastian was taken aback. He hesitated before responding. "I sincerely apologize," he said softly.

Shay finally looked into his soft gray eyes. She could tell that her words had come off as a rebuff. He appeared hurt. "I'm sorry, Commander," she said softly, "if my comment came out too harsh. I will, of course, help you in any way I can." She smiled. "I just don't see how that could be."

She realized that she had no reason to feel anger toward this man. She was genuinely sorry that her words had sounded harsh. It wasn't his fault that she felt whatever she was feeling for him. Nor was it his fault that she agreed to this meeting when she really should have declined or at least insisted that it be held in a more professional setting, like the police station. Yes, she thought, if he insisted upon meeting again, she'd do it at his office. She was sure she'd feel more relaxed there. Her face abruptly clouded at the thought that maybe there would be no other meetings. Damn, she thought, are you losing your mind?

Sebastian, carefully watching the changes in her facial expressions, felt anxiety. Had he done something wrong? Of course, he had. He should never have asked her here as if they were on a date. What was wrong with him? Was he losing his mind?

Shay smiled and attempted to focus on resting her coat on the chair Sebastian had pulled out. Ignoring the fact that he had expected her to sit closer to him, she had taken the chair as far away from him as possible.

Sebastian smiled and exhaled. "I admit I should have met with you at your office, but …" He didn't know how to complete the sentence. But what? he thought to himself. I want you so badly that I can't stand to be near you, yet when I'm near you, I can't stand it because

I can't touch or kiss you…what? Get a grip, he told himself. Pull it together now.

All the while, Shay just sat watching him as if she could read his thoughts. Maybe, as if she had the same thoughts, her quietly looking at him unnerved him even more. Pull it together; he thought to himself more strongly this time. What would give you the idea that she feels anything for you? She certainly hasn't said or done anything that would give you that crazy idea. Sebastian's thoughts ran rampant. He physically gave himself a small shake before speaking.

Shay watched the changes in his facial expressions and then lowered her head.

"Dr. Jackson," he started. He cleared his throat. "Do you mind if I dispense with the 'Doctor'?" he asked, feeling so close to her.

"Of course, Commander. The Doctor title is much more important to my husband than to me. You can call me Shay if you'd like. After all, I'm not a medical doctor. I have a Ph.D. Honestly, using the title has always made me a little uncomfortable," she admitted.

"Shay," Sebastian said and paused. Just using her first name brought on other feelings. Feelings he didn't want to be exposed. Clearing his throat once again, he continued. "There have been some additional occurrences recently. Do you know a couple by the name of Bradford?" he asked. His voice had almost returned to normal.

"Yes. I do." Shay volunteered no further information.

"Are you also familiar with Jennifer Bloom?"

"Yes." Again Shay offered no further information.

"It has come to our attention that you provided counseling to Mr. and Mrs. Grayson Bradford."

Again, no comment from Shay. However, she did not deny it.

"Were you aware that both Jennifer Bloom and Grayson Bradford died?"

Shay's eyes widened. "Oh, my God. No, I'm afraid I don't often get an opportunity to watch the news. That's terrible. I must contact Mrs. Bradford with my condolences. He seemed quite healthy the last time I saw him."

Sebastian could not help but focus on her full sensuous lips as she spoke. His heart beat faster. He couldn't believe he was aroused. He hadn't felt this way since the last time he saw her, he thought. He had to shake it off.

Sebastian, forcing himself back to reality, noticed that Shay was shaken. He briefly touched her hand, which was now ice cold. "Would you like something warm to drink?" he asked. When she nodded, Sebastian summoned the waiter.

"Tea or coffee?" he asked.

“Tea,” she said, still a little shaky.

Sebastian watched her for a moment. She looked so fragile. He wanted to take her into his arms.

“I know this is a shock. I’m sorry to have to be the one to tell you. I was hoping you’d already heard it on the news.”

The waiter brought the tea. Shay squeezed lemon in. Her hand shook as she picked up the cup and took a sip. The warm liquid seemed to calm her somewhat.

“I had to have this official conversation with you. It becomes more than a coincidence when two people seeking help from your practice die under questionable circumstances within days of each other.”

“Questionable circumstances?” Shay frowned. “What do you mean questionable circumstances, Commander? I thought John Raines died from some infection, and how has Grayson Bradford’s death led you to believe there were questionable circumstances?”

“He died from the same lethal medication that caused John Raines’s death.”

“Couldn’t both just have been a mistake on the hospital’s part? Maybe a wrong medication dosage, something.” Shay’s eyes pleaded with Sebastian to tell her it was all an accident, a mistake.

He could not.

The investigation was not complete, but they knew enough to

suspect that both people were murdered. He looked once again at Shay. He didn't give a damn as he covered her hand with his to try to comfort her.

Shay did not move. She looked up at Sebastian. Their eyes locked. Suddenly, Shay stood, almost knocking her tea over.

"I can't do this. This was a mistake," she said. "I should not have come here. I'm sorry, I have to go." She picked up her cape and purse and ran out of the restaurant. Once outside, she was totally embarrassed. She saw Sebastian through the window. Initially, he sat still, too shocked to move. Then, he reached into his pocket to put money on the table before running after her. The valet had not yet parked her car. The keys were still in the ignition. Shay jumped in and sped away. She had no idea what was happening to her, but she knew it was not right. She could not see this man again. If police business had to be conducted, it would have to be at the police station, or better yet; he could just send someone else to interview her. Meeting at the restaurant was a mistake.

"You knew that before you agreed to come," the voice in her head shouted.

Chapter 29

Shay drove around for at least an hour, unaware of her surroundings and still unnerved. Finally, she dialed her best friend, Saundra.

Please pick up, Shay pleaded silently. She needed the comfort and advice of her level-headed friend. They had been friends for over twenty years. Saundra was looking forward to celebrating her fifty-sixth birthday on April 8th of this year, and since Shay's forty-second birthday was April 10th, they had planned their Hawaii trip to celebrate both birthdays.

The two Aries women had always gotten along well. Even with the age difference, they were the best of friends. They had been friends since Shay was twenty and Saundra thirty-four. They had both briefly worked for the Detroit Police Department, and so had their friend Gwen. Shay had been a twenty-year-old social worker, studying at the time to obtain her MSW degree, while Saundra already had her MSW.

Hanging out her shingle as a psychologist had come later for Shay. They had worked well together, dealing with rape victims. They lunched together and shared everything. Saundra was Shay's maid of honor at her wedding, and Shay was Saundra's oldest son's godmother. Gwen was also in the wedding party and made sure the flowers were supplied. Whenever Shay needed to work something out in her head, Saundra and Gwen were the two friends whom she confided in.

Shay desperately wanted to talk to Saundra, so she tried calling her, but the phone went unanswered. However, she kept ringing her. Saundra finally answered on the fourth ring.

"Hey, friend, how are you?"

"I'm so glad you answered. I was about to hang up, and I really need to talk with you."

"I was on the phone with both my sisters, Christina and Sasha, and it was difficult to get off with both of them talking at the same time." Saundra laughed. "Family chitchat is all. But what's wrong?" she asked, more serious now.

"Saundra, I've just messed up everything!"

"I'm sure you haven't messed up anything, let alone everything. No matter what has happened, and I'm sure you'll tell me about it, everything can't be messed up. And whatever is messed up, you or both you and I can fix. It's as simple as that," Saundra stated calmly. She had a knack for being able to calm Shay down when she needed it.

"Okay, so let's have it."

"I really hope you aren't busy because I need to meet someplace. This is not a phone conversation. I just made a complete fool of myself."

"I refuse to believe it's that bad," Saundra said softly. "Where would you like to meet? I'd invite you here, but James and Gentry are both here. I don't expect you'd like to talk in front of them."

Gentry was Saundra's son, and no, Shay didn't want to talk about this in front of James or Gentry, or anyone else for that matter. She wasn't even sure she wanted to share it with Gwen. She was that embarrassed by her dramatic actions.

Calming down a little, Shay said, "Well, maybe it isn't quite as bad as I initially stated, but it is pretty bad. And no, I don't want to talk in front of James or Gentry."

Remembering she had run out of the restaurant before even finishing the tea she'd ordered, she asked, "How about we meet at Savannah Blue downtown? I'm starved."

The restaurant was conveniently located close to both of their homes. Shay could picture a comfortable table where she could discuss her dilemma and be cozy at the same time.

"Sounds like a winner. Where are you now? I can meet you at the restaurant. Just give me a time."

"I left Detroit about twenty minutes ago, and I'm on Interstate 75 now. I was just driving aimlessly. I can meet you in about twenty minutes if that gives you enough time," Shay said.

"That's perfect."

"I'm so glad you aren't at the animal shelter today," Shay said, referring to Saundra's new career. Saundra loved animals so much that she went back to school and now ran an animal shelter, where she offered affordable health insurance for pets but treated all animals, whether their owners could afford to pay or not. Her staff consisted of veterinarians, who offered their services for free, volunteer dog walkers, and dog trainers. She also sold healthy foods for all pets.

Only Saundra, Shay thought, would have been able to pull all the services a pet needs together under one roof. Saundra's husband, James, who loved pets as much as she did, was in perfect agreement to tapping their savings to open the shelter. The money was a good investment, and the shelter was thriving.

"You know I'm always here for you," Saundra responded.

"I'd find time to meet you. Luckily, I have good help now, so I don't go into the shelter nearly as often as I used to. Now I only go to pet my favorite fur babies. They actually look for me, and the wags of their tails let me know they are so glad I stopped in to pet them. It's a really great feeling," she giggled. "Now, back to the business at hand. You sound as if you really need to talk. If I arrive in the restaurant first, I'll grab us a table."

"Perfect. See you there," Shay responded.

Chapter 30

Shay pulled up to the restaurant precisely twenty minutes later, as promised. She hadn't realized that in her quest to get away from that darned police officer, she had driven so far. She recognized her friend's white Ford Super Duty truck in the lot. Saundra loved that truck. Using it, she was able to transport any number of animals, including horses, in an attached trailer. Besides, she'd confessed to Shay; the extra-large truck made her feel powerful. Shay smiled. She could always count on her friend. They'd named the truck the White Beast.

She hurried inside, immediately spotting Saundra waving to her from the table. The two women hugged.

Saundra asked, "So, what's the story?" She was eager to find out what could be upsetting her friend.

"I know we haven't talked much lately beyond the conversation we had about our upcoming trip, but you have to know some really crazy stuff has been going on. As a matter of fact, you could say deadly stuff," Shay responded.

"What do you mean?" Saundra said, wrinkling her brow. "Please stop the drama, Shay, and give it to me straight."

"Okay, first I counsel a couple, and the woman ends up stabbing the man, and she ends up in jail. Then they release her, he dies, and they arrest her again. Initially, I was told he died from some hospital infection. Then later, I was told that wasn't it at all. It was from suspicious circumstances, to quote the police."

Saundra opened her mouth to speak, but no words came out. Finally, she uttered,

"Police? And is there more?"

"Yes. Then I counseled a couple who was involved in a love triangle, and the mistress and the man both died. Again, suspicious circumstances. I finally caught up on the news and read that they both committed suicide. So, it looks as if people I counsel are expiring."

"Oh, my God. No wonder you're so frazzled." Saundra interrupted. "Wait, you mentioned a love triangle. I heard it on the news. Are you talking about that Grayson guy and the model Jennifer something?"

"You know I don't talk about my clients, even to you. But that's still not all," she said.

"Did someone else die?" Saundra asked, wide-eyed.

"No, no one died. It's…." Shay paused, not able to go on. The tears slid down her face.

Saundra stood and came around the table to comfort her friend.

"What's wrong, sweetie? Why are you crying?" she asked as she handed Shay some tissues she had quickly fished out of her purse.

"I've never seen you like this. You're always so pulled together. You know I envy that."

Shay blew her nose. Still sniffing, she told Saundra about Sebastian Crawford.

"I've never felt this way about anyone, not even Jeff," She said, ashamed. "And that's not all. Just a couple of hours ago, I embarrassed myself even more. The police officer asked me to meet him at the Whitney to discuss the case. He innocently put his hand over mine. I looked into those soft gray eyes of his, and suddenly I couldn't breathe. I knew the way I was feeling was wrong, and I had to get away from him. I had to get away that instant."

By this time, Shay was calmer. Sharing with her friend always made things better. She smiled as she said,

"Do you remember the old movies we used to watch together, where the leading lady would become upset in a restaurant, maybe because the guy gave her earrings instead of the engagement ring she had expected or something equally stupid, and she would run out of the restaurant?"

"Sure," Saundra responded, puzzled for a moment. "But what does that have to do with…." She stopped. "Omigod. Are you going to tell me you ran out of the restaurant for real?"

"That's exactly what I'm going to tell you," Shay said, lowering her eyes. "I didn't think. I just ran out. I looked back, and he was coming after me. I had only been in the restaurant a few moments, so the valet didn't even have time to put my car away. So, I jumped in it and sped away. I didn't even pay the valet. How's that for dramatics?" she said, giving a short laugh. "I am so embarrassed. Now I guess he'll put out a warrant for my arrest for fleeing without paying. And you are right. You know I'm not usually a drama queen. But this, this thing I'm feeling, whatever it is has me acting so out of character. I dream about him at night, when I can sleep at all, that is. And the guilt. I feel so guilty. You know I have a wonderful husband. How could I possibly do this?"

"It's okay. I'm sure you're safe from that scenario, and this is not the worst thing that could ever happen," her friend consoled her. "So, let's just think about what's going on and try to figure out how to handle it. Take some deep breaths. And you haven't done anything, so save the guilt. So, again, just calm down."

Shay heaved a big sigh, trying to slow her breathing.

"Saundra, I don't know what to do. I can't shake the feelings I have for this guy. He's in my dreams. He's in my thoughts. I love Jeff. He is so good to me. How could I feel like this about another man?" she ended sadly.

"It's probably just temporary insanity, and it will pass. Besides, you don't have to see him anymore unless, of course, someone else you counsel dies." Saundra couldn't help but throw that in with a little laugh.

Shay glared at her. "First of all, there is nothing remotely funny about this. I wish it were that easy. I know I don't have to see him in person. But I just told you," she said impatiently, "even when I don't see him, he invades my dreams. I think about him constantly."

Saundra reached out and squeezed Shay's arm. "Sweetie, I know you would never cheat on Jeff, so this will have to pass. There is no other answer. You will have to get a grip. You don't have a choice. Just think about our romantic Hawaii trip. I promise if you just focus on that, this will pass."

"You really think so?" Shay asked.

"Yes, I do. But I have something to share. I didn't want to interrupt you, so I kept quiet. But you know, because Arnie works for the police department, he always brings officers home for one of his mom's home-cooked meatloaf or lamb chop dinners. So, as it turns out, Sebastian has been to the house numerous times. Arnie thought he needed some TLC after his wife died, and boy, did he ever. He was in horrible shape. James and I got to know him quite well during that time. The last time I saw him, he was much better. He had been devastated by his wife's death. I was concerned he would never recover."

"Wow, that is so sad. You never mentioned him before. I wasn't aware that his wife had died. What happened?"

"Automobile accident. It happened just a block away from their home, and after they'd had some kind of argument. I sense that he felt as if it were his fault for the longest time," Saundra said as she picked up the menu. "Let's order some food, continue our conversation, and then put it out of our minds and go shopping for our Hawaiian wardrobe. Agreed?"

"Agreed," Shay responded, following Saundra's lead and picking up her menu.

"And guess what else?" she went on. "We'll drop your car off at your house. I'll drive, and once we're done with our shopping at the Somerset Mall, we can head to Bar Louie at the Great Lakes Crossing Mall, and you can have as many drinks as you'd like. You can drink until that guy's face is blurry. I insist." She laughed. "Then I'll drive you home."

Shay was able to laugh as well. "That, my friend, sounds like a plan," she said, grateful that Saundra referred to him as that guy without using his name. "Let's order," Shay said, feeling slightly more uplifted than earlier. Shopping at two malls, dinner, and drinks can uplift anyone.

Chapter 31

Returning home after her day out with Saundra, Shay felt almost normal except for having too much to drink. Shay rarely drank, so her three frozen daiquiris put her over the top.

She did manage to text Jeff and ask him to pick up whatever he wanted for dinner. Once she'd done that, she climbed the stairs, got undressed, and fell into bed. For the first time ever, she abandoned the nightly teeth-brushing routine she religiously practiced. She slept peacefully and soundly.

When she awoke the next morning, she discovered she had a slight headache, but her head was clear where the police officer was concerned. She would not see him again. That was that. She would, as Saundra had suggested, focus on their Hawaii trip.

Shay showered and dressed. She heard Jeff downstairs and smelled coffee. After a while, the smell of bacon wafted up. Shay dressed a little faster so that she could get downstairs to her loving husband and the coffee and bacon as she smiled to herself.

"Good morning, darling," Jeff said. "You seemed to be sound asleep by the time I got in last night. You must have had some day."

"Yes, I guess I did," she said, telling him about lunch, shopping, and Bar Louie with Saundra. "I picked up some great bikinis, sandals, and sun dresses for Hawaii. I found sandals and a couple of pairs of shorts for you. I'll do more shopping for you the next time," she promised.

"Thanks, that was kind of you, but I really don't need anything," he responded as he touched her face lightly and planted a firm kiss on her lips. "By the way, I met your Commander Crawford. Yesterday afternoon, he came to the office looking for you a little before three. He seemed kind of upset that you weren't there but finally settled for questioning me about the Raines woman and about Bradford and that model he was cheating with."

"What did you tell him?" she asked.

"What could I tell him? They were your cases, not mine. I told him we had discussed them as we discuss everything, but I had never spoken with or met either client."

Shay felt strangely uncomfortable and noted Jeff's emphasis on "Your Commander Crawford" and "We discuss everything."

Stop reading so much into Jeff's comments, she told herself. There is absolutely no way that Jeff could have any idea about my feelings or whatever they were." She sadly acknowledged that she wasn't quite sure what she was feeling.

She loved Jeff. There was no doubt about that and absolutely no chance that she could care for someone else, she told herself for the zillionth time. Shay was startled as she heard Jeff calling her name.

"Shay to earth. Where are you, darling? Are you okay?" Jeff asked.

"I'm sorry," Shay said hurriedly. She hadn't realized she had probably been staring into space. "I've got a lot on my mind with all that's happened. What were you saying?"

"I said that after grilling me, he asked if he might wait for you. I told him I didn't think you would be returning to the office and that you probably didn't have any more to tell him."

The strangeness returned. Shay felt a chill. Jeff didn't know she would not be returning to the office. She wondered why he would say something like that to Sebastian. She had not texted Jeff until she arrived home that evening. Shay said nothing.

"You look a little flushed, darling. Are you okay?" Jeff asked again.

"I'm fine, just maybe a little too much to drink with Saundra last night."

"Sit down and have some breakfast. I thought I'd pamper you this morning."

Shay's appetite suddenly disappeared. She drank a cup of coffee and picked at the breakfast of bacon, eggs, and toast Jeff put before her.

"I'd better get to the office," she finally said. "Thanks for breakfast. I'm sorry, I guess I'm not very hungry."

Before leaving, she helped Jeff clear the table and put the dirty dishes in the dishwasher.

"Are you sure you're okay?" Jeff asked. "The last time I remember you losing your appetite was when you first fell in love with me."

Shay looked up, startled by his remark. "I'm fine. It's probably the drinks from last night," she muttered again.

"What time is your first client?" Jeff inquired.

"Uh, eleven forty-five, but I just need to go over some notes," she stuttered.

She kissed Jeff on the forehead, quickly got into her coat, and left. Once she was a couple of blocks from her office, Shay spotted Jeff behind her. It was hard to miss the large black Navigator he drove. She could see him clearly once he turned into the Renaissance Center parking lot just a few seconds after she had. That's strange, she thought.

"Why didn't he mention that he was leaving only a few minutes after her?"

Shay scolded herself once more. "Stop it," she said out loud. "Are you so damned guilty that you've now become paranoid? Stop imagining things."

Once Shay arrived at the office, she waited for Jeff to enter. He did not. She knew he was behind her. Maybe he had another appointment out of the office, she reasoned. She tried to put it out of her mind.

As she hung up her coat and spoke with Gwen, Sam exited his office.

"Shay, you are just the person I need to see. How long will you be in the office today?" he asked.

"I'll be in the entire day. Why do you ask?"

"I received a call from Commander Crawford from the police department this morning. He wants to stop by to see me. I can't imagine why. I told him on the phone that I don't know any more about those two cases than what you told me. But he insisted he needed to stop by anyway. He said he would be able to kill two birds with one stone, as he needed to see you as well."

Shay was glad Sam was busy looking at some paperwork and not looking directly at her. She knew there was a panicked look on her face. She tried to smile as she asked,

"What time was he planning on coming?"

"I believe he's on his way now."

No sooner were Sam's words out than the door to the suite opened, and in walked the Commander. To Shay's horror, Jeff walked in right behind him.

Shay offered a weak hello and walked toward her office. Sebastian placed a hand on her arm to slow her.

“Dr. Jackson, do you think I might have a word with you once I’ve spoken with Dr. Roberts?”

“Well, I have a client coming in, and I’m pretty busy today, Commander….”

Shay was interrupted by Jeff.

“Darling, I thought you told me your first client wasn’t until later this morning. We don’t want to give the Commander the feeling that we aren’t being cooperative. I think you should speak with him.” Jeff smiled at both the Commander and Shay.

Shay had only heard Jeff sound so controlling on one previous occasion. A man Shay had gone to high school with whom she had not seen in years had hugged her after she and Jeff ran into him in a department store. Jeff actually invited, no insisted he come to dinner with them. The tone of his voice at that time was much like it was today. She remembered that Jeff had pretty much drilled her friend about his previous relationship with Shay, even though they had been no more than sixteen years old. Jeff wanted to know if they had dated. Shay got the impression that when the response to his question was no, he had not believed the answer. Shay couldn’t imagine what had gotten into Jeff.

Aloud Shay simply responded to her husband’s comment. “You are right, darling,”

Turning to the Commander, "When you are ready to speak with me, just have Gwen buzz me."

"Thank you, Dr. Jackson," Sebastian said.

Shay sat rigid in her office. She didn't know exactly what to make of Jeff's behavior. She didn't want to speak with the Commander. She sat twisting her wedding ring until the buzz of the phone scared her back to reality. Her stomach was in knots. Jumping at the sound, she grabbed the phone.

"Yes, Gwen?" she responded. Why can't this buzz be to tell me that the Commander got a phone call and he had to leave? Doesn't he have other cases? Aren't police officers always on call? Can't they be called off one case and to another needing more urgent attention? Shay's thoughts ran rampant in her head.

"Commander Crawford would like to speak with you now," Gwen said the dreaded words.

Shay knew there was nothing more for her to do. There was no escape.

"Send him in, please."

Shay braced herself.

"Good morning, Commander," she said without looking up.

All of a sudden, it seemed that Shay had a flurry of notes she had to write at just that moment. She began to write with a flourish.

Sebastian walked boldly over to her desk and put his hand over hers, stopping the obviously nervous movement. He could tell how tormented she seemed to be. He vowed at that moment to try to stay away from her. He could feel the synergy between them. He knew his instincts were not wrong. She wanted him as much as he wanted her. But he also knew she was not the kind of woman who would cheat on her husband. And before now, he had not been the kind of man who would pursue a married woman.

She had let his hand stay on hers longer than he had any right to hope she would. Finally, she slid her hand from under his and stood. She put her head down, but not before he saw the tears forming in her eyes.

Without thinking, Sebastian enfolded her in his arms.

"Please don't cry, Shay. I'm done," he promised. "I never intended to make you miserable. I can't stand to see you cry. I only wanted to love you," he said honestly. "I can't bear seeing you this way. I apologize."

He felt his eyes tear up as well. He actually felt pain for her. What am I doing to her? He thought as he held her for one more brief moment.

Neither heard the door to her office open and quietly close.

Sebastian's footsteps were heavy as he left the building. He could have sworn that he saw Jeff Jackson's office door crack and the man watching him as he closed the door to her office. Sebastian quickly walked away from the only woman other than Sara he felt he could love forever.

Chapter 32

Sebastian knew his feelings for a woman he had seen only three times made very little sense. How could this be logical thinking? Had he lost all of his police training? He was trained to be logical and not rely on emotion. How could he love someone he didn't know? Yet, he felt he did know her. He knew how she thought; now, he even knew how she felt in his arms. He knew how much integrity she had. He knew she would never leave her husband for him. He knew she would never carry on a sordid affair with him. But he also knew, without a doubt, that she wanted to. And he, well, he definitely wanted to. There was just no ignoring that.

The tears in her eyes confirmed her feelings. But they also tore at his heart. He had made one woman miserable because he would not give up a career he loved. He had no intention of making another miserable because he would not give her up.

He consoled himself, knowing that he certainly had enough to do to keep himself busy and his mind off her. He had relieved the detectives who were initially handling the Raines and Bradford cases, having decided to take them on himself. He now knew that to be a mistake, but it was too late to modify. Since he hadn't selected a partner to work the cases with him, that meant all the legwork was on him. And that was fine, he thought. Rubye, of course, would help with any research he required. Officially he would partner with Rubye.

Chapter 33

He swung into the Bonner Memorial Hospital parking lot. Walking into the building, he went over to the registration desk.

"I'm Commander Sebastian Crawford," he told the older woman seated at the desk.

He noticed that her perfectly coiffed silver hair was beautiful. She reminded him of his mom, to whom he remembered he owed a phone call.

"How can I help you, Commander Crawford?" she said, smiling at him.

"Ms. Stafford," he said, repeating the name he saw on her metal name tag. Sebastian knew people were always more responsive and receptive when you used their names. "I am here to investigate two cases." He gave the receptionist the names, and she directed him.

Sebastian walked down the long hall to the B elevators as he had been instructed. He first wanted to speak with the nursing staff who had taken care of Mr. Raines and Mr. Bradford at the time of their deaths.

At the third-floor north nursing station, he asked for Barbara Troy. He waited only moments before nurse Troy emerged from a patient's room and stood before Sebastian. She appeared to be a little less than five feet tall. She looked up at Sebastian, who stood six feet, six inches tall.

"Is there someplace we might sit and talk?" he asked.

She led him to a small room off the nursing station.

"How can I help you, Commander?" she asked.

"I understand you were in charge when Mr. John Raines was on this floor?" he asked.

"I was the head nurse, Commander. However, I had an emergency that day, and I called Della Perry to work overtime in my place. Even though it was her off day, she agreed to cover for me. If you hurry, you might be able to catch her before her shift ends. She is currently taking care of some business on the second floor. You'll find her at the second-floor nurses' station."

"Thank you kindly, Ms. Troy. You've been very helpful." Sebastian tipped his hat cordially. The nurse smiled after him.

Rather than wait for the elevator, Sebastian hurried down the one flight of stairs. Opening the staircase door, he almost ran into a pleasant-looking woman. He spied her name tag and knew that she was the nurse he needed to see.

Before he could speak, she reached out to him. Her curly mixed gray hair bounced as she shook his hand.

"I'm Della," she said. "I just received a page letting me know that a commander with the police department would be looking for me. I'm going to make a bet," she smiled, "that you are just such a commander."

"I am Commander Crawford, Ms.—"

"Della Perry, but call me Della," she interrupted. "Everyone does." She directed him to an office off the nursing station resembling the one he had briefly been in upstairs.

"How can I help you, Commander?"

"I understand that you were on duty the night Mr. John Raines died."

"I was, indeed. I had just checked on him about thirty minutes before it happened. Everything was fine."

"Was there anything strange that you might have noticed in or around his room?" Sebastian asked.

"No, not that I noticed," she answered.

"Did he have any visitors?"

"No."

"How about his wife? Did she visit him?"

"I've never seen his wife except on the news when they took her away from the emergency room in handcuffs."

"Can you take me to the room he occupied?"

Della led Sebastian to the elevator and pressed three as she got on. They got off and walked to room 328. He carefully looked around the room and the bathroom but saw nothing unusual.

"I'm afraid I haven't been very helpful." Della looked at Sebastian with disappointment showing on her face.

"You did fine, Della," Sebastian assured her. "There is one more thing that you might be able to help me with. I understand you were working when Mr. Grayson Bradford died?"

"Yes, I was."

"Can you take me to his room?"

Della led Sebastian back to the elevator and pressed four. They stepped off and walked down the hall to room 430 North.

"This is it," she said, opening the door and showing him in.

Sebastian looked around the room. "Is that the bathroom?" he asked, looking at the closed door.

"Yes, it is."

Sebastian walked over and opened the door. Spotting the exit door, he opened it and looked into the hall.

"Mr. Raines's room did not have an exit door leading to the hall from the bathroom. Do other rooms have one?"

"Actually, this is the only room in the entire hospital that has this door. I have no idea why."

"Is it kept locked from the inside?"

"No, it is kept unlocked as far as I know," she responded.

"Who else would be aware of such a door?"

"I don't know, everyone who works here, I guess?" Della frowned, and her eyes widened.

"What have you remembered?" Sebastian asked quickly.

"Nothing important, I don't think, but I did mention that door to someone."

"Who did you mention it to?"

"Well, to Dr. R."

"What's his full name?"

"I really don't know. We just call him Dr. R."

"Can you check the records of the doctors on staff and get me a name?"

"I'm afraid I can't. He is a doctor who visits here often but isn't actually on staff."

"Surely, he has medical privileges here, so there must be some record showing his entire name." Sebastian looked hopeful.

"No, I don't think he does," Della said nervously. "Have I done something wrong, mentioning the door to him? He's just a nice old man who comes in and out of the hospital and makes pop calls on people. He's harmless."

"Do you remember when you mentioned the door to him?"

"I think it was when Mr. Bradford occupied the room. The Bradford-Jennifer Bloom thing was juicy news to everyone. So, I kind of remember talking to Dr. R. about it."

"Who are the other patients he visits?"

Della thought for a moment. "I actually never noticed which patients he visited. I usually talked with him in the lobby or on the elevator. I'm sorry, Commander, I just never noticed him in any patient's room."

"Can you tell me what he looks like?" Sebastian asked.

"We call him the gray man. He's about five feet six, I think." She paused. "Actually, I don't exactly know how tall he is. You see, he walks bent over. He could be taller. He always wears a gray jacket and gray cap pulled down over the side of his face. He wears gray shoes and always carries a gray bag."

"A doctor's bag?" Sebastian asked.

"No, it's like a tote bag. I think it's made out of some burlap material. Oh, and he walks with a cane, and he has a dark red birthmark on the side of his face."

"Have you seen him since Mr. Bradford's death?"

"Actually, I don't think I have. No, I'm sure I have not seen him," she said. "One more thing, Commander. I had checked on Mr. Bradford and noticed that the IV bag was about a third full, so I knew I had to return shortly to refill it. But before I was scheduled to return, the alarms on his equipment went off. When I went in, I didn't immediately notice that the bag was fuller than the way I had left it. I first thought that maybe another nurse had done it. However, our nurses have strict orders that they are only to work with those patients to whom they have been assigned."

"Anyway, I dismissed that in lieu of taking care of the emergency before me. Mr. Bradford was not breathing, and he had no pulse. The appropriate staff was there, and the doctor on duty attempted to revive him but was not successful."

"It wasn't until the next day that I remembered about the bag and told the doctor. The coroner asked to see me. The doctor had reported what I'd told him. I retrieved the bag, which was still in the room. It smelled just like lemonade to me. That's all I know, Commander. You'd have to see the coroner and the doctor for more information."

"One more question, Della. When you got to Mr. Bradford's room that morning, did you see this Dr. R. anywhere near the room? Maybe in the hall or anyplace?"

"No, I'm afraid I didn't see him. But you can't possibly think that nice old man had anything to do with either Mr. Raines's or Mr. Bradford's deaths?"

"Thank you, Della," Sebastian said without responding. He handed the nurse his card. "If you should remember anything else, please give me a call. If Dr. R. should come in again, call me immediately. I'd just like to speak with him. Are you sure there is no one in the hospital who might know more about him—a full name, maybe? How about what his medical specialty is?"

"I'll call you if I think of or find anyone who might know more. However, I think I talked to him more than anyone," Della said. It was obvious she was now feeling a little nervous about her interactions with Dr. R.

"What about his vehicle? Did you ever happen to see him arrive in a car?"

"No, sorry," Della said. "But we do have valet parking. Maybe the attendants parked his car or at least noticed him arriving in the parking lot."

Leaving the hospital, Sebastian was hopeful. Even though he did not know who this Dr. R. was, he at least had a lead. The lemonade smell was also a connection to Raines. He remembered the coroner saying that Mr. Raines had consumed lemonade.

Sebastian's interview with the valet and parking staff turned up nothing concrete. The woman who manned the booth where cars entered couldn't recall seeing anyone fitting Sebastian's description of the elusive Dr. R.

Chapter 34

Returning to his office, Sebastian sat down, rubbing his eyes. Sensing movement, he uncovered one eye and saw his busybody assistant, Rubye, standing at his shoulder.

"Can I help you?" Sebastian said unenthusiastically.

"You could if you would get more sleep. You were doing well, but now you look like something the cat dragged in. Just look at you." Rubye put her hand under his chin. "Your eyes are blood red, and I'll bet you haven't eaten."

"Your bet would be correct. But it is also none of your business," he snapped, irritated at her intrusion. "And for your information, I'm just not hungry. I'm not a kid, and I eat and sleep when I want to."

"It is my business," Rubye said, ignoring his mood. "I was put on this earth to take care of you, and I suggest you deal with it instead of being annoyed. You know your moodiness will not make me go away." Rubye stood her ground.

She didn't want to tell him that his deceased wife, Sara, had always relied on her to take care of Sebastian at work. And take care of him, she intended to do. She couldn't care less how irritated he got. Taking one last look at him, she walked away and headed to the vending machine, returning with a chicken salad sandwich and a bottle of water.

"Eat it," she said, plopping them down in front of him.

Sebastian started to laugh. She was never going to leave him alone. He ate the sandwich and drank the water. All the while, she stood beside him with her hands on her hips. Anything, he thought, to get her to take her hands off her hips and maybe even get her out of his office. That would be better. He willed her to leave his office and return to her own. But no such luck.

When he was finished, she took away the empty bottle and the paper from the sandwich. Returning, she asked, "What have you been up to? You've been out of the office all day, and you haven't checked in." Sebastian didn't miss the accusing note in her tone.

"I've been doing my job, if you must know. I interviewed the nurse at the hospital where the Raines and Bradford guys spent their last days. I also spoke with Mrs. Bradford and Mr. and Mrs. Bloom, Jennifer Bloom's parents. And I spoke with Dr. Jeff Jackson and Dr. Sam Roberts. They are both partners at the Relationship Fix Group, Inc." Sebastian purposely didn't mention Shay.

"Did you come up with anything?" she asked.

"Maybe." He relayed what he'd learned to his assistant. "Mrs. Bradford received a text from her husband telling her they were going to commit suicide. Mr. and Mrs. Bloom, however, did not receive anything from their daughter. I also spoke with Jennifer Bloom's husband and with the nurse at Bonner Memorial. Apparently, there is an older man, Dr. R., who is all they know him by. He is not on staff there, and he has no medical privileges but seems to come and go often. He was there the days that both Raines and Bradford were there. The nurse happened to mention to this Dr. R that there was a back door leading to the hall from Bradford's bathroom. And that is the sum total of what I know about this mysterious Dr. R."

"Well, it's a lead. Maybe he will return to the hospital, and she will call you."

"Let's hope," he said. "Can you get me the coroner's report on both of the victims?"

"Right away."

When Rubye returned with the reports, Sebastian had one more thought.

"Rubye," he said quietly, "I need you to do something for me. You can help me with this investigation. Please call Dr. Shay Jackson and ask her a question for me. While you're doing that, I'm going to review these files."

Sebastian had promised her he would stay away. He would not break his promise by making contact with her, but he needed to clear up something that had occurred to him.

“Ask Dr. Jackson if she knows of any other of her clients that have recently died, of natural causes or otherwise. And if we need a warrant to get the names, we can do that. Just tell her that you are now handling the investigation.”

“Am I now handling it?” she said, giving him an odd look. When he did not answer her question, she didn’t push further.

His assistant was really cooperative when she wasn’t getting on his case about his sleep, his health, his food intake, and his life in general, he thought.

Sebastian closed his eyes. Something else was bothering him. He was pretty sure Shay’s husband was watching him as he left her office this morning.

Chapter 35

George looked at his cell phone. The caller ID showed that it was the Doc.

“Hello, Doc. What’s up?” George knew there must be something important going on. The Doc rarely communicated with him by phone. Normally they arranged to meet at the loft every Thursday evening. That had been their schedule for months.

“I need to see you earlier than planned. I’ve got something urgent I need you to do.”

“Are you at the loft? I’m just a few blocks away from there. I can come now.”

“Yes. I’ll see you as soon as you can get here.”

George drove the few short blocks to the loft. Using his usual mode of entry, he raised the garage door. He was greeted by the Doc.

“Come in and sit. I need to talk to you,” he said as he paced back and forth.

George had never seen him like this. “What do you need me to do?”

“Follow her,” was all he said as he continued to pace.

George frowned. “Who do you want me to follow?”

The doctor paced, mumbling incoherently.

“I know something is going on” were the only words George could make out.

“I know her. I know she wasn’t looking me in the eyes. I know something is going on.” The Doc paused and continued to pace.

George waited.

When after a few moments, the Doc said nothing, George proceeded to tentatively ask, “So, you want me to follow a woman?”

The Doc stopped pacing and stared at George. The angry look on his face said everything.

“I know the bitch has been cheating. I know who he is. I’ll take care of him. She was warned not to do it. She won’t get away with this. Cheating is never to be tolerated. Why would she do it?” he asked, not expecting an answer.

“Follow her,” he yelled.

The comment was so loud George jumped.

“Here’s a picture and the other information you’ll need. Let me know what she’s doing every moment of the day. Every moment of the day,” he repeated.

“I will.” George hastily made for the door, but the doctor stepped in front of him.

“I want to know what she’s doing. And then I will take care of her,” he said through gritted teeth. "My plan is to take care of her, but if something goes wrong, take this." He held out an envelope to George. "Open it."

Opening the envelope, George counted ten one-thousand-dollar bills. "What's this for?"

"I want her dead. It may play out that I will do it, but if that doesn't happen, or no matter what happens, I want her dead. So, if for any reason I'm unable to do it, you will. The money is yours either way. Do you understand?"

George nodded. Leaving the same way he had entered, he scratched his head. He actually didn't quite understand. So, the Doc plans to kill someone, but if he fails, I've been paid in advance to do it. George smiled. He had just acquired ten thousand dollars. And best of all, he got to keep it whether he did anything or not. More money to share with Gracie, he thought. Now he knew he'd be able to persuade her to return to him.

Chapter 36

Shay managed to sit through her counseling session. She was distracted and was grateful that the couple had been in many times before but were not difficult. A few prompts on her part were all that was needed to get them to open up. The session went smoothly. The couple left.

Shay sat quietly for a moment and then buzzed Gwen. “Is Jeff in session?” she asked.

“No, he isn’t. He actually left immediately after the Commander left.”

“Did he say where he was going or when he’d return?” Shay asked.

“No. He didn’t say anything to me. He left in somewhat of a hurry. Do you want me to check with his secretary? Sherelyn probably knows what was on his schedule.”

“Thanks, Gwen. It’s okay, don’t bother Sherelyn,” Shay said.

Jeff was acting strange. She texted him, but he did not respond immediately. When he texted her back, he said he was at home packing for their trip. Shay decided to shake her blues and go home and do the same.

When she arrived home, she found Jeff smiling and making dinner. He kissed her and continued to stir something that smelled like beef stew.

"Smells really good," she said.

"It won't be ready for about an hour. It needs to simmer," He looked at her. "Why don't you go upstairs and freshen up? I'll call you when it's ready."

Shay walked up the stairs. Feeling drained, she lay across the bed. She remembered how happy she and Jeff had been when they first met. They had a wonderful but at the same time, strange courtship. They had talked for hours, as they did now. They had done everything together. They went swimming, played golf, went to the park, and enjoyed going to the movies together.

But Shay found it strange that after six months of being a couple, Jeff had never made love to her or even tried to. He was affectionate, always holding her hand and kissing her, but never going further. She, on the other hand, wanted him so badly she couldn't see straight. But of all the discussions they had, none had included sex.

Then, out of the blue, he'd asked her to go on a romantic cruise. Shay was delirious, thinking this was where they would finally make love. What a romantic backdrop, she thought. He had just been planning this romantic getaway for them to have each other.

However, the moment the boat started to sail, Jeff got violently ill. He threw up continuously for the entire seven days. Nothing the ship's doctor gave him quelled nausea. Shay, of course, took care of him the best she could, feeling guilty that she was so disappointed over them not being able to make love while on the cruise. On the last evening of the cruise, he seemed a little better. He was finally able to keep food down but was still weak from having very little nourishment the entire cruise.

They had dinner in their suite, as they had the majority of the cruise, just in case Jeff couldn't keep the food down. He was able to eat only a little, but during the meal, he pulled out a red box. Apologizing profusely for being so ill during their getaway, he handed her the box.

"Open it," he said.

She did. It was a diamond engagement ring. Shay knew she loved him but had not expected this, especially under these circumstances.

"Please say yes. This isn't the romantic proposal I'd planned, but I love you. I don't want to live without you. Please marry me."

"Of course," Shay said. "Yes, I'll marry you!"

Once off the ship, and after Jeff recovered, they made love. Jeff was not the most romantic lover, but he was so kind, gentle, and generous that Shay found it difficult to complain about anything he did or didn't do. Just being held by him was all Shay needed, she told herself.

Chapter 37

Over the years, their lovemaking dwindled to fewer and fewer occurrences. Again, Shay didn't complain. They traveled and spent time together building their business. The business came first; Shay had consoled herself.

They had both put in eighty-hour weeks getting the business up and running. There were office staff to hire and equipment to purchase. Both Shay and Jeff participated fully in the marketing aspect of the business. They both offered seminars for couples. Some seminars were in their offices, and some were in other states. Shay enjoyed spending time alongside Jeff doing the business work. They were often both exhausted by the time they fell into bed. Much too tired to make love. That was the excuse, anyway.

Conversation between them was always plentiful but never about sex. And then, finally, it was. One night after they had been married for five years, Jeff finally told her that he was simply unable to make love to her any longer. Shay was certainly aware that it had been more and more difficult for Jeff to get and maintain an erection, but she didn't know how to start the discussion. When she had tried bringing it up previously, he'd shut her down.

"I can't discuss it," he'd said.

But one night, a few months after all sexual relations between the two had completely ceased, she had continued anyway.

"We can figure this out together," she pleaded. "We can visit Anna."

Anna was a good friend of both Shay and Jeff, and she also happened to be the best sex therapist in Michigan. Jeff had simply stared at her. He seemed to want to say something but could not. He had turned away from her, rolling over onto his side of the bed. Shay had touched him gently and felt him go completely rigid. Finally, he rolled back over.

"Shay, I can no longer make love to you, but I love you desperately. I've never loved anyone the way I love you," he'd said as he wiped tears away.

"I beg you to understand, and please don't leave me. But, more importantly, please don't cheat on me. I promise to give you everything else you could ever want. I'll shower you with gifts. I'll give you the world. Anything you want is yours," He was speaking to her through sobs at this point. He was visibly shaking.

Shay was crying as well. She loved this man, and sex or no sex, she would always love him. However, she had to make one last-ditch effort to get him to seek help.

"I do understand," she'd said. "And I love you too. I won't leave you, and I will certainly not cheat on you. But I implore you to seek help. There is help available. And it doesn't have to be with Anna."

Shay hoped maybe he'd consent to see someone that he didn't know personally.

Jeff shouted at Shay for the first time ever in all the years she'd known him. Through clenched teeth and with a face so distorted it looked evil, he said, "I will not discuss this again. Never, ever bring it up to me again. I am a psychologist, counseling other couples, for Pete's sake. How do you think I would feel admitting to someone that I can't make love to my wife? It's difficult enough sometimes to face you. I know you have desires. You're young. I can do anything else sexually you want me to do, but I just can't complete the act. I know what I'm talking about. I've researched it and done my own tests. It's hopeless. Shay, I'm warning you, do not bring this subject up again."

Shay watched his face turn even darker, and his eyes blaze. For a moment, she was frightened. Then remembering who her sweet husband was, she snuggled close, kissing his tears away.

"It's okay. We'll get through this together. We'll be okay. I will never cheat on you," she promised again and again.

They had both kept their promises. Jeff had showered Shay with expensive gifts and vacations. Shay had not cheated on or left Jeff. And she had never brought up the subject of sex again. But failing to discuss sex had done nothing to take the urges away. She wanted a normal sex life with her husband.

Shay, of course, knew how to satisfy herself when absolutely necessary. But, she thought, there was nothing like having the man she loved on top of her and in her, holding her, kissing her, exploring different positions. She felt the heat that could only be cooled by Jeff if only he could. Shay remembered numerous times that she had been so aroused just lying in bed next to Jeff that she'd rise and go into the bathroom. She'd always been careful to lock the door. The last thing she wanted was to hurt Jeff by letting him know that she was pleasing herself on the bathroom floor.

Shay's thoughts were interrupted by Jeff calling her down to dinner. To Shay, conversation between the two didn't appear to flow as easily as usual. Jeff admitted that he was tired but seemed to stare at her when he thought she wasn't looking.

"What did you do today?" Shay asked. "Gwen said you left in a hurry this morning."

"Yes. I had some errands to run, and I had a meeting with some potential clients," he said. "Then I returned home, and now I'm all packed for our trip. Aren't you the least bit excited, or would you rather stay close to home?" he asked.

Shay wondered if it was her imagination or if his tone was accusatory.

"Of course, I'm excited. We've been planning this trip with the Hunters for months. It will be good to get away," Shay said truthfully.

"I suppose your meeting with your commander went well?" Jeff said softly.

There was that word again. *'Your'* commander. Shay wasn't sure what Jeff expected her answer to be.

"It went fine," she said stiffly.

"There really wasn't anything else I could tell him. I'm sure he won't have any further need to interview me," Shay spoke with more confidence than she felt.

Jeff said nothing, but Shay could swear she heard him breathe a sigh of relief. *I'm probably being paranoid again*, she thought.

Chapter 38

The Metropolitan Wayne County Airport was noisy, as usual. Shay told herself she was excited and anxious to get away from the office. She couldn't help but think that she also needed to make sure she was far away from Sebastian as well.

Shay was glad she had come. However, thoughts of Sebastian continued to enter her head during the trip, and she diligently pushed them away.

"Darling, what are you thinking about?" Jeff asked Shay for the second time.

Shay looked at Jeff and realized he had been speaking to her. Get a grip, she thought to herself. She forced herself back to the present as Saundra quickly tugged at her arm.

"Let's look in this boutique," she said, pulling Shay away from Jeff.

"Sweetie, what's wrong? You aren't yourself, and I think Jeff is noticing. You haven't seen the Commander, have you?" Saundra waited as Shay was slow to answer.

"Only once, very briefly. He came to the office to speak with Sam and insisted on speaking with me. I tried to get out of talking with him, but Jeff was there and insisted I speak with him."

Saundra's brow furrowed. "That's odd. Why should Jeff care

whether you spoke with him or not?"

"I couldn't figure it out either. He said something about not wanting the Commander to think we weren't being cooperative. But I wish I'd been able to avoid him," Shay said sadly.

"Why, what could have happened in the office?" Saundra asked.

"Shay, what happened?" Saundra asked again when Shay didn't answer immediately.

Then, looking over at Jeff, who was watching Shay and Saundra intently, Saundra smiled and picked up a purse, holding it out to Shay.

"Please smile, Shay," Saundra said through clenched teeth. "Jeff is watching us."

Shay took the purse Saundra held out to her, examining it as she pasted a false smile. Shay continued to talk. "I teared up, and he put his arms around me and held me for just the briefest of moments. I haven't seen him or heard from him since. I think he realized how much strain I was under, and I hope he's decided not to come near me again." She continued to smile. "He promised he wouldn't."

"It will all work itself out, Shay. But you've got to pull yourself together and stay in the present while we are on this vacation. Let go and enjoy yourself. At least you know while you are here, there is no chance of seeing the Commander. Now, get it together, girl, before Jeff thinks there's something fishy going on." Saundra smiled.

"I think he already suspects something. He's been acting slightly different, but I just can't put my finger on what he's thinking."

"I'm sure you're imagining things. Now let's spend some money in this wonderful boutique. I assure you it will make us both feel better." Both women laughed. "Then we can go take a plush seat in the first-class lounge until it's time to board our plane."

Stepping off the plane in Maui diminished all of Shay's inhibitions. She had been to Hawaii a couple of times before, and Maui was her favorite island. The feeling was wonderful but indescribable. The calmness captured her the minute she stepped off the plane. The flowers and greenery were so beautiful. And, of course, being met by tour guides placing leis around your neck signaled fun and relaxation. Mahalo, she thought.

Once they were checked into the resort, Shay was the first to change into her bikini and jump into the pool. She immediately swam up to the pool bar. Jeff, Saundra, and James waded after her.

For two weeks, the couples played golf and tennis, swam, ate, and drank. Nothing could be better, Shay thought. She felt more relaxed and hoped that Jeff did as well. But she again caught him watching her when he thought she wasn't looking. It unnerved her, but she forced herself not to show it.

They took an inter-island plane over to Kuai and Kona. Shay felt all the islands they visited were exquisite. Her favorite part of all was the rainforest. She had never had a more beautiful and relaxing experience ever. Jeff held her hand as they walked amongst the trees and greenery and whispered in her ear that he loved her. The quiet peace lulled Shay into a calmness she had not felt in weeks.

The late dinner on their last night was wonderful. The restaurant overlooked the water, and the food was superb. They ordered champagne. Both couples chatted comfortably and laughed easily.

Returning to Detroit, Shay felt a little depressed and anxious. Saundra watched her friend and once again pulled her aside at the airport.

“We’ve had a great time these last two weeks. Hold on to that. Don’t sink back to that dark place you were in before Hawaii. Dismiss it. Dismiss him. Do you understand me?” Saundra sounded like a mom.

Shay had to laugh. “I’m okay, Mommy,” she said.

After dropping Saundra and James off, the Metro Car Service headed for Shay and Jeff’s house. Shay could feel that something was wrong between them. But what was she to say? Jeff, are you upset because I have feelings for another man? Shay smiled sadly to herself. She didn’t know what to do except convince Jeff that she loved him. She slid closer. He put his arm around her as they traveled the three miles to their home. His embrace was particularly strong. He held her so tightly it was almost painful. But she said nothing.

Once the car dropped them off at home, they both headed back out to pick up Pam and Kimberly Alice at the animal hotel in Rochester Hills. The location was a little far from their home. Shay and Jeff had interviewed several pet hotels for their sweet fur babies. They both agreed that the one they selected was the best. They always went together to pick up their pets after having been away.

Once they got the pets and returned home, the ice between Shay and Jeff seemed to be broken.

Shay's first day back at the office brought a flurry of messages. One message Shay could not possibly ignore was from Detective Rubye Weaver. Shay dialed the number. The call was answered on the second ring.

"Detective Weaver," Shay said pleasantly. "My name is Shay Jackson. I've been out of town for the last two weeks; I see that I have a message from you. How can I help you, Detective?"

"I just have one question for you. I do understand the legalities involved with your divulging information. However, I just need you to think about my question."

Shay could not help wondering if Sebastian had turned the investigation over to someone else because of her. It's just as well, she thought. I'm glad he did, she tried to convince herself.

"Dr. Jackson, are you aware of or have you attended any funerals for someone who has died in, say the last several months?"

Shay was stunned, at first. Then she slowly answered. "I went to a funeral a couple of months ago for a woman named Janice Blakely, if that helps you, Detective. I wouldn't be able to tell you anything more than that."

"Thank you, Dr. Jackson. You've been a big help. Thank you for speaking with me. Please enjoy the rest of your day," Rubye responded.

Chapter 39

Rubye buzzed Sebastian. Before he could answer, she rushed out of her office and into his.

"You'll be surprised at the call I just received," she said excitedly.

He looked up. "Will I really?" he responded.

"It was from Dr. Jackson. You remember you told me to call her two weeks ago, but she had left for the day by the time I tried her office. She went on vacation for two weeks and just had an opportunity to return my call. You do remember asking me to call her, don't you?" she asked, out of breath.

Sebastian swallowed hard before responding. The knots had returned to his stomach at the mention of Shay's name. "Yes, of course, I remember," he answered, sounding somewhat agitated.

"Well, what got under your butt this time?" Rubye asked, picking up on the agitation in his voice. "Oh, never mind, I don't care what's bugging you, but whatever it is, you need to get a grip. You've been this way for the last few weeks. Get a grip," she said more sternly this time.

"I'm sorry, Rubye. I'm just tired. What did you get from Dr.… her?" he asked, not wanting to say her name.

"Well, as it turns out, Dr. Shay Jackson and Dr. Jeffrey Jackson both attended a funeral for Mrs. Janice Blakely. The doctor did not say, and I did not ask her if the deceased had been a client, but I did some checking."

"It seems that Mrs. Blakely had not been ill but died suddenly. I talked to her husband, Ted Blakely, and he said they were estranged and were considering divorce. According to Mr. Blakely, he asked his wife to please seek counseling to see if their marriage could be saved. And guess where they went? Yep, the Relationship Fix Group, Inc." She rushed on without allowing Sebastian to respond.

"He said that during the session, Mrs. Blakely admitted to having an affair. She, in fact, had confessed to having several but claimed that she wanted to start fresh. But before they could actually get back together, she died. Mr. Blakely told me that both Dr. Shay Jackson and Dr. Jeffrey Jackson had attended the funeral. He thought that was very kind and caring of them since the couple had only visited the Relationship Fix Group once."

Rubye went on to tell Sebastian that Mrs. Blakely had gone to Bonner Memorial Hospital for a simple procedure that had been scheduled a month before. She was admitted to the hospital the evening prior to receive preparation for the procedure. She never received the surgery. By the next morning, she was dead.

"And, get this," Rubye went on. "She had discussed the procedure during the counseling. It seemed Dr. Jeffrey Jackson wanted to schedule another counseling session for the day she was to stay over at the hospital. The session was then scheduled for another day, but of course, she was dead by then."

Sebastian looked thoughtful. "Was there an autopsy done?" he asked.

"It turns out, there was. Mr. Blakely said he needed to know what had happened to his wife. But nothing significant turned up that would answer his questions."

"Can you get me…"

Without letting Sebastian go on, Rubye placed the autopsy report on his desk. She smiled smugly and walked back into her office.

Shay's face blurred Sebastian's vision as he perused the autopsy.

"Focus," he said quietly. He then placed a phone call, making an appointment to see the coroner who had conducted Mrs. Blakely's autopsy.

Upon interviewing the coroner, Sebastian discovered that the only thing significant about Mrs. Blakely's autopsy was that she had consumed lemonade. This proved interesting, as she was to have had nothing by mouth prior to the procedure, which was to be conducted the next morning. Sebastian gave the coroner, Dr. Matt Hollins, a surprised look but said nothing.

There it was again, 'the lemonade.' Della had also said she smelled lemonade in Mr. Bradford's room.

"Dr. Jefferey R. Jackson, Jr., was here to look at the report. He found nothing out of the ordinary," Dr. Hollins said, almost defensively.

"Why did Dr. Jackson look at the report?" Sebastian asked. "He's not a medical doctor."

"I have no idea," Dr. Hollins said quickly, now looking nervous. "You'd have to ask him that."

On the way back to the office, Sebastian once again stopped at Bonner Memorial. He sought out Nurse Della once more. She appeared glad to see him.

"Hello, Della," he said pleasantly. "Just wondering if you've seen Dr. R. again?"

"Actually, I have not. He's usually in and out more often, but he hasn't been in since you and I spoke. That was a couple of weeks ago. I'm sorry. I would have called you if I had seen him," she said anxiously.

"Another question. Are you familiar with Dr. Matt Hollins?"

Della frowned before answering. "Yes, we know Dr. Hollins well. He is not generally liked around here. He's always trying to borrow money, even from the nurses. Don't you think that's a little strange? A well-paid doctor trying to borrow money from a nurse. I hear he's a gambler. I guess he has some gambling debts."

"You've been very helpful, Della. But I've got one more thing I need from you. If I send our sketch artist over to you, do you think you can help him sketch a picture of Dr. R.?"

"Sure, Commander. I can do that. I know just what Dr. R. looks like. I've been seeing him around here off and on for years."

"Thanks for your cooperation."

As he strode out of the hospital, Sebastian realized something else was bothering him. He couldn't put his finger on what was nagging at him at the moment, but he knew sooner or later, he would. As he drove, he went over all of the conversations he'd had with both Della and Dr. Hollins.

"Bingo," he said out loud. Dr. Jeffrey R. Jackson, Jr. That's what Dr. Hollins had called him. Sebastian had taken Jackson's card when he interviewed him. There was no Jr. on his card. He'd also dug into and found information on the Relationship Fix Group, Inc. There was no Jr. listed on the website or on any other documents he had viewed. Was there a son? he wondered. Or was Jackson a Junior? He wasn't sure whether it was important or not, but he'd find out. Sebastian intended to leave no stone unturned with this case. After all, this was the third death, and all the victims had two things in common: lemonade and the Relationship Fix Group, Inc.

Back at the office, Sebastian buzzed Rubye. Instead of answering, she came out of her office and stood before him, looking at him questioningly.

“Can you see what you can pull up on Dr. Jefferey R. Jackson, Jr.?”

“Sure thing,” she said, turning to go back into her office. “On second thought, can I do this tomorrow?” she said, looking at her watch. “I’ve got to pick up my nephew, Murphy, from school. My sister has a doctor’s appointment. She couldn’t schedule it any other time.”

“Sure, tomorrow’s fine.”

Chapter 40

Sebastian contacted the sketch artist and sent him over to Bonner Memorial to meet with Della.

Looking up from his desk less than an hour later, a tall thin young man stood before him. He was wearing a red jacket and matching red pants. Sebastian looked down to see red tennis shoes and red socks as well.

"Hey, Ralphie," Sebastian greeted him. "That was quick."

"I know, right? It was the easiest job you've ever sent me. Della was great. No hemming and hawing about eye color or anything else. She knew exactly what this guy looked like. She's been seeing him, she told me, in and out of the hospital for many years."

"Okay, so what have you got?" Sebastian said anxiously. "Let's see it." This had to be it, Sebastian thought. If this guy had been in and out of the hospital frequently for years but hadn't been seen in over two weeks, it had to mean something. He hadn't been seen since the day Bradford died. Sebastian had already checked with other staff in case he'd come in on Della's day off or on a later shift. No one remembered seeing him in the last couple of weeks.

Ralphie carefully laid the sketch out in front of Sebastian. "Dr. Roberts!" Sebastian gasped. "It looks a lot like Dr. Sam Roberts, one of the partners at the Relationship Fix Group. The age is about right. He sometimes uses a cane. But he doesn't have a birthmark on the side of his face. I can't be sure," Sebastian said slowly. "The gray cap is pulled down over one side of his face, and what's showing on the other is the birthmark, which could be fake. The other question is the height. How tall did Della say Dr. R was?"

"That was the only thing she was kind of unsure of. She first said he was about five-six or so. But then she decided that she really did not know how tall he was as he always walked doubled over, using his cane."

Sebastian checked his notes on his interview with Della. She had definitely also told him she was unsure of Dr. R's height. Sebastian thought about Dr. Roberts. He had not walked bent over and he had not used a cane while in Sebastian's presence. However, Sebastian remembered seeing a cane by the door. Dr. Sam Roberts could indeed be a suspect.

R, for Roberts, he thought. Well, he decided, there was nothing he could do until early tomorrow morning. Roberts had mentioned that he arrived at the office early and left early. He would certainly be gone by now. In addition, he did not want to run into Shay. He intended to keep his promise. He'd have a talk with Dr. Roberts early tomorrow morning, hopefully before Shay arrived.

He had promised Rubye that he would start eating better. Anything, he thought, to get her off his back. He would stop at the market for fresh broccoli, skinless, boneless chicken breasts, and salad greens. That should be healthy enough for her. His mom had made sure he and his brother knew how to cook. She wanted to make sure they could take care of themselves in case they didn't find anyone as good as she was at taking care of her man, his mom had added.

But Sebastian had found someone as good. Sara was certainly as good at taking care of him as his mom was at caring for his dad. But he had lost her. He then thought of Shay. He'd never gotten the chance to know her. He'd lost Shay before even having her. He knew that statement made no sense. He could still feel her hand under his and her soft body in his arms. He only touched her fleetingly, but he remembered. He could still smell her clean fragrance. He knew the scent, Dolce & Gabbana Light Blue. He knew it well because he wore the men's version of the fragrance. Damn, she smelled good. He remembered her body quivering against his. The embrace had only been a moment, but he could remember how aroused he had become with her body that close to his. She had fit snuggly against him.

Sebastian looked at his watch. He hadn't realized he had been stuck at his desk that long. It was now after seven o'clock. Sebastian rose from his desk and put on his jacket. He had given so much time to the recent murders that he had gotten behind in some other administrative duties, which he caught up on tonight.

Grabbing his hat, Sebastian took the stairs to the first-floor lobby. He needed to stretch his long legs after sitting at his desk for hours. He exited the building through a side door that led him to where his car was parked. He took note of the occupied black vehicle parked across the street but stopped walking as his cell phone rang. He answered, saying hello several times, but no one responded. Just as he disconnected the call, a vehicle's lights blinded him, lights that were coming right at him. As he ducked behind a nearby car, the car nearly missed Sebastian but scraped the car ahead of the one Sebastian had ducked behind. Sebastian turned quickly to look for a license plate.

There was no plate on the car.

Chapter 41

"I hear you had a scare last night," Rubye said as she touched his face and smoothed back his hair, examining Sebastian for cuts and scrapes.

"Will you stop it? I'm fine. How did you know?"

"You went back into the station after it happened. You spoke with Christopher Maddox, who works the evening shift. You knew his desk was right by the window near the parking lot, and you wanted to know if he had seen anything from his window. I always have my sources," she said as she smiled and winked.

"Do these guys report to you or to me?" Sebastian laughed, shaking his head.

"Both," she said, still smiling. "So, what do you think that was, an accident, or are you getting too close to something?"

"No accident, for sure. I think a call came into my cell phone to distract me. The number was restricted, so I'll see if our tech geeks can do anything about capturing it. I paid a visit to Dr. Sam Roberts early this morning. As much as Della's sketch resembles him, my instincts tell me that he is not the one, but we'll keep working on it. I haven't dismissed him yet."

"Do you think he'd be dumb enough to use his own last initial at the hospital? I mean, really," Rubye said, hands on hips. "Using R for Roberts. That doesn't strike as very smart to me."

"He also doesn't have a birthmark on the side of his face, but that could have been cosmetics. I spotted a gray coat hanging in his closet, but lots of men have gray coats. I have one myself." Sebastian smiled.

"Have you come up with anything on Dr. Jeffrey Jackson, Jr?"

"I'm working on it now," she assured him.

Thirty minutes later, Rubye stood at Sebastian's desk holding the newspaper article she'd printed.

"Whatcha got?" he asked.

"Take a look. Maybe something, maybe nothing. It seems Jeffrey Jackson, Sr., is, as we speak, still in prison for killing his wife and sodomizing his young son, Jeffrey, Jr. No wonder he dropped the Junior. I'm sure he would not want to follow that act."

"Or would he?" Sebastian said.

"What do you mean?" Rubye asked.

"Nothing, I don't know. Probably nothing. Just thinking out loud."

Sebastian continued to pore over the news articles.

It appeared that Jeff Sr. killed his wife because she cheated on him. According to the newspaper article, as he was being taken away in handcuffs, he was screaming these words to the fourteen-year-old Jeffrey Jackson, Jr,

"Son, never allow a woman to cheat on you. Your mother was a lying, cheating slut. Never allow a woman to cheat on you."

The article concluded that the senior Jackson had screamed these words to the young boy over and over as he was being led away. And, of course, that young boy was Dr. Jeffrey Jackson, Jr.

A follow-up article stated that Jeffrey, Jr., had initially been sent to a number of foster homes until, some three years later, his mother's sister and her husband took him in.

After Sebastian read this, the article troubled him more and more. What if Jackson surmised that Sebastian and Shay were cheating on him? How would he react? He wondered if Shay even knew the story of Jeff's father. It wasn't exactly the type of story most men would share.

This made him more concerned for Shay. He kept thinking about her safety. He found it difficult to concentrate on his work. He would start to follow a lead and become totally distracted. He swore he could still smell her perfume.

Chapter 42

Relaxing in front of the television, Shay sat up straight as she saw Sebastian's face come across the screen. He was being interviewed about the recent attack on his life.

Shay sat up straighter. "Oh my God," she said aloud.

She needed to see him, to touch him, to know he was okay. But she couldn't, could she? What if she just went to the police station? *What if?* She was frantic.

Feeling defeated, she slumped back against the sofa cushions. There was nothing she could do but pray that he was okay and that he would not be harmed.

She found it difficult to breathe. This situation was impossible. She blamed herself. How did she let it get this far? She seemed to have no control over her feelings when it came to Commander Sebastian Crawford. She may have little control over her thoughts, but thank God, she did have some control over her actions. She had allowed him to touch her hand and to hold her, but nothing more and only for a split second.

"That was enough."

The small voice in her head was back again. "You know you shouldn't have done that. But you enjoyed it," the voice taunted.

"Especially since you are a married woman." The small voice, which was not really so small, continually reminded her of the obvious. There seemed to be no way to shut the voice off.

Rising from the sofa, she turned off the television. She felt as if she were losing her mind. She hoped she didn't look the way she felt. She couldn't let Jeff see her this way. She sent him a text telling him she was tired and that he should pick up something for himself for dinner. She told him that she was turning in early.

Shay dragged herself up to bed. She was still awake when Jeff came in, but she closed her eyes and adopted steady breathing as if she were asleep. She lay there feeling guilty for deceiving her husband in more ways than one, she thought. She felt Jeff climb into bed.

By the morning, Shay believed she had gotten possibly an hour of sleep. She lay awake most of the night thinking about Sebastian and the hopeless situation in which she found herself.

Shay heard Jeff shaving in the bathroom. She didn't rise. She heard him as he walked over to the bed. Shay kept her eyes closed. Finally, he gently touched her arm. She opened her eyes.

"Good morning, darling," Jeff said, smiling down at his wife. "You were sound asleep when I came to bed last night, so I didn't disturb you. I heard someone tried to kill your Commander Crawford last night."

There it was again, "Your Commander Crawford."

"Yes, I saw it on the news last night." Shay decided not to deny knowing about the attack.

"Are you sure that's how you found out?" Jeff asked. His voice was soft, but the words were cutting.

Shay sat up groggily. "What do you mean?" she asked. "How else would I have found out?"

"Are you sure he didn't contact you to let you know what happened?"

He was scaring her now. Shay tried to answer with a calm voice. "Why would you possibly think he would contact me? I don't really know him."

"He seems like a nice enough fellow. Wouldn't you like to get to know him? Why don't we have him over for dinner?"

"Darling," Shay said, forcing a calmness she didn't feel into her voice. "I don't think it's necessary to invite a perfect stranger over for dinner. This is nonsense," she said with a laugh. "Why don't I get up and fix you some breakfast."

"No, you look tired. I'll fix you some and bring it up on a tray. Would you like that?"

"No, that's not necessary. I'm getting up now. You go on down. I'll be down shortly." Once Shay heard Jeff's footsteps on the stairs, she slid out of bed and went into the bathroom, locking the door behind her. She wasn't sure why Jeff was acting so strange, but she sensed it had something to do with Sebastian. She needed to convince Jeff that she lov… She started to say "loved him" but found it difficult to get out.

She needed to release some tension. Her head ached. She felt as if she would burst if she didn't do something.

Quickly throwing on a gray and pink jogging suit, she went downstairs. Jeff had started breakfast. He was listening to music and did not hear her when she came up behind him. She put her arms around him and was shocked when he turned around and grabbed her roughly.

"I'm sorry, darling," he said. "You scared me. I didn't hear you. I apologize. Did I hurt you?"

"No, of course not. I didn't mean to scare you," she said, rubbing the arm he had grabbed. "I'm going to take Pam out for a run. I should be back before breakfast is ready," she said, kissing him on his cheek.

Again, Shay's jog turned into a run. She had to release the pent-up energy. She didn't know what to make of Jeff's behavior. As she neared the dog park, she slowed. Taking Pam's leash off, she let her mingle with the few dogs that were in the park. Shay sat down on a bench.

She'd always known that Jeff was afraid of losing her. Somehow, she had to convince him that he would not. She had said her vows when they were married, and she meant them. Even the way she felt about Sebastian could not change that. He had nothing to worry about.

Now slowly walking home, Shay went over what she'd say to Jeff.

She entered the house. Taking Pam's leash off, she fed her and Kimberly Alice. She took a few minutes to rub the white cat before going in search of Jeff. She found him sitting in the four seasons room with his head in his hands.

He looked up when she came in. His eyes were red. Shay went over and sat next to him. She took him in her arms. "We are married for good," she said softly. "There is no way you are going to get rid of me. I said my vows to last a lifetime." Putting her finger under his chin, she forced him to look at her.

"Do you hear what I'm saying? I've never lied to you in all the years we've been married, and I need you to know that I'm in it for the long haul."

Jeff looked doubtful. Shay could swear that anger flashed across his face, but then he smiled. She felt or at least hoped he had accepted and believed what she said. She hoped he hadn't noticed that she did not tell him she loved him. For some reason, the words still wouldn't come. Her feelings for her husband seemed to have diminished.

Shay refused to accept that the cause was a certain police commander. She admonished herself. How could a perfect stranger impact her enough to alter her feelings for the man she'd pretty much loved all of her adult life? A wonderful, loving man who was always good to her, she added.

Chapter 43

Sebastian finally sat up in bed. He'd tossed and turned all night, having gotten absolutely no sleep. So, get out of bed, he urged himself. There was something that had nagged at him the entire night. It was the report he'd read on Jeff Jackson's father. He had no reason to think that Jeff would harm Shay as his father had harmed his mother, but even the thought scared him shitless.

He realized he was living without Shay now, and the feeling was more painful than he could describe. But living without her because someone had hurt her would be unbearable. Discovering that she had been hurt or worse would certainly do him in for good this time. He couldn't lose yet another woman he'd loved because of a senseless crime.

Yes, loved, he thought to himself. He loved this woman. It might be crazy, but Sebastian could not control his feelings. He knew that loving someone should bring sunshine, but this could only bring clouds. Even so, he loved her. And when Sebastian Edison Crawford loved, he loved hard. The fact that he had known her for such a short time did not come into play. There were just certain people who could invoke feelings even the first time you met them. Shay was one of those people.

Because of the promise he'd made to Shay, he wouldn't contact her unless he had damn good reason to think that her life was in danger. He was pretty well convinced that Jeff knew, saw, or sensed something was going on between Sebastian and his wife. His fear was not knowing how that knowledge would play out. His instincts told him that Jeffrey Jackson, Jr., was a jealous man, desperately trying to hold on to his woman. Sebastian's instincts also told him that something wasn't quite right in their marriage. He just didn't know what it was.

Standing up, he slowly walked into the kitchen. He put on some coffee and scrambled some eggs, adding a little cheese. The combination always made him feel better. I know what I need to do, he thought, jumping up. First, he cleaned up the mess he'd made in the kitchen. Both Sara and his mom had pounded cleaning up after himself into his brain.

Once he was done straightening up the kitchen, he took a hot shower. All the while, his brain was working. I've got it, he thought, stepping out of the shower. He needed to get to police headquarters.

Once arriving, he called out to Rubye as he strode into his office.

"What is it? You haven't even taken your coat off, and you're yelling for me already. What's wrong with quietly buzzing me?" She smiled.

"Sorry, but I've got something on my mind," he said, taking his jacket off and hanging it on the back of his chair. "See if you can find any more stories on Jeffrey Jackson, Sr. Also, see if there are any relatives around in the area that I might speak with. This was about forty years ago, so anyone who was Senior's age might be in their eighties now. But see what you can rustle up, will you, Rubye?"

Rubye opened her mouth to give a smart retort but looked at Sebastian's face. There was strain there. She wasn't surprised. Someone tried to kill him a couple of nights ago, and he was more embroiled in the murders than she thought he would be—or should be. It was obvious that he was no longer just doing his cousin a favor. There was something else driving him. She just didn't know what it was.

Aloud, she simply said, "I'll get right on it."

Forty-five minutes later, Rubye once again stood in front of Sebastian. He was on a phone call but motioned to her to sit down in the chair next to his desk.

Ending his call, he asked anxiously, "What do you have for me?"

"Well, there was an aunt who took Jeff, Jr., in, who is dead now. But there was also something else. It seems there was a younger sister. She would have been about twelve at the time of her mom's murder. Her name is Dorothy Jackson. She's a photographer and lives in Lansing. The sister was never mentioned in the article written when they carted Senior off to prison. However, Senior had gotten some kind of award a couple of years earlier. At that time, a newspaper article showed a picture of the family. That picture included Dorothy, who was about ten at the time the picture was taken. I have an address for her."

"That's great. Thanks, Rubye."

"There's more."

Sebastian turned and listened intently. He knew he could not effectively do his job and solve the murders or even investigate the attempt on his life until he knew that Shay would be safe.

"There is also Jackson, Sr.'s sister. She's in a nursing home on Evergreen and Thirteen Mile in Southfield. She's unable to walk and kind of weak, but according to what I could find out, she does not have dementia, so she just might remember what you need. Her name is Maggie Jackson Clark."

Almost before the words were out of Rubye's mouth, Sebastian was shrugging into his jacket.

"I'm on my way to Evergreen and Thirteen Mile."

Rubye watched as he moved swiftly through the door. Something else was going on with him, she thought. She had worked with Sebastian long enough to know when something wasn't right with him. She knew him sometimes, she thought, better than he knew himself. Suddenly, she slapped her forehead.

"It's a woman," she said aloud. She hadn't thought of that before because he hadn't looked at another woman since Sara died. Many officers, including Rubye, had tried to set him up with women. Sebastian adamantly refused.

Rubye had also seen some of the most attractive women go in and out of his office, attempting to get him to notice them. Their attempts had all been in vain. He was oblivious to even the most ardent and shameful advances. Rubye laughed as she thought about the woman just a few months ago who went so far as to pretend to lose her balance and fall into Sebastian's lap. He politely helped her up and escorted her to the door as if he had no idea of the game she was playing.

She'd also overheard women ask him out on dates. He was always polite when he refused, but he left no doubt that there was no point in trying again.

Chapter 44

Sebastian didn't worry about breaking speed limits. He needed to get to the nursing home fast.

"I'm Commander Sebastian Crawford, Julie," he said to the woman at the front desk, reading the name on her name badge. "I'd like to see Mrs. Maggie Jackson Clark, please." He held out his badge for the woman at the desk to see.

"Mrs. Clark went to the lab for tests earlier, but I believe she's back now." The young woman at the desk smiled at Sebastian. "Let me check her room," she said, turning to pick up the phone. Her voice was perky, and her blond ponytail bounced as she talked. Now turning back to Sebastian, she said, "She is in her room, sir. Her room number is 222-A. Take the hallway to your left and then keep going around to the right. The building is just one big circle. You can't miss it. She's a very nice lady and will enjoy having someone to talk with. She hardly has any visitors. We just get a check to cover all of her expenses every month," the young woman volunteered.

Sebastian did as she said, walking around to the right until he spotted room 222-A. He walked in.

A woman of eighty sat straight up in her wheelchair. She smiled and greeted Sebastian.

"Commander, Julie called and told me you would be dropping in. It is so nice to see you. If I were in my own home," she said wistfully, "I would certainly serve you tea."

"That would be really nice, ma'am," Sebastian said politely.

"Why have you come, Commander? I never have visitors. Of course, I don't really mind. They keep us pretty busy here. They have games, and I learned how to knit, and we have movie night and popcorn." She stopped and took a breath. "And, of course, I always go to the dining hall for my meals. You wouldn't believe what interesting people they have here. There is a scientist, a meteorologist, several teachers, and even a psychologist, just like my nephew—"

Sebastian cut her off before she could start on another subject. He could see that she enjoyed having someone to talk with.

"That's just who I'd like to speak with you about. Could you tell me about your brother and your nephew?"

"What would you like to know, Commander? I guess you know where my brother is. He's been in prison for a really long time. Has my nephew gone and done the same thing?"

Sebastian was taken aback. "Why would you think he would do the same thing, Mrs. Clark?" Sebastian asked the elderly woman softly. His heart was pounding in his chest. He recognized the feeling as fear.

Mrs. Clark shook her head. “Oh, I don’t know. It’s just that he was so angry about everything. I was always afraid that all that hatred would get the better of him. But then I stopped worrying for a while when he met his wife, Shay. Such a sweetheart she is. I thought it odd that Shay had never visited me here. She visited me often when I was at my home. She’d bring lunch or take me out to lunch. I so enjoyed her company,” she said with a wistful look in her eyes. “Oh well, it’s okay. Jeff told me the one time he visited me that, he had not told Shay I was here. He said it would make her sad to see me here. He loves her dearly, and I thought he had finally come to grips with all the stuff that was thrown at him at an early age. But then I got a visit from my niece Dorothy, and she says, for some reason, the hatred is back.”

“When did Dorothy tell you this?” Sebastian asked.

“She was here a few days ago. At least, I think it was a few days ago. When you get my age, Commander, you lose track of time. What I do remember is that she was the first visitor I’d had in ages. Dorothy lives in Lansing, you know, which is about ninety miles from here. She’s visited a few times, but I can’t expect her to come that often. She works hard at her photography business. I’ve seen some of her work. It’s very good. And now, of course, she is taking care of my niece. Jeffrey, Jr. only came here one time, and that was when he brought me here. But it's okay." She smiled. "He pays for me to be in this very nice place."

"What else did Dorothy tell you?" Sebastian prompted.

"It's so sad. Her daughter is ill. She has an inoperable brain tumor. Dorothy just thought that maybe Jeffrey, Jr., would like to see her as she only has maybe a few months left to live. He said he would think about it, but she wasn't very hopeful that he would. The child is twenty-eight years old now, and he's never seen her. She's actually no longer a child. But twenty-eight is so young to die. Her name is Mona." Her eyes teared up, and Sebastian reached over and handed her a tissue. "Thank you," she said, dabbing at her eyes. "Dorothy was hoping that since she never got married, Jeffrey, Jr., would be the man in Mona's life, but because of what happened, Jeffrey, Jr., just couldn't do it."

"Why would he not want to see his own niece?"

"Oh, don't you know? Jeffrey, Sr. not only sodomized Jeffrey, Jr., but he also raped Dorothy, and she gave birth to a baby at the age of twelve years old. I've always been afraid for Jeffrey, Jr. because instead of getting help, he simply buried all of it. He buried his mother's death at the hands of his father. He buried the fact that he had been sodomized. And he tried to bury the fact that his dad had raped his baby sister. But he couldn't totally bury that one because there was a child to remind him. This is why he's only seen Dorothy a few times in all these years and why he refuses to lay eyes on her child.

She stopped and looked at Sebastian. “He even dropped the ‘Junior’ from his name. I’ve been afraid for Jeffrey Jr. because I just don’t think you can continue to bury that kind of drama all your life. It has to come out in some way, and I’ve always been afraid that there would be more violence when it does.”

Sebastian’s heart beat even faster. He took a breath to calm himself before speaking. “Why do you say that?” he asked weakly.

“Because certain things trigger this hatred Jeffrey, Jr. carries.”

“What kinds of things?” Sebastian asked his mouth now as dry as cotton.

“Well, when he was in his freshman year of college, he found out that the affair his mom had resulted in a child. She had an affair while married to Jeffrey, Jr.’s dad, that resulted in her becoming pregnant. She managed to conceal the pregnancy from Jeffrey, Sr. You see, she had a sick sister who lived way up north in Marquette, Michigan. Her sister was in the last stage of breast cancer. So, Gretchen went up to take care of her. She was there for five months and delivered the baby there. She, of course, had concealed the pregnancy for four months before she left. Gretchen was kind of a large woman, so at four months pregnant, you could barely tell. Jeffrey, Sr., of course, missed her. They often spoke on the phone, but he was working and taking care of Jeff, Jr., who was only about six years old at the time, so he never went up north to be with Gretchen during that time." She now paused and looked as if she were reliving the incident now. With a small shiver, she continued.

"Gretchen had arranged to give the baby to a distant cousin who was unable to have children. Jeffrey, Sr., never knew about it until just before he killed her. It seems Gretchen's child was about eight years old when she fell ill and needed a bone marrow transplant. The cousin wasn't a match. So, of course, the cousin called Gretchen, the natural mother, to see if she was a match. Gretchen took the test, and sure enough, she was a match.

"I guess she couldn't figure out how to carry this one off in secret, so she confesses to her husband, begs his forgiveness, and says she must do this for her child. My brother told her he understood, but the night she was to leave to go to donate the bone marrow was the night he killed her.

Jeff Jr. didn't find out about this child until he was in his freshman year of college. He ran into the cousin, who was extremely bitter because her child had died without Gretchen being alive to provide the bone marrow. She told Jeffrey, Jr., the whole sordid story.

"After finding out, Jeffrey, Jr., was walking down the street, so full of anger that he struck out at a perfect stranger. Just hit him right in the face. Then he was consumed with uncontrollable crying.

Luckily, this man got up and actually tried to help my nephew. The man was a psychologist and knew immediately that this young man needed help. Jeffrey, Jr., was only about eighteen years old then. He told the stranger, right there on the street, part of the story. The stranger never called the police but made Jeffrey Jr. promise to come to his office for help. Unfortunately, Jeffrey Jr. didn't give the stranger his correct name, nor did he go for help. But I often thought that the stranger was the reason Jeffrey, Jr., became a psychologist."

"And as far as you know, has he been alright up to now?" Sebastian asked hopefully.

"Not exactly; there's more. There was another incident while he was in college. I believe this time, he was in his junior year. That's right. He didn't meet Shay until his senior year. He was dating a girl that he really liked, but he found out that she was cheating on him. According to Dorothy, whom he shared it with on one of the few times they got together, it seems he came up behind her and pushed her down the stairs. He continued to beat her even though she was unconscious. She never saw her attacker. He escaped punishment, as the crime was blamed on the boy with whom she was cheating, on Jeffrey with. It seems the young woman and the new boyfriend had argued violently the night before, and the boyfriend had raped her. So, it was believed that he was her attacker. As you can see, certain things just trigger terrible violent behavior in my nephew. I'm telling you this because I hope you can help him."

By now, Sebastian was finding it difficult to breathe, but he knew he needed to get out of there fast and find Shay. He had to warn her.

“Thanks for your help, Mrs. Clark,” Sebastian said as he hurried from her room and down the winding hall.

Chapter 45

Sebastian's mind was racing. Fear gripped him as he stepped out into the cool Michigan day. The sweat collected on his brow ran down his face and wet the collar of his once crisp uniform shirt. The cold air did nothing to cool him off.

Jumping into his vehicle, he called Shay's office. Gwen answered. Sebastian tried to sound calm.

"Is Dr. Shay Jackson in?" he asked.

"Yes, she is, but she is in with a client. Is there a message?" Gwen asked.

Sebastian breathed a sigh of relief. "No, there's no message," he said. At least for now, she was safe, but he had to figure out how to get to her to warn her. He had to figure out what he would say.

"Is Dr. Jeff Jackson in?" Sebastian decided he needed to keep tabs on him.

"No, I'm sorry, he isn't in."

"Do you know where I might find him?" Sebastian held his breath. He knew there was no reason for an assistant to divulge that kind of information. Yet, he did not want to tell her who he was. He knew it would spook both Shay and Jeff for different reasons.

Gwen, recognizing the Commander's voice, said, "Dr. Jeff Jackson is on his way home. If you'd like I can contact him there and have him phone you," she offered politely.

"No," Sebastian said quickly. "That won't be necessary. This can wait. Will he be in tomorrow?"

"Yes, he has an eight-thirty appointment."

"Thank you," Sebastian said, ending the call.

He had to think. He had to protect her. He decided to text her. She had to be warned.

"Shay, I said I wouldn't bother you again, and I promise I won't. But I need you to google Jeffrey Jackson, Sr. I don't want to scare you, but I want you to be extremely careful. You have my cell number. If you need me, please call." Sebastian pushed the send button and prayed this would be enough to alert Shay.

In the meantime, Sebastian decided he'd make his way to Shay's office. He was twenty-six miles away and in heavy rush hour traffic. At that moment, the traffic was standing still. He had to get to her. He'd follow her home if necessary. He'd sit outside her house. He'd do whatever he needed to do to keep her safe. But she needed to be aware that she might be in danger.

Now he used his cell phone to call his assistant. "Rubye," he said hastily when she answered. "You are a master at getting information for me. So, put your magician's hat on and pull the names of some of Dr. Jeff Jackson's clients out of that hat."

"I can do this in my sleep. I know just what to say. Are you looking for any particular client?" she asked.

"No. But I've got a hunch that some of the Doc's clients might have come to harm just as Raines and Bradford did. Find out what you can, will you? And do it fast." Sebastian didn't wait for a response from Rubye. His phone was now ringing. The caller ID told him it was Shay. He answered quickly.

"Shay. Where are you? Are you okay?"

"Sebastian, I don't understand. Jeff told me both his parents were dead. He said they died together in a car accident. How can what I googled possibly be true? Is Jeff's dad still alive and in prison? That can't possibly be true," she insisted.

"Believe me. It is true. Please believe me," Sebastian pleaded. "I just left his Aunt Maggie. She's in a nursing home on Evergreen and Thirteen Mile Road in Southfield."

There was a pause before Shay responded, "No, that can't be. Jeff told me Aunt Maggie moved to Atlanta to be with her sister."

Shay sounded confused, "The article said Jeff was sodomized at fourteen years old. How could he not have shared this with me?"

"I'm afraid that's true as well," Sebastian said. "According to his aunt, Jeff has buried the truth so deeply for years that he couldn't share it with you. He's done it for so long that he probably believes whatever he's told you. He couldn't face the truth and seldom allowed himself to be in contact with anyone from his past that would remind him of the horror. I'm surprised that he had allowed you to have any contact with his aunt."

"I don't think he meant for me to have any. She found us. She just showed up at our door one day. So, he could hardly keep her a secret. She had actually hired a private detective to find us. She's such a sweet lady. I used to visit her often at her home. She never told me any of this." Shay sounded even more puzzled.

"I'm sure she was afraid that if Jeff thought she might divulge anything to you, he wouldn't have allowed her in your life. And as it is, it appears he wasn't sure he could trust her not to say anything. Hence his putting her away in a nursing home and telling you she moved to Atlanta."

Sebastian added, "I'm worried about you because his aunt made it perfectly clear that certain triggers cause Jeff to become violent. If he thinks you and I are—"

Shay cut him off. "But we aren't."

"I know that, and you know that, but even if he thinks that we are cheating, that could be enough of a trigger to cause him to become violent, and I don't want you anyplace near him if that happens. Shay, I can tell you are upset. You've been pushed to the limit by the newspaper article and all that I'm telling you. But just think about it. You're a psychologist; you know this is possible as well as I do."

"Sebastian, I've been married to this man for fifteen years. And as a psychologist, if there were something violent in Jeff's character, I'd have picked up on it, Sebastian," she said, repeating his name.

Whenever he heard her say his name, he melted. She was wrong but too deeply involved to think rationally. If she were counseling another couple, he was sure she would see it and probably give them the same warning he was giving her. She was too close to the situation to deal with it. And he was scared to death that it was going to get her hurt or worse.

"I'm still in the office, but I'm putting on my coat now. Jeff is home, and that's where I'm headed. I'll be home in less than ten minutes. I need to talk with Jeff. I promise I'll be careful, and I'll leave and call you if anything doesn't appear right."

"Shay, please wait until I get there. I'm on my way to your office now. I'm on the John Lodge Expressway. Please just wait ten minutes."

"I know you think I'm not thinking clearly. And I'm sure I'm not. This has hit me hard. My stomach is doing flip-flops, and I am totally confused. But you tell me, what do you think will happen if I wait for you? What shall we do, walk in together and try to convince him we aren't having an affair? What kind of trigger would your being anywhere near cause?"

"I agree, but you still cannot go into that house alone. If you wait, I could get my assistant to go in with you. Maybe you could say she is an old friend from grammar school or something. Anything," Sebastian pleaded. "You could tell him she lives in another state and will just be spending one night in your guest room. Please just think about it.

"Sebastian, I have to do this. I need to talk with him. I wouldn't be able to do that with a guest in the house. Look at it this way. Jeff has hidden this stuff for what—thirty years—and he's not been triggered yet. I don't know why you think something will trigger him tonight. Just let me have a conversation with him. Now that I know the facts, I know how to handle it. Trust me. I'll be fine. And I promise to text you as soon as my husband and I talk."

Her words coupling her to her husband cut Sebastian deeply. But he knew he could not convince her to wait for him. All he could do was put his siren on and move down the road as swiftly and safely as possible. He had to get to her house.

Sebastian decided to try one last effort. "Shay, please do something for me," he finally said. "Go across the street to the Gaming Commission. You've probably passed the building countless times without really noticing it. It's on Jefferson just east of your office on the north side of the street. Go there when you leave the office and ask for Commander Quinn. He's a good friend of mine. He'll be waiting for you with a small package. Take the package. When you arrive home, before entering the house, simply press down on the envelope. Then as you enter the house, leave your front door unlocked. I promise once I arrive, I won't come in unless it feels as if I should. After all, I am the police, you know," he said, trying to put some humor in the situation. "You can't stop me. If I were there, I'd probably arrest you to keep you safe. When you arrive home, you can leave what Quinn gives you in your purse. Just set the purse near wherever you and Jeff are in the house. It doesn't matter how far away from the two of you it is. As long as it is in the home, it will transmit."

Shay's sigh was audible over the phone. "I don't think it's necessary, but okay, if you insist, I'll pick up this package and leave the door unlocked."

Chapter 46

Sebastian had to let her go.

Now his phone was buzzing. It was Rubye.

"What did you find out?"

"Let me give you the run-down. It seems there are at least three people, and possibly more. In 2017, Sharon Goodman died of an accidental overdose. And guess who she and her husband were seeing before her death?"

"Dr. Jeff Jackson, Jr.," he said quickly. "Go on. Who else?"

"In 2018, Kevin Dandridge died in the hospital of a heart attack. And guess who he and his long-time live-in girlfriend were seeing before his death?" She didn't wait for a response. "And lastly, in 2017, Richard Fountain was run over by a hit-and-run driver. It happened as he was leaving his business. It seems he got a phone call distracting him from a restricted phone number. Does that sound familiar?" she said, reminding Sebastian of his own near hit-and-run accident and the phone call at just the right time to distract him.

"Very," he said, pushing his foot down harder on the accelerator. He had to get to her. "Thanks, Rubye. Don't know what I'd do without you. I'd thought Jeff was only someone who might hurt his wife, but obviously, he is the suspect for all of these, quote, unquote, accidents and the deaths of Raines, Bloom, and Bradford."

Rubye had no idea how much fear and anger she'd aroused in Sebastian with her words. "If he touches one hair on her head, I'll kill him," Sebastian swore.

Rubye silently hung up after hearing his last words. They weren't meant for her.

Chapter 47

Shay entered the house quietly, unlocking both locks as she entered. She didn't feel it was necessary, but she'd oblige Sebastian anyway. She just hoped he wouldn't burst in with guns blazing. What am I thinking? she said to herself. He's a police commander. If he needed to come to their door, she was sure he would have a good story available to share with Jeff about why he needed to speak with them. After all, Jeff knew that Sebastian was still investigating the case.

Shay heard Jeff moving around in his home office. She walked in quietly and took a seat. She gingerly set her purse containing the package she had gotten from the gaming commission officer on the sofa cushion next to where she was seated. She had pressed on the package as instructed as she entered the house.

She now sat watching Jeff as he paced around the office they'd just remodeled in their home. She needed to get him to talk to her. She wasn't stupid. She was, after all, a psychologist. This was her business. She agreed with Sebastian that she was not exactly on her game and thinking as clearly as she should when it came to being so close to what was going on with her husband, but she still believed—naively or not—that she could handle it—handle Jeff, if necessary. She felt numb. She still wondered how she could have lived for so long with a man who had endured so much pain and not known.

She wanted to help him. Somehow, her feelings had changed. She didn't actually know how she felt about Jeff any longer. But one thing would never change. He was her husband, and she would continue to be his wife no matter what. She did not blame him for all the lies and half-truths he had told her. She understood that these were his defense mechanisms. He might not have been able to go on without them.

And in spite of what Sebastian may think, Shay would never believe that Jeff would hurt her or anyone else for that matter. In fact, she now knew that she had no choice but to stay with him. He had been through a terrible ordeal. She wanted to help him. She had to help him. She had married him for better or for worse.

"Jeff?" she called timidly. He had not realized she was in the room as he paced.

Now he stopped and looked at her. The look on his face showed anger.

"Darling," she said, now standing, "why don't I make us some dinner, and then we can talk? We need to talk."

He continued staring at her. He said nothing but showed her a sinister smile. She noticed the curl of his lips and the chipped tooth that had endeared him to her when he smiled on their first date. But this smile was not sincere.

"Why are you angry? Have I done something to cause you to be angry with me?"

"Have I done something to cause you to be angry with me?" He repeated her words angrily through clenched teeth as he moved toward her menacingly.

Shay backed up. "Jeff, I've done nothing."

"I've done nothing?" He repeated her words again questioningly. "Of course, you've done something. I asked you never to cheat on me."

"But I haven't cheated on you. I swear. Jeff, I would never ever cheat on you. You have to believe me." Shay's voice was shaky.

"I saw you, Shay."

"What do you mean? What could you have seen when I've done nothing?"

"Now you are lying to me. I won't allow you to get away with it. No one should get away with cheating. Cheating tore my family and my life apart. I won't allow anyone to get away with cheating. I have to make it better for the other partner. The cheater doesn't deserve to live. Raines didn't deserve to live. I won't allow a woman to cheat on me," he said, remembering his father's words as he was led off to prison.

"But Mr. Raines had an illness. It wasn't his fault that—"

Before she could finish her sentence, Jeff struck her with the back of his hand. The brute force sent her backward and then to the floor.

“How dare you defend him,” he said with venom. “But then again, I guess you would defend him. You are a liar and a cheater, just like him. You don’t deserve to live any more than that Bloom woman and her lover, Bradford. They tore their families apart. And you remember your first case ten years ago when we first opened the office?” He didn’t give Shay an opportunity to respond before rushing on. “What’s his name, Jay something. You actually believed he’d had a sudden heart attack.

Well, he didn’t. I helped it along. His partner was better off without him. He was never going to shape up. He deserved what he got.”

Shay lay on the floor, frozen, the wind knocked out of her. She started to cry. She could hardly believe what she was hearing.

“Jeff, what are you saying? Please don’t do this,” she pleaded.

“It was actually so easy to make sure they all got what they deserved. That includes all those who came for my help with that senseless nonsense. They all had ‘accidents.’” He used air quotes. “One was hit by a hit-and-run driver. One died of a heart attack. Another was stabbed by some robber. So many I can hardly remember now. Two died of an overdose of medication in their IVs. Potassium chloride stops the heart and is undetectable. It barely changes the body’s overall potassium level. Come now, don’t look at me like that. They are all gone, and those they cheated on are better off now."

Shay continued to lie on the floor, staring up at Jeff, as frightened as she'd ever been in her life. Her entire body was shaking. Sebastian was right about Jeff hurting her. But did he already know that Jeff was responsible for who knew how many other murders? Talk to him, she thought. Try to calm him down.

Shay sat up. "Jeff, why didn't you tell me about your dad and your mom? We could have and still can work things out together," she pleaded.

"No, we can't. It's too late for that now. It was too late when you cheated on me, Shay. How many times have you done it before?"

"I've never cheated on you, Jeff. Never."

Jeff yanked Shay up off the floor by her hair and shoved her into a chair.

"Liar," he screamed. "Liar, Liar, Liar." He repeated the words over and over, his eyes wild. He was standing right over Shay as she sat in the chair. "I saw the two of you. I saw the way he looked at you. I saw the two of you in an embrace in your office. I saw you, and yet you still lie. You are no different than they are."

"Than who?" Shay whimpered.

"Then my cheating mother and father. They both cheated. She cheated and brought another child into this evil world. Then he cheated and raped my baby sister. They both tore our family apart. I can't stand to look at him or his bastard incestual child now."

"Jeff, don't do this. I can help you," Shay pleaded once again.

"No, I'm going to help myself. You don't deserve to live," he said, striding over to his desk and taking something out of the top drawer. Shay was horrified to see it was a gun. He pointed it at Shay.

Chapter 48

Shay closed her eyes, praying to herself. She did not hear Sebastian enter. She didn't hear Sebastian identify himself as the police, demanding that Jeff drop his weapon. She heard the shot but felt nothing. When she opened her eyes, Sebastian was holding her. Sebastian reached over and turned off the recording device.

"You're okay," he said soothingly. "You're okay." Shay looked at Jeff lying on the floor. "Is he…"

"I'm afraid so. I got here just in time. He would have killed you." Sebastian's voice shook as he briefly pulled Shay close to him. "I radioed ahead for another squad car to get here, but the traffic and getting through the gate slowed them. Since I was coming from the opposite route, the traffic opened up better for me. I got here in time," he said, still holding her. "My heart was pounding so hard in my chest when I heard him hit you over the device. For a minute, I thought I was having a heart attack. But I knew I couldn't. I had to get to you. I don't know that I've ever felt as much rage as I did today."

Rising, he helped her up and shielded her from Jeff's dead body as he got her out of the room and then out of the house. They sat in his car and waited for other law enforcement officers to arrive. Shay wept openly as Sebastian held her tight.

"I can never return to that house," she said through sobs. "But I have to make some kind of arrangements for my animals. I can't just leave them in there," Shay said weakly.

"Don't worry. I'll have one of the officers take them to the pet hotel for the night, and then you can make other arrangements tomorrow," Sebastian said as he pulled out his phone to call the officer guarding the crime scene. His name was Larry Craig, and Sebastian knew he was fond of animals. He'd take good care of them. Shay gave Sebastian a grateful look.

Once the reports were taken and all paperwork completed at police headquarters, Sebastian insisted that Shay return to his house.

"No, I can't stay at your house. I can call my friend Saundra or my friend Gwen who works in our office. You remember her."

"Shay," Sebastian said, looking at his watch, "it's two a.m." He knew he couldn't let her go like this. He had to take care of her, at least for tonight. "You've been through a lot. I just want to keep you safe and make sure you're alright. I don't think you want to wake either of your friends at this hour and lay this experience on them."

How could all of this have been brewing in him for years without her having a clue? She thought a while later, sitting in Sebastian's house. "How could I have missed this?" She looked tearfully at Sebastian.

"It's not your fault. He had buried his feelings so deep inside that unless there was a trigger to bring them to the surface, he had pretty much blocked all of this out," Sebastian said as he tucked Shay into the bed in his guest bedroom. He smoothed the covers and touched her face.

He looked down at her. He knew she was strong, but at the moment, she looked so weak and fragile. What she went through tonight tore at his heart. It had not been his intention to kill Jackson, but he couldn't say he regretted it either. Her eyes closed. He knew she was exhausted and needed sleep. He turned the light out and went to his bedroom. He lay in bed but couldn't sleep.

He heard a scream. He was up in a flash and by her side in an instant.

"I'm sorry," she said. "I guess I was reliving what just happened in my sleep. I didn't mean to disturb you. I'm fine. Please, go back to bed."

"I can't do that," he said softly, looking down at her. His heart felt as if it would burst. "I'll just sleep on the chaise lounge," he said, pulling it closer to the bed—closer to her. "I need to be near you."

That was what he said, but what he felt was all the love and caring a man could have for a woman. Yet, he knew this was not the time to discuss it. He knew a little about psychology himself. He knew she would need time. And he had all the time in the world. He wanted this woman so badly.

But I'll wait, he thought. I'll wait for as long as it takes. He would do nothing to frighten her or push her into a relationship with him before she was ready. But until she was ready, he knew he had to at least see her. He had to be there if she needed him. He had to be whatever she needed from him. And one day, he knew she'd be ready.

Chapter 49

Shay slowly opened her eyes and sat up. Looking around at the room decorated in shades of brown and orange, for a moment, she didn't know where she was. Reality hit, causing her to fall back against the pillows. Next to her on the chaise lounge, Sebastian stirred.

Shay stared at the large sleeping man for a moment. All of the events of the night before returned to haunt her. Tears flowed silently. How could last night have been anything other than a nightmare?

Moving quietly, Shay pulled the covers back and got out of bed. She went into the bathroom. Looking into the mirror, she almost didn't recognize herself. Her eyes were puffy and red. Her face had a dark bruise on the left side, which she now rubbed. She all of a sudden felt dirty. She hoped Sebastian wouldn't mind if she took a shower. She turned on the faucet.

Shay jumped, startled, as Sebastian knocked on the bathroom door.

"Shay. Are you alright?" he asked softly.

"Yes," she lied, feeling as if she'd never ever be alright again.

Who could live through something like last night and come out unscathed? Her husband, whom she believed to be sweet and kind, had been only a moment away from killing her when Sebastian had burst in and shot him.

‘Killed him,’ she thought.

The knowledge that Jeff was actually a sociopath saddened her even more. Her tears continued to flow. It was all so surreal.

“I’m just going to take a shower, if that’s okay,” she said to Sebastian.

“Of course, it’s okay. There are towels in the linen closet, and body wash in the shower. There are also new toothbrushes in the top drawer. Can I get you anything else?” he asked.

“No. I’ll be fine.”

“You should probably take a long bath. There’s a Jacuzzi tub in there. Enjoy it.”

Deciding that sounded better than a shower, Shay prepared the bath water. She made it as hot as she dared. Whatever was making her feel unclean would surely dissolve in that hot water. The tub filled quickly. She stepped in, sat down, and tried her best to relax against the back of the tub. She turned on the jets. Within a very few minutes, she knew she could not relax even in a tub of hot water. It wouldn’t take the uncleanliness she felt away.

Her husband was dead. Not only had he not been the man she thought he was, but he had killed others. She repeated that aloud, “He killed others.”

With those words came uncontrollable shaking. She managed to get out of the tub and used the large towel she had removed from the linen closet, and started to dry her body. Then she used the towel to scrub as if she could scrub away all that had happened. Finally, she forced herself to stop. There was no way a towel could do the job. Sitting down on the side of the tub, she wrapped the towel around her and took several deep breaths.

Again, she looked in the mirror, "He was also going to kill you," She continued to stare at herself. "How can I ever put this behind me?"

"Shay," Sebastian called to her. "Breakfast is ready. I'm keeping it warm for you, so take your time."

When she didn't answer, Sebastian walked to the bathroom door and knocked. There was still no answer. He wasn't quite sure what to do. He certainly didn't want to just burst in on her. He knocked once more. Finally, he slowly pushed the door open. Seeing her sitting on the side of the tub sobbing tore at him.

Thinking his heart would burst with love, he gathered her in his arms. Holding her as she cried, he knew he had to have this woman in his life. Finally, the tears subsided.

"I'm sorry," she apologized. "I just don't seem to be able to get control."

"You don't need to apologize," he said, looking at her tenderly.

"You've been through a lot. I'll be here whenever you need me. I won't let anything happen to you. I…" Sebastian wanted to say more, but he knew it wasn't the right time.

Shay looked down at the towel she had wrapped around her and this man with his arms around her. She felt slightly embarrassed. She hardly knew this man. Yet, she did know him. She knew his embrace. It felt comforting. She felt protected.

"You have no right to feel this way about this man." The tiny voice was at it again. "You just lost your husband. What would people say?"

Seeming to read her thoughts, Sebastian abruptly stood. "Breakfast is ready whenever you are," he said. Now he felt a little embarrassed. What am I doing? he thought. Don't move too fast, he warned himself.

Shay quickly dressed. Walking into the kitchen, she asked, "Can I help you with anything? It smells wonderful."

"No thanks, everything is ready. Just have a seat, and I'll serve you."

Looking at the muffins Sebastian took out of the oven; she asked, "Did you make those?"

"Not really," he confessed. "They were frozen. I just popped them into the oven." His smile seemed to ease her pain.

Shay sat, and her tears started flowing again. This felt just like the many breakfasts she'd shared with Jeff. Breakfasts that he had also prepared and served her.

Sebastian watched from afar, afraid to move toward her, afraid to scare her off by taking her into his arms again, yet not knowing what else he could do. He simply watched her silently. His heart ached for her. He had to take several breaths to gain his own control. Watching Shay was also painful for him.

Soon, Shay used her napkin to blow her nose. "I'm sorry, but I'm just not hungry. I've got clients scheduled this morning. I will have to cancel them. I have to go home and change clothes."

Sebastian watched a panicked look cross her face at the thought of going home. This time, he couldn't help himself. He strode across the room, gently pulling her up out of the chair and taking her into his arms again. She melted against him. This had to be okay, he thought. She didn't pull away. Please, God, he prayed a silent prayer, let her want this as much as I do.

With that, he gently pulled himself away. He knew he was taking advantage of her in a weak moment. Promising himself he wouldn't do that, he gently pushed her back down into the chair. He sat in the chair next to her.

"I can go to the house with you if you'd like?" he said, ending with a question. "When it's allowed, that is. The police won't let anyone in yet."

"Oh," was all she said. "I guess it is a crime scene." She had, of course, heard that on television. "I can't stay here, and I'll need clothes."

Sebastian wanted so much to tell her that she could stay here with him. But he knew better.

"I need to call my best friend, Saundra. I can stay with her for a few days." She looked around for her purse and her cell phone. "Have you seen…?" Sebastian quickly handed her the purse that he'd quickly grabbed the night before as he led her out of her house.

"I want you to stay here, but I've got to go into headquarters. I just got a text. It seems Internal Affairs wants to speak with me."

"I don't understand. Don't they only come in when something isn't done properly?" Shay asked, her brow furrowed in worry.

"Please don't worry. It's routine. I'll return as soon as possible. Please don't worry," he said once again. "The meeting is set for this afternoon. It's barely seven a.m. now."

Chapter 50

Shay fished in her purse and came up with her phone. She noticed her battery was low. There were numerous messages from Saundra, Gwen, Sam, and her mom. It pained Shay to have to call any of these people who she knew loved her. She hated to think how worried they were. She knew they had all seen the gory details on television.

She looked around for an outlet. She plugged her charger in and let her phone charge. She'd start with Gwen first, she thought, dialing her number. It wasn't quite eight-thirty yet. Gwen was probably on her way to the office. There was barely a whole ring before Gwen picked up.

"Oh my God," she cried. "Where are you? I've been calling and calling ever since I saw the news last night. Are you at least safe?"

"Gwen," Shay said. "Take a breath. I am safe. I'm with Commander Crawford at the moment. I need you to cancel my appointments for today, probably for the rest of the week. Beyond that, I haven't figured out what I'm going to do. But I will be alright eventually. I'll call you as soon as I figure things out. Please don't worry about me."

"That's kind of impossible. Just call me as soon as you can. If you don't, I'm going to be burning up your phone again."

"I promise," Shay said, ending the conversation as quickly as she could.

Next, she called her mom. She knew her parents were probably out of their minds with worry. Again, the phone barely rang before her mom snatched it up.

"Shay!" Her mom was crying. "I'm so glad to hear from you. I saw the news on television last night and tried to call you. Your father and I have been so worried. We, of course, don't have the entire story, just what we heard on the news. But we find it difficult to process any of it. I don't want to process it. What kind of man was Jeff? We thought he was so sweet and gentle. He fooled us all and almost killed our baby," she said, crying again. "If that police officer hadn't killed Jeff, your dad would have. Your dad is here beside me, and he's ready to come and get you if necessary. I don't care how you get here, but sweetheart, please come home."

Shay's parents would not let her off the phone until she promised to be on the first plane to Virginia. Shay promised. She hardly knew what else to do.

Before placing the call to Saundra, Shay looked around for Sebastian. He appeared to have quietly left the room to give her some privacy. Then she heard the shower.

Shay quickly dialed Saundra. She didn't want to keep her in suspense and worried for a moment longer. Saundra was at least not sitting on top of the phone as the others had. Her phone rang twice before she picked up.

"Honey, please tell me that was fake news I heard last night, as Trump calls it. Please tell me none of it is true," she begged.

"I wish I could, my friend. I wasn't exactly in any shape to sit up and watch the news last night since I was 'the news.' So, I have no idea what they said. But I guess the gist of it is true." Shay paused, fighting tears. She could hear Saundra crying on the other end.

Shay continued slowly. "Jeff committed murders of those who cheated. His family history, of which I knew nothing, had a lot to do with it. Then he thought Sebastian and I were having an affair, so I was to become his next victim. And he would have succeeded had Sebastian not gotten there just in time. So, Jeff is now d—" Shay couldn't bring herself to say the word.

"Shay, of course, I'm curious about what happened, but I love you, my friend, and I can tell how painful it is for you to talk about it. So, don't. Just come over here and let me and James take care of you. By the way, where are you? I went to your house last night after I couldn't get you on the phone. It was crawling with police. This morning, it was quiet."

"I'm with the Commander. I stayed in his guest room last night. I was almost hysterical, and he was very kind."

"I can come and get you. Just say the word," Saundra offered.

"I think the Commander will take me home. I need to get things out of the house, and I'm probably only going to be able to get in if I'm with him. It is a crime scene," she said softly.

The mere words started both her and Saundra crying again.

"Then what will you do?" Saundra asked, cutting off the tears, even though her voice showed concern.

"I'm going to stay with my parents in Virginia for a while. I need some downtime. They'll take good care of me if they don't smother me," Shay said, giving a short laugh.

"Good for you. You certainly do need some downtime. When you feel better, be sure to stop in and visit my favorite sister, Sasha. Do tell her I called her my favorite. Sasha, Jordan, and the baby are a perfect family. I'll let them know you'll be in Virginia. They will be so glad to see you. In fact, Sasha and her sweet, happy family may be what you need to uplift your spirits. You'd be surprised at how well she's adjusted to being a wife and mother. She rarely, if ever, even mentions her mediation career." Saundra knew she was chattering on and on but couldn't seem to stop.

"You are probably right about Sasha and her family uplifting my spirits. Of course, you are usually right. Once I've settled in with my parents, I will definitely give Sasha a call. But, Saundra, in the meantime, I need a favor."

"Anything."

"Sebastian arranged to have Pam and Kimberly Alice taken to a pet facility last night. I need you to take care of them while I'm gone."

"Is that all? Of course, I'd love to take care of them. It would be my pleasure. They're both calm, sweet fur babies. You know I love them. After all, you did make me their godmother. Of course, I will care for them. Just let me know where to pick them up."

Shay managed a smile. "Oh, here's Sebastian now," Shay said, looking up to see Sebastian, tall and striking in his uniform. Even as confused as Shay felt, she didn't miss the crisp creases in his pants, the snow-white shirt, and all the brass on his shoulder. She stared.

"I've got my best friend, Saundra, on the phone. She's going to take care of Pam and Kimberly Alice while I'm gone. Can you please tell her where she can pick them up?"

Sebastian took the phone. "This is Sebastian, Saundra. If you tell me where you want Pam and Kimberly Alice, I will go get them and bring them to you."

"That would be great. Thank you for being so kind. And most of all, thank you for saving my best friend's life." Her voice cracked.

"No one could be more grateful that I got there in time than me," he simply responded. "I'll have Shay's babies to you within the next couple of hours."

He smiled at Shay after ending the call. "Does that do it for all the calls you need to make?" he asked.

"Yes, all except Sam, but I just can't talk about this anymore. Give me a minute. I'm going to text him."

She brought up his name and typed. "Good morning, Sam. I know you've heard the horrible news by now. I'll be alright." Shay refused to lie and say she was alright because, at this exact moment, she was not. But she knew she would be one of these days. "I need you to check with Gwen." Shay continued her text. "There are only three cases in the coming week that I don't want to postpone; I wonder if you could handle them. We've already discussed all three. Please don't worry about me. I'm going home to Virginia to see my parents. I promise to call you as soon as I can. Take care."

That done, Shay looked up at Sebastian. "Do you think I could get into my house if I'm with you?"

"You can, but I'd rather you didn't," he said hesitantly. "It's not a good place to be, Shay."

"I'll be fine," Shay said bravely. "I really need clothes and to pack. I'm going to Virginia to stay with my parents for a while. I've booked my flight, and I'm on the three o'clock plane. So, that gives me plenty of time to get through this."

Sebastian knew Shay's leaving was for the best but couldn't help asking, "For how long?" Please say only a day or two, he pleaded silently. He didn't think he could be without her for much longer. Now smiling at her, he knew that thought was ridiculous.

"I'm not sure," she responded. "At least a couple of weeks, maybe more. I've asked Gwen to cancel most of my cases, and I've asked Sam Roberts to handle the three that I don't feel I should cancel. I spoke with my friend Saundra and my parents. I know there are a lot of others I should contact, but I can't. Not right now. I'm going to take it one day at a time and one issue at a time." She said the last words with more confidence than she felt. Then she placed a firm eye on Sebastian. "I need you to promise me that you will make sure Willa Raines is released since we know who—" Shay didn't complete the sentence.

"Already done. In fact, I took care of that last night."

"Thank you. Now I really need to get to my house to pack."

"Shay, I really don't think it's a good idea for you to return to that house."

"Sebastian. I have to do this. I'm just going to throw a few things in a piece of luggage and go to the airport."

Sebastian gave in, and they were soon headed for Shay's house. As they got closer, Shay had to take deep breaths to calm herself. Sebastian looked on but said nothing. He didn't want this scene for her but realized he couldn't protect her from everything.

There were two police officers standing in front. They knew Sebastian and gave him a warm hello as he got out of the car. Going around to the other side, he helped Shay out. He could feel her shaking. As usual, he wanted to put his arms around her and shield her from everything negative. She managed to stand, and he kept his hand under her elbow. She seemed so fragile.

They walked slowly to the door. The officers both said good morning and stepped aside to let Sebastian and Shay in. As he had last night, Sebastian stayed between Shay and what was now the police outline of a body on the floor. Shay kept her eyes averted as she headed upstairs. Sebastian followed.

Once they reached the top of the stairs, Shay swayed. Sebastian steadied her.

"Okay?" he said.

"Okay," she said weakly.

Shay took as little time as possible to get her luggage out of the closet and literally threw clothes and cosmetics in. She would normally have folded everything so neatly. She dismissed the thought that she also used to fold Jeff's clothes.

Shay was sure she hadn't packed nearly enough, but she could stay no longer. All of a sudden, she couldn't breathe. She picked up the luggage, which Sebastian immediately took from her. She rushed down the stairs and out the door. Breathing in the fresh air, she swayed again. Sebastian put a firm hand on her arm and guided her to the car. She could no longer stay in the house she'd always loved. She couldn't even look back as Sebastian's car pulled away. She never wanted to return to that house or to any of the memories it held. She'd replace anything she needed that was locked inside.

The officers watched as the couple departed.

"Would you mind taking me to see Pam and Kimberly Alice? I can't leave without seeing them. And then would you mind taking me to the airport? I'm going to change my flight. I'd like to leave earlier," she said, already making the changes on her phone.

Sebastian was hoping to spend just a little more time with her. It was barely ten o'clock. His Internal Affairs meeting wasn't for hours. Sebastian didn't argue but drove Shay to the facility which housed her pets and then on to the airport. He wanted to kiss her goodbye but was again afraid he'd scare her off. This was not the time.

She checked in with Delta Airlines. Turning, she kissed Sebastian on the cheek. “I’ll call you,” was all she said before turning away. She didn’t want to give Sebastian the opportunity to say anything. It was too soon.

This was not the time.

Chapter 51

Sebastian stood watching her walk away. Not until she was completely out of sight did he move. Slowly, he got into his vehicle and headed to his office.

When Sebastian pulled into his designated parking space at police headquarters, he didn't immediately get out of the car. He felt—Actually, he thought, I don't know how I feel. Yes, I do. Admit it, Sebastian Edison Crawford, you love her, and you feel as if something has been lost now that she's gone. Well, he said to himself, you might as well get a grip. You've got to go in here and face Internal Affairs.

Sebastian had told Shay the truth. An IA investigation could be routine or not. Rubye greeted him as he entered his office.

"Where have you been?" she asked, sounding a little angry.

"Why?" he asked. "Who put a bug up your ass?"

"Internal affairs, that's who," she answered through clenched teeth.

"Why would that bother you?"

"Why? I'll tell you why." She lowered her voice to a whisper. "Internal Affairs has been buzzing around here asking questions since seven this morning. Has he ever mentioned Mrs. Jackson to me? Was he having an affair with Mrs. Jackson? Did he ever say anything that might indicate that he would like to get rid of Jeff Jackson? You've been acting a little strange, so I knew it was a woman. I just didn't know it was the good doctor," she hissed.

"Don't be ridiculous. There is nothing going on between Dr. Jackson and myself. Why would anyone think that?"

"Well, for starters, how about I heard the IA interview by phone, the police officers standing guard over the Jackson house. I heard them ask the officers if anyone had been to the house. This cleared up for me why they then asked me if you had told me you would be with Dr. Jackson this morning. They wanted to know, didn't you usually let me know where you would be when not here? Did you happen to mention you would be stopping by the house with Dr. Jackson? Does that answer your question?" she hissed again.

"Look," Rubye continued, "I'd be the last one to begrudge you a life. I've been trying to get you to find one for the last five years. I want you to be happy. I want you to fall in love and get married again. I just don't think you want to do it with the wife of the guy you shot and killed." This time she softened her voice.

Sebastian did not respond.

Rubye's phone rang. She let it ring three or four times before taking her eyes off Sebastian. Finally, she turned to go into her office to answer the call.

Sebastian sat back in his chair. His brain was numb. He didn't think. He just sat there. He'd just have to see what IA had to say to him.

Sebastian handled a few calls. He couldn't tell you afterward exactly what he'd said. He walked to the vending machine and walked back without purchasing anything.

Rubye watched him. She did not want to see him in a battle with IA, and she did not want to see him hurt by what were obviously feelings he had for this woman.

Sebastian returned to his seat empty-handed. At exactly one o'clock, Rubye buzzed him. "IA is here," she said simply.

Chapter 52

Sebastian stood and buttoned his jacket. He shook hands with both men. He knew them both—Christopher Johnson and Harold Smith. Sebastian had worked with them many times, just never regarding anything he did.

"Hello, gentlemen," he said, surprised that his voice sounded so calm. "Can I offer you some coffee?"

"No thanks," they said in unison.

"We'll get right to it, Commander. No sense in beating around the bush. What do you know about this?" Harold said, throwing a piece of paper down in front of Sebastian.

Sebastian read the note. His face showed no sign of emotion.

This is not something I want to do, but I find I have no choice. I told her not to cheat on me. I told her over and over, but she didn't listen. I saw her with the Commander. I saw his arms around her.

I will not allow any woman to cheat on me. So, her fate has to be sealed the same as so many other cheaters. They all had to die, and I had to be the one to kill them. She must also die. I will have to be the one to kill her. My fate is also sealed, as I cannot live without her.

Sebastian could tell both men's eyes were focused on him.

He looked up calmly. He'd let them ask the questions.

"What are your questions?" he said.

"Would you like to have an attorney present?"

"No, thank you, I would not," Sebastian responded.

"Have you seen this note before?"

"No, I have not."

"You know Dr. Shay Jackson?"

"Yes."

"Did you know her prior to last night when you killed her husband?"

"Yes."

"How did you meet Dr. Jackson?"

"I met her when one of her clients, Willa Raines, had been arrested for murder."

"Is it customary for you, Commander, to handle cases such as this?"

"I have on occasion."

"How did you make the decision to get involved in this particular case?"

"Mrs. Raines is a neighbor of one of my cousins. He called and asked if I could look into it."

"But you didn't just look into it, Commander; you actually took over the entire investigation alone. Is that not true?"

"I did take over the investigation, but not alone. I had help working the case with my assistant, Lieutenant Rubye Weaver."

"What made you take over the investigation?"

"I had a gut feeling about the case."

"Did this gut feeling come before or after you met Dr. Jackson?"

"It actually came before. I interviewed Mrs. Raines before I went to see Dr. Jackson. That's when I got the feeling that she wasn't guilty. My instincts told me she was not. And my instincts are usually right. I'd say they were right this time as well. Mrs. Raines did not kill her husband."

"After you looked into the case and spoke with Mrs. Raines, why didn't you turn the case back over to your detectives?"

"Because they were convinced that Mrs. Raines was guilty. I decided to take the case to prove her innocent, not guilty."

"Again, I ask you, Commander, did this revelation come before or after you met Dr. Jackson?"

"Before."

When was your initial contact with Dr. Jackson?"

"Maybe two months ago. I'm not sure. I'd have to check my notes if you want the exact date."

"What was your initial conversation?"

"I knew she was bound by client confidentiality, but I wanted to at least find out if Dr. Jackson could say no to Mrs. Raines ever saying she would kill or like to kill her husband."

"And was she able to substantiate that Mrs. Raines had not expressed a wish to kill her husband?"

"As a matter of fact, she was."

"Did you have occasion to see Dr. Jackson again?"

"Yes."

"When was this and why?"

"Mr. Grayson Bradford's death was also ruled a homicide, which occurred shortly after Mr. Raines's murder. And again, the Bradfords had sought counseling from Dr. Shay Jackson. Consequently, I once again questioned Dr. Jackson about Mr. Bradford."

"What is your relationship to Dr. Jackson?"

“We don’t know each other well, but I guess you can say we have a mutually respectful friendship?”

“How friendly, Commander?”

“If you want degrees of friendship, I’d say when you have only known someone for the short period of time that I have known Dr. Jackson, the relationship couldn’t possibly be very deep.”

“Then tell me if Dr. Jeff Jackson’s comment in this note pertaining to finding you with your arms around his wife is true.”

“It’s true.” Sebastian did not hesitate to answer. “Dr. Shay Jackson became emotional while I was in her office, and I just attempted to comfort her. There was nothing more to it.”

“Where were you before coming into the office this morning, Commander?”

“I took Dr. Jackson to her home to pick up some clothes and pack luggage for a trip. She said she needed to go there. I first tried to dissuade her. When she insisted, I offered to take her. Otherwise, she would not have been able to get to the crime scene. I assure you that the crime scene was not compromised by her visit.”

“How did you and Dr. Jackson make contact this morning?”

Sebastian once again did not hesitate before responding. “Dr. Jackson stayed in my guest room last night. She was terribly upset after almost being killed by her husband, and I offered to let her stay in my guest room, knowing that she could not stay in her home."

"Is it customary, Commander, for you to allow witnesses to stay in your guest room? Especially witnesses who are present when you kill their husband?"

"What happened here was a clean shoot. You can make whatever you want out of my courtesy to Dr. Jackson, who had almost been another homicide at the hands of her husband. But the reality is that it was after two o'clock in the morning when the paperwork was completed, and Dr. Jackson had nowhere to go without waking someone in the wee hours of the morning. It was obvious that she could not return to her home, the crime scene."

"We understand that Dr. Jackson had in her possession a recording device that was activated to allow you to hear what was going on in her home. How did that come about?"

"My assistant, Rubye Weaver, who was working the case with me, came across some information that led us to believe that Dr. Jeff Jackson might be contemplating doing harm to his wife. So, I made contact with Dr. Shay Jackson to warn her.

"In spite of the evidence Lieutenant Weaver had discovered, Dr. Jackson insisted she was going home to talk with her husband. I felt that was a dangerous move and tried my best to talk her out of going there without the police. When she continued to insist, I directed her to the Gaming Commission across the street from her office to pick up the device. I had advised her that I would contact a scout car in the area to be there, who would be directed not to enter unless something was heard that would give a reasonable cause. She had agreed to leave the front door unlocked so that once the car arrived, an entry would be possible if necessary."

"And did you contact a scout car in the area, or did you just decide to proceed alone?"

"The scout cars in the area happened to be busy. I was not able to garner one until fifteen minutes later. There was a hockey game, a basketball game, and a convention that caused extensive traffic in the downtown Detroit area that made it difficult for the scout car to get through on Jefferson Avenue, even with sirens. Consequently, I arrived maybe two minutes before the two officers."

"So, you arrived far enough in advance of the officers so that they did not see the actual shooting?"

"That is correct. They arrived not more than two minutes afterward. On the way to the house, I heard Dr. Jeff Jackson confessing to Dr. Shay Jackson that he had killed people because they were cheating. He accused her of cheating on him with me. She, of course, denied it because it was not true. But I'm sure this is redundant from here because I'm sure you've listened to the tape. When I arrived and ran into the house, Dr. Jeff Jackson was holding the gun on his wife and appeared ready to pull the trigger. I had no choice but to shoot immediately before he did."

"Did you identify yourself as a police officer?"

"I did. I'm sure you heard me on the tape."

"Why did you find it necessary to shoot Dr. Jeff Jackson in the head rather than wound him?"

"After the confession, I heard on the recording, I believed that Dr. Jeff Jackson, even if wounded, would still have attempted to kill his wife. When I identified myself as a police officer, he did not lower the gun; he did not take his eyes off of his wife. My decision was based on my best professional experience. And now, reading his note, I believe that the call was accurate. Actually, Dr. Jackson's head was most prominent, as I was standing to the side, and he was standing directly in front of Mrs. Jackson. Dr. Jackson was prepared to die at either the hands of the police or his own. Consequently, I believe nothing I said could have deterred him. Had I shot him in the arm or the leg to injure him, I felt he would still have managed to shoot his wife."

"I'm sure Lieutenant Weaver has filled you in on the information she obtained regarding Dr. Jeff Jackson, Jr., and Jeff Jackson, Sr., who is in prison in Lapeer as we speak. He killed his wife for cheating on him, impregnated his twelve-year-old daughter, sodomized his fourteen-year-old son, and advised the boy never to allow a woman to cheat on him. That boy was Dr. Jeffrey Jackson, Jr."

"I also interviewed Jackson's aunt, Mrs. Maggie Jackson Clark, who advised me that Jackson had buried the facts regarding his father killing his mother, impregnating his sister, and sodomizing him, and had been known to become violent before when triggered. I believed the fact that he believed in error that his wife was cheating on him was that trigger. I have no more to say. Are we done here, gentlemen?"

"Yes, Commander, we are done. You'll be hearing from us." With that, the IA officers left the building.

At that point, Sebastian felt exhausted and didn't care much about what the bastards thought or did, for that matter. His need was simple. He needed Shay. And a good night's sleep wouldn't hurt. The chair next to Shay's bed wasn't the most comfortable way to spend a night. But Sebastian knew that for Shay, he'd sleep on rocks to be close to her.

Chapter 53

George turned off the TV newscast he'd been only half watching until Doc's face appeared on the screen. Sitting up and finally taking notice of what the reporter was saying, he couldn't believe what he was hearing.

"The Doc is dead," he said out loud. I just saw him two days ago, he thought. The same guy his wife was cheating with killed him. Looking at the envelope filled with money lying on the table, he smiled. He had only spent a couple thousand. Most of that was spent sending gifts to his wife. He still hoped to get her back. Now that he'd taken care of the slimeball she'd cheated on him with, he knew he had a better chance of that happening.

He realized he was close when she'd accepted his gifts. He had tried sending gifts before, only to have her return them to Aunt Edna's house. This time she hadn't done that. He had watched her from afar at the cheater's funeral. He could tell she was vulnerable. She was crying. He'd make it up to her and dry her tears. She'd be glad the guy was gone in no time. She'd be back in his arms. He'd done her a favor by getting rid of him.

He'd, of course, made it look like an accident. No one would ever know that the large FedEx truck he used to take care of Doc's business had also been useful for him. She wouldn't miss him.

George had followed him late one night. He had been watching him for months. George was aware that he took a dark, unpaved road home from work every night. There was rarely anyone on the road at that time of evening. A simple nudge to the small Kia he drove sent it rolling over and over. He watched as the car became engulfed in flames. There was hardly any damage to the truck. The Doc hadn't even noticed.

He smiled again. Now, he just had to finish what the Doc had paid him to do. He remembered again how intense the Doc was when he made him promise that if he didn't succeed in killing his wife, George should finish the job. So, he would.

He'd been kind of romantically involved with Gail Brown for the last few months. It was mostly for sex. After all, it had been a long time since he'd been with his wife. Besides, Gail had been hired by the Doc to work in the TRFG office so that she could keep tabs on things. Now she'd told him that the Doc's wife would be leaving for Virginia. He'd take care of her when she returned.

He'd need to know what her schedule would be so that he could keep his promise to the Doc. There was no hurry. He needed to do this right and make sure nothing could be traced back to him. That also meant, unfortunately for Gail, that he'd have to get rid of her as well. Now that the Doc was dead, Gail was the only connection between himself and the good work he and the Doc had done. He was aware that Maverick Jones had been arrested, but he had been very careful when dealing with him. Maverick had never seen him and did not know his real name. Even so, Maverick had provided good information via his investigations. The final good deed would be seeing Dr. Shay Jackson dead.

Part II

Chapter 54

Shay was both emotionally and physically exhausted. She'd slept through the entire flight. Now stepping into the airport, she followed the signs to pick up her luggage by rote. She placed a call to her dad as she walked. He would pick her up.

She managed to get her one piece of luggage with the help of a young man who snatched it off the turnstile when he saw her struggling to drag it off. Shay thanked him profusely. All of a sudden, she felt weak and didn't think she would have been able to lift the suitcase had he not assisted her.

Pulling up the handle, Shay slowly rolled the luggage to a bench. She needed to sit. All of a sudden, she felt like crying. Sniffing, she shook herself. Get a grip, she thought. She knew she could not let her family see any signs of distress. She sensed they would know that she couldn't be doing well after the ordeal she'd been through. But Shay knew staying strong for them would also keep her stronger. Besides, she was afraid that if she broke down, she'd delay getting herself together. She knew she wasn't thinking like a psychologist. But it was the best she could do at the moment.

Forcing herself up off the bench, she walked toward the exit. Once outside, she looked for her dad's red Lincoln MKX. She smiled as she realized that her mom, dad, one of her sisters, and the dog were all in the car. Her mom was holding the small poodle in her lap. As she saw Shay exit the airport door, she immediately put the puppy down, jumping out of the car to greet her daughter. Her dad and sister Suzanne all followed suit, converging on Shay. There were only two family members missing from this reunion, Shay's sister Juliette and Juliette's twin brother, Julius. Of course, they both had families, and she hoped they were home with them. Shay wasn't certain she could take any more attention.

She had to admit, other than a little too much attention, it felt good to be home. While she appreciated how the family continued to pamper her, at times, she felt smothered. They appeared to watch her every move, looking for what Shay wasn't quite sure. She guessed they were looking for any signs of her mental and emotional state after the ordeal. Consequently, Shay continued to hide any signs that would make her family worry or uncomfortable.

Once the entire family arrived, including Suzanne's husband and son; Juliette, her husband and their twin daughters; and Julius and his wife and daughter, Shay was ready to run back to Detroit for some air. She found it difficult to breathe.

She wasn't sleeping but did not divulge this to anyone. She wasn't eating, but at mealtime, under the watchful eyes of her family, she managed to force herself to eat enough to satisfy them.

Shay took to going for long walks. Initially, a family member would come with her. But Shay wanted to be alone and discovered if she got up just before the sun rose, she could get away alone. She started reading old novels she found on the bookshelf in her room. She wasn't particularly interested in books, but reading was a way to have uninterrupted silence. Whenever a talkative family member started near, she would pick up her book to avoid conversation.

Chapter 55

She was well aware that she was not handling things well. She needed assistance. However, she did not want to worry her family. So, this, too, caused her to find a way to seek professional help without arousing her family's suspicions.

But most of all, she really needed Sebastian. Within the first few days of her visit, she had received at least six phone calls from him. She did not answer them. She wanted him, but it really was too soon. She texted him to let him know she had arrived safely and that she was coping. But she knew coping was not what she was doing.

Shay thought about phoning a practicing psychologist with whom she had gone to school. Then decided against it. Then thought of all the torment Jeff had gone through when he failed to seek help. With help, Jeff might not have come to the conclusion that he needed to take care of his problem with his wife by using a gun. Shay found it difficult to even think of what Jeff had tried to do to her. She needed help, and she'd seek the assistance she needed. Making contact was the first step to getting better, she knew.

Shay called her friend and former schoolmate, Janet Lacoste. Janet answered on the third ring.

"Shay," Janet said, surprised to hear from her old friend. "Yes, you are still saved in my contacts. It's been years, and you're still there." She laughed. "What can I do for you?"

"For starters, you can have lunch with me tomorrow. I'm in Virginia."

"Tomorrow is Saturday, and for once, I don't have a consultation, seminar, or anything planned. I'd love to have lunch with you. Why don't you come here? I'll whip us up something." Pausing, she said, "I'm sorry to hear about what happened with Jeff. I suppose that's why you called. And I'm not trying to make you feel guilty. I'm just glad to hear from you, and if I can help, you know I will."

"I do feel guilty about finally making contact under these circumstances. Janet, please forgive me."

"There is nothing to forgive. Shay, we will always be friends whether we see each other or talk or not. We've got it like that, girl. And after all, we've both been busy. I feel a little guilty as well. I didn't reach out either. So, I guess that makes us even," Janet said softly. "Just get here by twelve thirty tomorrow. We'll eat, drink wine, and talk."

"I'll be there," Shay said, hanging up. The first step accomplished, she thought and actually smiled. It was pretty much the first smile that wasn't forced since the incident. She'd simply tell her family she'd be lunching with an old friend. That was true.

The lunch Janet prepared was excellent. Janet had a real sweet tooth, so Shay knew it would conclude with some decadent dessert. Janet didn't disappoint. The moist fudge brownies with whipped cream and vanilla and raspberry sauce surrounding the plate were heavenly. Shay found that, at least with this meal, her appetite had returned.

She spent the next four hours with Janet. It felt good to see someone other than her family. She loved them but confessed to Janet that they were smothering her. She also couldn't be herself with them. A smile had been plastered on her face ever since she'd arrived home. She knew she wasn't really fooling anyone, but she just couldn't completely open up to her family.

Initially, the two women took time to catch up and renew their old friendship. Later they got into allowing Shay to express a few of her fears and her guilt. They agreed she would start seeing Janet professionally on Tuesday.

Shay arrived home in time to share dinner with her family. She felt more like her old self than she had since the ordeal. She'd made an appointment to return for a more professional session at Janet's office. That alone helped. She knew it was only the first step, but everything positive started with being able to take that first step.

Shay was anxious to speak with Sebastian but spent the rest of the evening watching some television program with her family. She knew little of what it was about. Her mind was on Sebastian. She couldn't help it.

After the ten-thirty news, Shay managed to slip away from her family and head up to her bedroom. In the privacy of her room, she started to dial Sebastian's number. Pausing, she thought about all of his calls she had ignored. But she had ignored them long enough. She could no longer deny that she had feelings for him, so it was time to at least have a conversation. She was convinced that she needed more time before delving into any relationship, but she was sure that when the time was right, he would be the man she would be with. She continued dialing.

"Hello, Shay." He sounded breathless.

"Did I get you at a bad time?" she asked.

"Shay, there could never be a bad time for you to call. Are you alright?"

"Actually, I am a little better than I had been."

"I've been praying to hear your voice," he said. "I'm not pushing or rushing you. I think you know how I feel. I just wanted to hear your voice. To know that you're okay. I haven't been able to think about anything else. I apologize for all the calls. I promised myself I'd give you some space, that I wouldn't rush you, but I couldn't seem to help myself. I just needed to know you were at least making progress with getting back to normal."

"That's very sweet of you," Shay said. "And I really appreciate your friendship. This just isn't the time right now. I'm doing what I need to do to get back to normal, whatever that means. And yes, I also wanted to hear your voice."

Sebastian melted with those words. "Shay, when do you think you'll be returning to Detroit?"

"I'm not sure. I think it will be at least another few weeks. I'm getting some counseling while here. It's something I feel I need to do," she said softly.

It felt good to share that she was seeking help from someone. She had not yet shared it with her family or even Gwen or Saundra. She knew they would worry about just how bad things were if she, a psychologist, had to resort to seeking help. She knew they'd be glad she was getting help but would worry even more knowing she needed it.

"I'm glad. Just know that I'll be here waiting for you for however long it takes."

"Thanks, Sebastian. I just wanted to call. I'm going to try to get some sleep now. Please take care of yourself."

"I will. You do the same."

Shay found a relaxing sleep that night, the first in weeks.

Chapter 56

Sebastian sat quietly at his desk in police headquarters. His thoughts were, of course, on Shay.

"Penny, for your thoughts?" Rubye said, smiling at him. She'd been much nicer than usual lately. She hadn't been on his back about sleeping, eating, or any of the many demands she usually bombarded him with. She seemed to sense something was going on with him. It was time he talked about it, she decided.

Prodding him to get out of his seat, Rubye helped Sebastian into his uniform jacket as she pushed him toward her office. Once there, she picked up her purse and continued propelling him toward the exit.

"Do you mind if I ask where we're going?" Sebastian asked.

"It's quitting time. We're going to dinner, that's where. Your treat," she said, smiling.

Her "I mean business" tone caused Sebastian not to argue. Secretly, he was glad. He'd wanted to talk with Rubye for a while. She was, in fact, his best friend at the office. She always had his back. He also knew she would keep his confidence.

"I'll drive," she said, heading toward her red sports car. Sebastian once again did not argue. Rubye waited for him to fold his long legs into the small Ford Mustang and fasten his seat belt before taking off.

“Where are we going?” Sebastian asked.

“Just relax,” she said. “It’s time for you to let someone else take the lead. Don’t you get kind of tired of always being the boss and calling the shots? I know you do,” she continued without allowing Sebastian to answer. “I know something is going on with you, and I’m holding you, hostage, until you tell me what it is.”

Sebastian was silent as they pulled up to Cliff Bell’s Jazz Club located on Park Avenue. The club had actually been a speakeasy in the prohibition days. Rubye loved the history.

“I figured it wouldn’t hurt you to have some food, a few drinks, and listen to some jazz. You can relax, and we can talk,” she said, emphasizing the “we.”

Sebastian held up his hands in surrender as they exited the car and headed into Cliff Bell’s, one of the world’s oldest jazz clubs, having opened in 1935. Sebastian was aware that some really great jazz musicians had played there and at Baker’s Key Board Lounge, another Detroit club that opened in 1934. Sebastian loved jazz as much as Rubye did and was even aware that the Green Mill Jazz Club in Chicago made its debut in 1907. All great history.

Once they were inside, Rubye moved with purpose as Sebastian followed. She said hello to the staff, who seemed to know her, and went to a large comfortable sofa located at the front of the club and on the right side of the room. She slid into the booth as Sebastian again followed. I guess she was serious about my following instead of leading, he thought.

Sebastian looked around. The rich wood paneling gave the place a warm, comfortable feeling. He liked the ambiance. The long bar was inviting, but the sofa to which Rubye had led him was comfortable and definitely promoted conversation with its high, secluded back. The furniture was upholstered in soft gray suede. The entire setting was relaxing.

Once seated, Rubye called the waiter by name and ordered two bourbons. "Make it Blanton's if you have it," she said, smiling. "How are the kids, Howard?" she asked before the waiter could move away from the table.

"They're fine, Rubye. Thanks for asking." The waiter beamed.

Sebastian watched the interaction. Rubye made friends easily and cared about everyone. It was like her to ask about the waiter's family. She was always genuine. You knew she was sincere and that she really cared. She was a caring person. She raised three younger siblings after her mom passed. She also took good care of her dad until he died of lung cancer a few years ago. Having no children of her own, she was a perfect and doting aunt to her sister's three children.

Chapter 57

Now turning toward Sebastian, she stared him straight in the eye for almost a full minute until he blinked first. He laughed.

"What do you want from me?" Sebastian demanded.

"I want the truth, dammit. You've been acting strange ever since before the shooting. The guys think killing someone is what's on your mind. But I know differently. I know you better than you know yourself." She laughed.

"I've left you alone for weeks even though I knew something was going on," she went on. "I'd hoped you would come to me. But I'm tired of waiting. It's time you spilled the beans right now. You aren't getting out of here without talking to me. I already know part of it. It's a woman, so you might as well admit it and talk to me."

The drinks arrived. Sebastian took a long swallow. "Smooth," he said. "Okay, something is going on. It's not like me, but I fell for a married woman." He paused, ignoring Rubye's raised eyebrows and loud cough, and then continued.

"We don't have some kind of sordid affair going on, but I can't get her out of my head, and I think she feels the same. But it's even more complicated than that." Sebastian stopped.

“Take your time,” Rubye said softly. “But I’m waiting.” She turned to make sure she was squarely facing Sebastian.

“It happened the first time I went to question Shay Jackson.”

Rubye sputtered as she was in the middle of taking a drink. “I’m sorry,” she said, cleaning the droplets off the table with her napkin. “I think I didn’t hear you right.”

“You heard me. The woman is Shay Jackson. There were sparks between us. I know that’s cliché, but there really were sparks. I couldn’t stop thinking about her. I couldn’t sleep. It was as if I wouldn’t be able to breathe any longer if I wasn’t able to see her. And nothing has changed,” Sebastian said, lowering his head.

Rubye interrupted him. “You are speaking of Dr. Shay Jackson, the wife of the man you killed?”

“Well, when you put it like that, it really sounds bad. You’ve just managed to make things sound even worse than the Internal Affairs guys did.”

“I’m sorry. But do they know about all of this?”

“Not all of it, but I answered the questions they asked me honestly. I even admitted that I had taken Shay home with me to sleep in my guest room after the shooting.” Rubye gasped. Sebastian shrugged. “Well, they asked. You know, they were aware that Shay and I had both arrived at her house together early that morning. So, they wanted to know how the two of us had connected so early in the morning. I think they actually asked how we made contact. I told them. They asked what our relationship was, and I told them I guess we were friends but that we had not known each other long, so we couldn't be really deep friends. Deep was the only word I could think of at the time." He sighed.

"It seems that Jeff had left a suicide note. His intention was to kill both Shay and himself. The note stated that he had repeatedly told her not to cheat on him. And, of course, he thought she had cheated with me. He mentioned that he had seen her in my arms."

"Sebastian, no," was all Rubye said, her eyes widening.

"Calm down. It wasn't like that. She was terribly upset the last time I was in her office. She was actually crying, and I just held her briefly to comfort her. That's what I told Internal Affairs when they asked if what Jeff had written was true about me holding her. I didn't lie. But that was also the last time I had seen her before the shooting. What I didn't tell IA was that I believe her tears stemmed from the internal struggle she was having over me."

"Again, we didn't have any affair, but I believe she felt the same attraction I did. When I saw what my coming around was doing to her, I swore I would stay away. And until you gave me the terrifying information about Jeff and I went to visit his aunt, who really had a lot to say, I had not and would not have contacted her. But I had to warn her. And even so, I simply texted her and asked her to Google Jeff, Sr.'s name. Jeff had told her the man was dead. No mention that his mom had been murdered by his dad. He told her that his parents were killed in an automobile accident." Sebastian took a deep breath and a large swallow of the warm bourbon.

"Then what happened?"

"Once she knew, she felt as if she had to go to Jeff. I guess she felt as if she could both comfort and counsel him. I tried to get her not to go, and you know the rest. You have the copy of the tape with him threatening to kill her."

Rubye hugged Sebastian and lightly rubbed his back. "I am so sorry this happened. What's happening with the two of you now?"

Sebastian sighed. "Shay left and went home to her parents' place in Virginia. We've talked briefly, but she wasn't returning my calls for the most part. I don't really know when she'll return to Detroit. And I don't really know what the future holds for us. I just know I really want her. I think she feels the same, but I don't know if she'll be able to go forward with me because of what happened." He paused and then said, "I need her, Rubye. You know better than anyone how I've agonized over my guilt about Sara's death. I haven't felt any kind of emotion; been numb for years. And to meet someone who unlocked feelings that I never thought I'd have again has been difficult to ignore. I need her," he said again, rubbing his forehead.

"I know you do. You've needed her for a long time. I think it will all work out. Just give her some time."

Sebastian looked at his friend and confidante gratefully. He'd really needed to get this out by venting to someone. And there was no one better to confide in than his long-time partner. He knew he could trust Rubye and that she would give the best advice when he needed it.

Rubye reached out and touched Sebastian's arm. "I'll be here whenever you need to talk, you know that. Don't keep everything in like you do. Promise me that."

"I promise," he said, downing the last of his drink and ordering another. He felt lighter than he had in weeks. The two sat for the next hour, listening calmly to the melodious jazz music. Sebastian looked around him and took a deep breath. He felt, as Rubye had said, that it would all work out. At least, he hoped it would. He had a fear that Shay might stay in Virginia. He didn't know what he'd do if that happened. He refused to give the thought credibility by admitting his fear to Rubye.

Chapter 58

After being silent for a while, Sebastian asked shyly, “What do you think Sara would think of all this?”

“You want the honest truth?”

“I do,” he said, afraid of what Rubye would say.

Seeing the look on his face and reading his thoughts as usual, she covered his hand and leaned closer.

“She would want you to be happy. I never told you this, but she asked me to take care of you. You know she was afraid for you working this job?” She looked up. “Of course, you know. But what you don’t know is that she and I had numerous conversations. This is why I can say this without any fear of contradiction, she would have liked your choice of Shay Jackson, and she would want you to be happy with her. You know I’m always honest with you, don’t you?”

“Of course I do.” Sebastian nodded.

“So, when I say this, I want you to listen carefully. Do not for one minute let what you think Sara would think hold you back from living your life. She is gone, and I know that hurt. You can’t have her back. I’ve watched you hide away and mourn for what you can no longer have long enough. It is past time for you to get on with your life. So, get on with living with the person who is here, or at least I believe she will be at some point. The minute she returns, don't you dare waste a minute before going to her." She smiled at him, suddenly remembering another tidbit she'd never shared with him. Years after Sara's death, it was now funny. But, while the pain was fresh with him, she knew he wouldn't have thought so.

"Okay," Rubye said, "I need to tell you something else about my conversations with Sara. Do you remember that big-butt girl you dated before you and Sara became serious?"

"Not exactly." He looked puzzled.

"Well, Sara told me if something ever happened to her, she'd want you to get married again, but not to her. The girl's name was Laura. Do you remember now?"

"Vaguely," he laughed. "I can't believe the two of you had conversations like that." He shook his head. "You're always worrying about me. What's going on with you? How's that dog you adopted?"

"Fanny is wonderful. She keeps my feet warm at night." Rubye laughed.

"I thought Jack Roberts was the new man in your life. Doesn't he keep your feet warm?"

“I’d like him to, but he hasn’t had the balls to ask yet. He’s a little shy. However, I have a plan. The next time he visits, I’ll just drag him upstairs. I know he wants to. I can tell by the bulge in his pants each time I kiss him. And get that, I kiss him. He is really that shy. It’s kind of cute, actually, but it makes getting what I need from the relationship slow going. You know, at first, I didn’t even like him because of his potbelly. But now I actually think it’s cute. I really do want him.”

“I’m sure you’ll figure out a way to get what you want,” he assured her. “You always do.”

Sebastian and Rubye continued bantering until Sebastian stood. “I’ve really got to try to get some sleep. I haven’t been sleeping well lately. Tossing and turning and counting Shays is really a bitch.” He smiled wanly.

Chapter 59

The Doc's wife had been gone nearly two months when Gail informed George Hayden that even though she was still in Virginia, Shay Jackson had purchased a new condo in Michigan. Gail gave him the address. Gail's placement in the TRFG office certainly came in handy, he thought to himself.

He pulled the white truck out of the garage. He'd already affixed the Smithers Alarm Co. sign to both sides of the truck. Pulling up to the condo a short while later, he boldly got out of the truck and walked up to the door. He had coveralls with Smithers Alarm Co. printed on the back. So no need to sneak around.

Standing at the door using his tools to enter seemed perfectly normal for someone who was there to install an alarm system. He moved into the house and installed only one tiny bug in the corner of the foyer that would pick up every sound throughout the house. Once done, he looked around. Finding the master bedroom, he made a mental note. He'd take her during the night, so he needed to know which bedroom she'd be in. Exiting the house, he continued to use tools on the outside of the home, pretending to complete the alarm installation. He then walked boldly down the stairs and hopped back into the truck.

The neighbor across the street smiled as she straightened her window treatment. The new owner had been making a lot of changes. She'd never seen her but had heard she had purchased the home while out of state. There had been furniture delivered. And now she has an alarm system installed. Better to be safe than sorry when moving into a new area, she thought. Perhaps she should think about an alarm system for her home. Things weren't as safe anywhere as they used to be. Yawning, she stepped away from the window and returned to reading her morning paper.

Chapter 60

Shay made contact with her office on Monday. Sam was handling things well and had hired an associate to help. He and Shay had discussed the idea a week after Shay had left Detroit. Shay knew the woman he had brought on part-time very well.

Angela Nelson had recently closed her own office in an effort to start retirement. But Sam had talked the attractive sixty-eight-year-old widow into accepting the idea of working part-time at The Relationship Fix Group, Inc. She would only take on a partial caseload and still reserve time for the golf and travel she had planned on doing once closing her office.

Shay suspected there was a little something more than work going on between them, and she was glad. She knew that Sam and his wife had been good friends with Angela and her husband. They had both suffered the loss of their spouses around the same time. Shay smiled, thinking that perhaps these two could get together. They had a lot in common. They both liked to golf and travel. Of course, Sam had not been doing any traveling since he lost his wife as his travel companion. Shay hoped that would change now that Angela was in the picture.

Chapter 61

On Tuesday, Shay started her first session with her friend and psychologist, Janet Lacoste. Shay was anxious to get on with her life and felt blessed that she could seek help from someone she knew and trusted.

She arrived at Janet's office at eight a.m. sharp. She was surprised at how anxious she was to lay out her entire life to Janet. She knew that this was exactly what she needed. She had divulged only the minimum to her family and was glad they hadn't pushed for more. She sensed they recognized how difficult it was for her to talk about what had happened. At the same time, Shay felt guilty because they were her family. They deserved to know. But she just couldn't talk about something so horrendous with them.

Shay was waved into Janet's office by a professional-looking young man who appeared to have a handicap. He had one leg shorter than the other and walked with a cane. Janet was wearing a bright purple dress with a black jacket. Purple was one of Shay's favorite colors. Janet hugged Shay before directing her to the comfortable black chaise lounge across from where she was seated.

"Shay, I want you to talk to me as me, your friend who cares about you and in whom you can confide. There will be no judgment, only help. Our goal is to help you to return to some semblance of normal and to know that this is possible. It doesn't matter how you're feeling at this moment; just hold on to the fact that normal is possible, and it will come."

Shay smiled and nodded.

"Now, let's start at the beginning," Janet said. "The beginning will probably be the start of your life with Jeff."

Shay started talking stiffly at first, remembering large issues about her marriage with Jeff, like the absence of sex and his adamant refusal to seek help. She then started remembering smaller, more subtle things that had happened.

"Jeff was controlling, but I never noticed. No, that's not true, I noticed, but I didn't mind. He became more controlling any time I was near another man. In fact, he wasn't keen on me having a close relationship with anyone, not even women. Any time I wanted to see my friends, Saundra and Gwen, he managed to come up with something else he and I needed to do. He was okay if he was able to come along, like our dinners with Saundra and her husband or our vacations, but he balked when I just wanted to see my friends without him. I really didn't think much of it at the time. I'd just see my friends for lunch during work hours or when Jeff had something else to do.

I also now know that the absence of sex was more debilitating than I let myself admit. I usually just tried not to think about it. I had convinced myself that our marriage was good enough, that he was good enough to even withstand something like that." Shay shook her head sadly. "But I loved him, or at least I thought I did."

Janet made a few notes, nodding as she did. "We need to get started here because it allows you to examine some things that may still be bothering you about your life with Jeff. But I want you to know that the way to get back to normal now will not be to vilify your marriage. I do believe you loved Jeff, and in his way, he loved you.

"He was ill, and without treatment, his issues had to play out in some violent way. At some point in your marriage, Jeff would probably have found a reason to believe you were cheating on him. He had been programmed that way because of his experience with his parents. However, many men who want to make love to their wives but who cannot will sooner or later believe that she will be satisfied or is being satisfied by another man."

Shay spent the next few days mulling over Janet's words. Shay did remember looks from Jeff and questions whenever he saw her simply speaking to another man. All signs she had ignored. But signs that Janet convinced Shay could never have led her to uncover Jeff's real problems. Jeff's problems weren't her fault. The end result was that the feelings she now had for Sebastian were not wrong.

Chapter 62

Shay's next visit with Janet was a week later.

"I'm feeling a little guilty," Shay said to Janet. "I still have not shared with my family that I am seeing you on a professional level. They all know you and simply think you and I are just hanging out as friends. I'm concerned that if I told them I was seeking counseling, they would then be sure that I was still extremely troubled. I guess I just don't want them to be concerned about me," Shay confessed.

"They are going to be concerned about you regardless. It's okay if you don't want to tell them. But if it is going to make you feel this guilty, then maybe you should think about telling them. I'm sure they are concerned about you and know that you have to be deeply troubled after what you've been through—anyone would be. Telling them you're in counseling might just reassure them that you are trying to help yourself."

Shay continued visits with Janet, becoming more and more confident that she could now function in spite of what had happened. Janet was great at drawing her out and getting her to see that life really does go on. After four months of counseling, Shay decided it was time to return to Detroit and perhaps to Sebastian.

She had discussed her feelings for Sebastian with Janet. She couldn't deny they existed. She had denied her feelings while Jeff was alive, but there was really no reason to deny them any longer. Shay realized she had done nothing wrong. She had fought feelings that were so strong that she could easily have allowed Sebastian to make love to her.

This was difficult for her to say, but the feelings were there and had been since the first time he entered her office. But she had done the right thing. She was married to Jeff, and she had not given in to her impulses. No matter how she felt about Sebastian, she was confident she would never have cheated on Jeff with Sebastian or anyone else.

"Are you so sure about that?" The little voice said. Shay dismissed it. She had to believe that she would have never cheated on or left Jeff. And now, not only was Jeff no longer alive, but he had also intended to kill her. He would have killed her had it not been for Sebastian. Shay knew that had all of this not happened, she would have continued to be faithful to Jeff, no matter how she felt about Sebastian. This time the little voice remained silent.

"The part of your life you shared with Jeff is now over. You are free to do whatever makes you happy. You now need to move on. Move on without the guilt, my friend. There is no guilt attached to having feelings for someone else," Janet reiterated over and over to convince Shay that she must move on—and that moving on with Sebastian was okay if that was what she wanted to do.

During the four months of counseling, Shay had also dealt with how, as a counselor herself, she could have missed the signs that Jeff was hiding this deep-seated hatred and anger for his parents and for anyone who would cheat on their partner. These deeply buried feelings were Jeff's downfall and almost Shay's as well. Jeff was certainly a master at hiding his feelings and had long ago learned to believe that his previous life before age fourteen never existed. He was deeply troubled. Shay could not blame herself for the feelings Jeff chose to bury. This was his choice, not Shay's. Yet, initially, Shay carried a nagging feeling that, as a good wife, she should have recognized that Jeff had problems other than just not being able to perform in bed.

"I know without a doubt that if Jeff had ever confided in me, I would have supported and helped him as much as possible. I would have been there for him. It's too late now, but how I wish he had been able to face his demons. We would have faced them together."

"I believe as well that you would have been supportive and helped him," Janet said. "But that wasn't how it played out. The reality is that Jeff would never have confided something that he had buried so deeply. I think he had convinced himself that as long as he buried the tragic parts of his life, he would be okay. That wasn't your fault, Shay."

Shay also knew that absent Jeff sharing his deep-seated problems with her, there would have been no way for her to have guessed what was going on. She sensed that Jeff's aunt Maggie, who was the only one of Jeff's relatives she had met, might, over time, have divulged some information. But Jeff had made sure that didn't happen by lying about his aunt's whereabouts and hiding her away in a nursing home.

Shay was finally able to control and dismiss, when necessary, the thoughts of Jeff and everything that had previously happened. She would now focus only on whatever was to come next—her future.

Chapter 63

It was now July. In a few months, Detroit would once again hunker down for cold, snow, and ice. Shay preferred warmer weather, but for some reason, this year, she was looking forward to winter. She found herself thinking about what it would be like to snuggle up with Sebastian in front of a fire. Prior to counseling, such thoughts made Shay feel guilty and extremely uncomfortable.

Because of her counseling, she no longer allowed herself to feel guilt. Shay was aware that four months of counseling couldn't erase all the trauma she'd experienced. Her recovery wasn't perfect. She still jumped when she heard loud noises. Once in a while, she dreamed that she heard the sound of the gunshot. There were still times that she'd awake paralyzed, closing her eyes as she'd done that day. But she was much improved. It was time to return, not to her old life, but to her new one.

Shay dialed Sebastian's number, letting him know she was on her way back to Michigan.

Again, Shay's mom, dad, sister, and the poodle all escorted her to the airport. This time she was leaving to return home. She had come broken, but she was leaving a reasonably normal and whole woman. Or at least as normal and whole as one could expect to be after such an ordeal. She actually felt happy as she thought of Sebastian meeting her at the airport. It was now time to breathe again…now time to live again… and possibly love again.

Stepping off the plane, picking up her luggage, and heading to the exit, Shay couldn't stop smiling. She didn't know exactly what the future held with Sebastian, but him taking her into his arms in public at the airport finally felt as if it were okay. They still needed to take things slow, but it felt right. In an effort to take it slow, he simply hugged her to him hard. But he didn't kiss her. He was proud of himself. He'd played things just as he'd rehearsed after her call last night.

"I'm glad you're home," he said, still hugging her. He knew he should release his embrace, but he couldn't. He loved her, but he didn't say it. Again, just as rehearsed.

Hold back, he commanded his brain and his body. Don't scare her off.

I don't know how long I can do this, his mind argued.

You can do this, he argued back. She's back in Detroit. You'll have lots of time to just be with her. You don't have to say everything you feel. I can't hold it back for long. I will hold it back, he thought to himself over and over. His thoughts were scattered. Shutting them off, he said, "I've waited for you for over four months. You are finally here in my arms, and I can't let you go."

Oops, he thought, that wasn't as rehearsed. His thoughts were so jumbled. He waited for her reaction to his words.

"And I don't want you to," was all she said, looking into his warm gray eyes.

Being with Sebastian feels right, she thought again.

Chapter 64

Once back in Detroit, Shay met Gwen and Saundra for dinner twice. Shay always selected the location. The fact that the restaurants were always miles away from downtown Detroit was not lost on her friends. They, however, were ultimately just glad to meet her wherever she wanted.

Both women loved her and wanted whatever made her comfortable. Their first meeting was at Seasons 52 in Troy, more than twenty miles from Detroit. Their next was even further at Cooper's Hawk Winery in Macomb County. The reunions were light. Gwen and Saundra noticed Shay's improvement from the conversations they had with her over the months she spent in Virginia.

They were also pleased that she had found a beautiful condo overlooking the water in Lake Orion. Everything was new and shining, including the furniture. The beautiful furniture she and Jeff had filled their Detroit home with was long gone. The location of her new home was forty miles away from the old one.

Gwen and Saundra had both overseen the sale of the furniture and the home. Shay had donated all of the expensive paintings and some of the furnishings to DuMouchelles Art Gallery on Jefferson Ave. near the office. Per Shay's instructions, many expensive pieces of furniture had been donated to Habitat for Humanity and other charitable organizations that helped individuals who were certainly less fortunate than Shay. Any gifts that Shay received from Jeff were packed away in the office storage room by her friends. They didn't want anything left around that would cause Shay to have bad memories. Like Sebastian, they felt their friend's pain.

Shay's reunion with Pam and Kimberly Alice was as happy as the one with Saundra and Gwen. Shay had known all during her time in Virginia that returning to her beloved animals would put a smile on her face. While avoiding the return to her office, she used the time to walk Pam and cuddle with both animals whenever possible.

She'd even found time to read a good novel and do some shopping. She almost felt like herself, apart from one glaringly obvious factor: she was avoiding going to the office. Her work had been a big part of her life. Everyone she counseled was special to her, and she liked doing it. Building TRFG had been first and foremost in her mind for years. Now she felt as if she were abandoning her business and her clients.

Shay felt her anger rise. *How dare Jeff take that away from her?* But then, she forced herself to calm down and think rationally; she remembered he was ill. 'Besides, no one can take anything from me unless I let them.' She repeated the thought again out loud this time.

Chapter 65

Sebastian's alarm sounded like an explosion. Rolling over, he turned it off and sat up. Unlike usual, he did not hit snooze. He was anxious to rise and start his day.

He did something he had not done often in over five years. He smiled. The memories of Shay flooded his body, providing both warmth and energy. He almost wanted to pinch himself to make sure he'd remembered her words at the airport correctly. He smiled, remembering how he was holding her. But the best part was that she'd told him she didn't want him to let her go.

Thinking of those words invigorated him. Most importantly, they'd talked for hours. That night was perfect. After dinner, they walked around Greektown. The July evening was warm and balmy. The seventy-five-degree temperature had prompted them to walk. He took her hand to help her over a rough sidewalk and kept hold of it as they walked.

He was careful to hold back some of what he was feeling. He didn't want to tell her just yet that he knew from the moment he had laid eyes on her that he wanted her – that he wanted to marry her; that he wanted her by his side always. He never thought after Sara that he'd ever feel this way again. He did not want to scare her. He remained cognizant of what she had been through. The thought of the pain she must feel was almost unbearable for him. He could physically feel her pain.

Instead, they just walked and made light conversation. He listened to every word she said. But in reality, she could have been reciting *"Mary Had a Little Lamb," which* would have been fine. He just needed to hear her voice — he just needed to know she was by his side. He never wanted the night to end. But of course, like all good things, it had to. He finally took her home to her new condo. She gave him a glass of wine before he left. He knew when it was time to leave. When he became aroused just looking at her curled up on the oversized sofa she'd purchased, he knew he needed to get out of there quickly.

Now, he looked forward to seeing her today. He hadn't seen her for what felt like ages. Knowing she was back in Detroit and not seeing her every day was difficult. He wanted to be with her every moment. But she'd mentioned at dinner that she needed to catch up with friends. He knew he couldn't monopolize all of her time, but he sure wanted to.

He had only been away from her a few days, and the good part was that he would see her today. He'd asked her to meet him at headquarters, and he'd take her to lunch. He was thrilled when she'd said yes. He wondered if he dared take her back to the Whitney so they could finish their first encounter. He didn't quite know how she'd feel about that. She had been pretty upset with him that day.

Sebastian pulled back the covers and got out of bed. He shaved and showered in no time. He was ready to start his day with her. He needed her so badly that it frightened him. He hadn't felt this way in so long. *Oh hell,* he thought, *I've never felt this way*. "Just admit it. You've never felt this way." This time he said it aloud. He gazed upward. "I'm sorry, Sara," he said softly.

Sebastian was at the office and seated at his desk when Rubye walked in.

"Good morning," she said, giving him a strange look.

He knew why. He was never in the office before Rubye unless he had stayed there all night. After Sara's death, he stayed at the office for many nights, not wanting to go home. Rubye knew about those times. She had often made one of his favorite meals and left it in the lunchroom fridge so that he'd have something to eat.

This time, he gave her a big smile to let her know everything was fine with him. She smiled back and walked over to his desk.

"So, I guess from that goofy smile you're wearing, things must have gone well when you picked Shay up at the airport a few nights ago? It's been so busy here for the last few days that I didn't have a chance to ask you about it. But you've been smiling lately and not grouchy, so I assumed things went well. Did you tell her you need her to work with you on tying up the loose ends of the case?"

"Not exactly."

"And what might not exactly mean, Sebastian? Then what exactly?" Rubye asked, hands on hips again.

"Things were going too well to bring up anything concerning such negativity in her life. I just couldn't go into detail. But I did ask her if she'd meet me for lunch today. We can discuss it then."

Rubye just shook her head. "Lovesick," she mumbled as she walked away.

Sebastian looked over some reports, spoke with some detectives, and gave some directives. All the while, he was watching the clock. When Shay finally walked through the door, she took his breath away. It was another warm sunny day in Detroit. Shay looked like a breath of sunshine in a lemon-yellow skirt and jacket with a crisp white blouse. Her shoes and bag matched the outfit, and she carried a white hooded raincoat across her arm. You never knew in Michigan when warm and sunny would turn to cool and rainy.

"Good afternoon." She smiled.

He smiled back. "Good afternoon. I'm ready to go if you are?"

"Well, I'd like to say hello to Rubye first. She was so kind to me that night I was here. I just wanted to say thank you."

On that note, Rubye walked over to Shay. Rubye had ears like an eagle, and heard everything said at Sebastian's desk.

"Good afternoon, Dr. Jackson."

"Rubye, please call me Shay. I just wanted to thank you for your kindness when I was here some months ago. I brought you a little gift from Virginia."

Rubye smiled as she took the small gift bag. "That wasn't necessary, but such a sweet thing to do. Thank you."

The gift was a gold holder for Rubye's business cards, which Rubye opened as the two women talked easily. Shay simply wanted to show her appreciation. She knew she had been a wreck that night. Rubye had hugged her and brought her hot tea.

Sebastian sat back and watched the interaction between the two women. *Wow. They are both really important in my life. I'm glad they like each other.* The thoughtfulness on Shay's part made him love her even more.

After the two women had been chatting for about fifteen minutes, he finally cleared his throat.

Shay looked up. "Ready to leave?" she asked.

Sebastian's answer was simply to pick up his jacket and take Shay's arm to propel her away from Rubye.

"Do you think we might go back to the Whitney again?" Shay asked, smiling. "I promise to be more relaxed this time. I'll probably even stay long enough to have a meal." They both laughed, remembering.

Rubye watched the couple walk out. They look good together. Both tall, both great looking, both smart, and both in love, she thought. Why not? Although she kind of wished they'd cool it until the final Internal Affairs report came in.

Chapter 66

Shay looked around as they entered the Whitney. She wondered if anyone there now would remember her last exit scene. She giggled as the waiter showed them to their table. She was sure no one would.

"What's funny?" Sebastian asked as he pulled out the seat for Shay. He loved the sound of her laughter.

"Just remembering running out of here the last time. Hope no one here remembers. I was more embarrassed about the cheap theatrics than I believe I've ever been in my life. It wasn't so funny then. Actually, without counseling, it might not be so funny now. But I've really learned to relax. It's amazing what a few months of counseling can do for you. I'm starved," she said, opening her menu.

Sebastian couldn't help but drink in both her beauty and her energy. There was a new airiness about her. Her entire mood was lighter. It was almost as if a weight had been lifted. He did not want to dull the mood by talking about murders. However, he needed her help to track where Jeff had been.

The FBI had recently been brought into the investigation. Jeff was now believed to be a serial killer, leaving a string of dead spouses who had cheated, along with unsuspecting family members. It was also now known that he had two partners who had participated in many murders.

Sebastian continued to stare at Shay, unable to take his eyes off her. He was also having a difficult time starting the conversation he needed to have with her about Jeff. He was afraid that if he told her what the FBI had discovered, it might in some way impact the progress she'd made with her counseling. Yet, he knew he needed to share the information. He needed her help.

The waiter took their lunch orders. Sebastian had the salmon, and Shay had a Caesar salad with shrimp. Sebastian sat silent as they ate. Shay talked about her parents and siblings and how much she loved Virginia. Sebastian still had not spoken more than a couple words.

"Sebastian, is something wrong? You've been so quiet. Does it have anything to do with the Internal Affairs investigation?" Shay asked anxiously.

"No. It'll be alright. I told them the truth," Sebastian said.

"Then why so quiet?" she asked, laying her hand on top of his.

Her mere touch caused him to become aroused. Visibly shaken, he reached for the glass of water the waiter had placed on the table. He drank the entire glass down before looking at Shay. He was not able to ignore the feelings this woman elicited in him. Setting the glass down slowly, he looked at the ceiling but not at Shay.

He knew that once he looked at her, he would not be able to think straight, let alone talk. Keeping his eyes averted, he started. “I don’t exactly know how to start this conversation. You’ve made so much progress and recovered well after all you’ve been through. I just don’t want to bring it all up again, but I need your help. Actually, the FBI needs your help. And I thought maybe I could start the conversation in a less aggressive way than perhaps they would. It’s about some discoveries made about Jeff and what he’s been doing for the last few years.”

Chapter 67

Keeping her hand on Sebastian's, Shay watched him for a while before speaking. She took a deep breath.

"What do you mean the last few years? Do you mean Jeff has been doing this for years? He lay beside me in bed and had been killing people for years?"

Sebastian watched her before speaking. He noted that despite the words she spoke, her voice was even. She wasn't panicked. She was just inquisitive, albeit shocked.

"Yes, it has been over a number of years. If this is too much for you right now, I can always stall the FBI for a while," he offered.

"No, no, that won't be necessary. This won't be easy, but I want to help if possible. I just don't know what I can tell you. I still find it difficult to believe that Jeff could hurt me or those people, but it's obvious that he did." Taking another deep breath, she asked, "So how can I help?"

"Let's start with the fact that there were many more murders than those he mentioned." Sebastian stopped short of sharing with Shay that the FBI had now classified Jeff as a serial killer.

"How many more?"

“We’re not sure yet. Were you aware that Jeff had another office where he saw clients?”

“Another office? No, of course not. Where would it have been?”

“He leased an office in the name of Dr. Rogers. It was located off Jos Campeau in Hamtramck.”

“I don’t understand. It sounds almost as if Jeff was leading a double life. When could he have practiced out of that office? How?” Shay was totally shocked.

“Well, it seems he was not there all the time. He would often arrive just moments before his clients showed up. He didn’t have a secretary or receptionist. He was always there to greet them himself. It appears he saw no more than one or two clients there per week. We ascertained that he was there mostly on Thursdays. The landlady said that every now and then, he would return in the evening around five o’clock. He’d stay for maybe an hour and then leave. He received mail there, which is how we tracked down two of his clients. He received thank-you notes from two of his clients whose spouses had died. It seems he attended the funerals. He also received invoices and payments through the mail.

Shay’s brain was whirling. “You said Thursdays. He volunteered at an Eastside clinic on Thursdays. I always thought that was really nice of him. I’d even offered to come and volunteer with him. He dissuaded me by telling me it was a really rough area and that I should just leave it to him. I was really busy myself, so I really didn't think much of it. He made a point of letting me know he was simply volunteering and didn't take any money for his services. I guess that was also a lie," she said, picking up her water glass.

"According to our investigation and interviews with the spouses, the invoices only arrived after the victims were dead. We believe he hired someone to commit some of the murders. The money he was paid was used to pay the person he hired. That person is named Maverick Jones. He's currently in prison and will be there for a long time. He functioned as a private investigator. He followed those who cheated, took pictures, and often disposed of them when requested by Jeff."

"By disposed of," she swallowed, "you mean killed?"

"I'm afraid that's exactly what he did. It seems that Jones was initially a cellmate of Jeff Jackson, Sr., Jeff's dad. He was hired by Jeff, Jr. to kill Jeff, Sr. He actually beat him and cut Senior badly and left him to die in his prison cell. But before he bled out, a corrections officer just happened by and found him. He lived, but he was unconscious for weeks."

"During that time, his attacker was actually released from prison. Of course, the authorities didn't know that he was the attacker when he was released. So, Jones was out of prison for three weeks. During that time, he was hired by Jeff Jr. to kill three people. The three all had only one thing in common: they received treatment at the Rogers Counseling Center. And, of course, they all cheated on their spouses." At the questioning look on Shay's face, Sebastian explained.

"The Rogers Counseling Center is the business Jeff set up to seek out couples who needed his help. It seems that Maverick followed those who were cheating and reported back to Jeff. The invoices instructed them to deposit the payment into a bank account. The instructions gave the name of the bank and the account number. That account actually belonged to Maverick Jones. In the meantime, Jeff Sr. comes out of his coma and tells the prison authorities that it was Maverick Jones who attempted to kill him and that he thinks the order came from his son, none other than Jeff Jr." Sebastian kept his eyes on Shay. "Is this too much for you?" he said gently. "If it is, I can stop. I don't have to tell you everything we now know."

"So, people paid Jeff to kill their spouses?" Shay asked incredulously.

"I'm afraid they did. Well, some of them, anyway. There were some, like Willa Raines, and others who were unsuspecting. We believe that Jeff committed crimes out of Michigan as well. That's where you might be able to help us. If you could tell us even the approximate time when Jeff was not in Michigan and where he went, it would help. None of his whereabouts were mentioned on his office calendar or computer."

"I'd have to look at my calendar. I normally wrote the times he'd be away on it." Shay pulled her phone out of her purse. She clicked her calendar open and scrolled through the months.

"He didn't do a lot of traveling. Actually, the only dates I know about are from four years ago. The first date was on the second Thursday in February. He was in Cleveland, Ohio. The next date was the second Thursday in July, and he was in Milwaukee, Wisconsin, and the next was the second Thursday in November when he was again in Cleveland. All of these were in 2019." Shay looked up from her phone. "Does the fact that all these dates fall on the second Thursday have any significance?"

Sebastian shrugged. "I actually don't know. The FBI might have some idea, but they only share bits and pieces of information on a need-to-know basis with the local cops. But if anyone knows, I guess they would. They were the first to ask about Jeff's travel. We checked with Gwen, but she didn't have the dates on her calendar, and we couldn't find anything on Jeff's computer. We also checked with Jeff's secretary, Sherelyn, and she didn't have any dates that he was out of town."

"Actually, Gwen wasn't working in the office all of 2019. In 2019, we used a temp service. So we had several different receptionists that year."

"Why did Jeff say he needed to be out of town during those dates?"

"He said he was doing seminars." Shay's voice sounded weak. "I stayed here to cover his clients at the office."

Sebastian put his hand over hers. "That's all for now. I've browbeaten you enough. I'm sorry about all of this. I would never have put you through this if the FBI wasn't insisting. As I said before, I thought it would be better if I asked the questions rather than let the FBI do it. But it wasn't easy to convince them to let me have a stab at it first. I think I've gotten them enough information for now. Actually, that's not totally factual. Even if the FBI weren't involved..." He stopped to formulate his words.

"The truth is, I personally believe the unknowing spouses and other family members of all the victims have a right to know what really happened. And, of course, we're still investigating those who actually solicited the deaths of their cheating partners. So I might need you to work with me to put it all together," Sebastian said timidly.

Shay's face clouded. She then mustered a smile. "Of course, I'll do whatever I can. But they must know Jeff was sick. The things that happened to him as a child apparently affected him deeply. Please make sure they know that," she pleaded.

"I will make sure they know," he assured her.

"Could I just ask one more question?" Shay asked timidly.

"Of course; what is it?"

Shay swallowed before speaking. "Did Jeff actually kill any of those people, or did he contract all of them out?"

Sebastian hesitated. He knew his answer would be hurtful to Shay.

"I'm afraid he killed or participated in the murders of a fair amount of those who died. There is one additional person who the FBI knows was involved, but they haven't been able to determine who that person is yet. I'm sorry."

"Don't be. And thank you for being truthful."

"Look, let's order some drinks,"

Sebastian said, waving the waiter over.

"Bring the lady a chocolate martini, and I'll just have tea. I'm still on duty."

This time, Sebastian took Shay's hand in his. He kissed her fingers and then quickly leaned over and kissed her. "I'll let them know Jeff was sick," he promised.

She looked surprised but did not pull her hand away. She smiled. “I like that,” was all she said.

Sebastian let out a breath. He hadn’t wanted to do anything to scare her off. His feelings were so intense for her that it was difficult holding them in check and even more difficult knowing when and how much to share.

Shay stared into Sebastian’s gray eyes. As if reading his mind, she said, “I care for you, and I know you feel the same. I know after what happened and how little time has passed since… “Shay paused briefly. “I want you to know that I’m interested, and I want to see where this relationship goes. It’s just difficult to know when to proceed. You’ve got the Internal Affairs thing hanging over your head. I certainly don’t want them thinking we were carrying on prior to….” She paused again.

“Let me worry about that. They heard the tape. They know how dangerous Jeff was. They know what his intentions were. I did what I had to do. If they were going to make more of it, I would have heard about it by now. I’ve got friends all over the police department, including in Internal Affairs. So, you can relax. I want to see you. I have to see you, but I can wait. If we could just continue having lunches and dinners for now and maybe talk on the phone?” This was a question.

“Yes. Of course, we can do that.”

"I promise I can go at any pace you say. But I need to see you. I need to hear your voice."

Shay smiled. "I feel the same."

The drinks arrived. They sipped them slowly, talking quietly, not about crime, but about themselves.

Finally, Sebastian realized he had to end his lunch with Shay and return to headquarters. Upon his entering the office, Rubye came out of her office and threw her arms around him.

"What's that for?" He laughed.

"The IA report is back," she whispered. "I know I shouldn't have opened it, but I couldn't help it. Are you mad?" she said, loosening her grip on him.

"Rubye, you may not know this, but I've always known that you open all of my mail, even that which is marked private. No, I'm not mad. But do you think I can take a look at it now?"

Sebastian sat down and quietly read over the report Rubye handed him. He blew out a long breath of relief. He had been cleared of any wrongdoing.

The first thing he did was to place a call to Shay to let her know. She'd seemed really worried about the outcome. Putting her mind at rest was first and foremost on his. They made a date to celebrate at another Detroit jazz club, Baker's Keyboard Lounge. Sebastian was pleased that Shay seemed to like jazz as much as he did.

Chapter 68

Returning to his office the next morning, Sebastian received a call from the FBI. They wanted to update him, they said. The call took him by surprise since working with the FBI had not exactly been a piece of cake. Updating him had not appeared to be on their agenda. Most often, they demanded all of the information the Detroit police had regarding the Jackson case but withheld most of what they knew. They only parted with tidbits when they needed something from him. So, to now be updated, Sebastian found it mildly amusing. Nevertheless, he was interested in what they had to say.

Sebastian had, of course, relayed to the FBI the states Shay had given him that Jeff had visited in previous years, along with the dates.

"We just wanted to update you," Agent Bradley now told Sebastian.

"Our agents questioned everyone who worked in the office except a young woman named Gail Brown. She did not return to work or call after Dr. Jackson was killed. We located Ms. Brown, however, not at the address she had on file at TRFG. As it turns out, Ms. Brown had a record and was on parole. We got her correct address from her parole officer."

"We caught up with her at her apartment, where she seemed to have been packing to leave on vacation, she claimed. She apparently didn't realize that she would bring more attention to herself if she left her employment than if she had stayed. The FBI simply wanted to talk with her as they had the other staff, to see what she might know about Jackson's comings and goings and anything he might have divulged about his feelings that his wife was cheating on him."

"She claimed to have no knowledge of anything her previous employer might have done or felt. She admitted to having been hired by Jackson himself, rather than through the employment agency the other staff advised that TRFG usually utilized for hiring."

"She did divulge that Dr. Jeff Jackson had often asked her about things that were going on in the office, including anything she had noticed about his wife. She, however, claimed that she didn't know why he would ask her. She appeared nervous, so we leaned on her further until she finally said that she had overheard Dr. Jeff Jackson talking about Mr. Maverick Jones, whom she didn't think was a client. She also provided an address of a location in Hamtramck. She said she had found the address written on a piece of paper in the waste basket. That, she said, was all she knew."

"We released her but not without a tail. We believe she knows a lot more than she was divulging at the time."

"At the Hamtramck address, we found freezers containing body parts that were waiting for disposal. But we have not as yet found Jackson's third accomplice." He stopped to clear his throat, and Sebastian used the time to question him.

"What all do you know about the third accomplice?"

"Well, we talked to Maverick Jones. Fortunately, he was recently locked up for another reason. Upon questioning him, we know there had to have been someone else, but we don't know much else. Jones said he only acted as a private investigator, following those who had been cheating and taking pictures of them in the act. He took his orders from Mr. John Smith. He knew that wasn't his real name. He said he'd never had a conversation with the doctor."

"The owner of the Hamtramck location, Edna Crombie, was questioned and released. Even though she rented the property to the doctor, it was clear she had no knowledge of what was going on. She honestly thought the man she knew as Dr. Rogers was simply a psychologist."

Sebastian waited silently. He knew the FBI had not divulged all this information for no reason.

"You know this town better than we do. We need more on Gail Brown and anyone she might be connected with. Just keep your eyes open and let us know if you come up with anything. Also, see what Shay Jackson knows about Gail Brown."

"I will indeed, Agent Bradley."

Chapter 69

Sebastian hung up the phone on his desk and sat quietly. This was obviously not over yet. He phoned Shay to update her and shyly ask for another date. She sounded happy that it was finally over. He didn't tell her it wasn't. He was happy that she said yes to the date.

Shay and Sebastian went to their favorite restaurant. The Whitney had become their place. Sebastian was always so happy to see Shay that he usually glowed. However, tonight he was having a difficult time shaking off the feeling he got thinking that he could have lost her. It seemed that this was far more involved than he had at first believed.

He willed himself to return to the moment and enjoy the evening.

"How are you?" he asked. His smile was bright. He only needed to look at her, and he was once again in the moment, loving her.

"I'm fine," she volunteered quickly.

"No, I mean really. You mentioned last night that you were hesitant about returning to work. Is there anything I can do? Do you want to talk about it?" he asked cautiously.

He was always conscious of overstepping his bounds with her. After weeks of being with her and spending every waking moment thinking about her and what he could do to make her happy, he still wasn't quite sure where he stood.

He knew she wanted to warm up to him, but her experience with Jeff was holding her back. He couldn't and didn't blame her for that. After all, he was right there with her when the worst happened. And afterward, he knew it had affected her so badly that she wisely decided she needed counseling.

But now that she was back, he wanted her. He ached for her. But most of all, he wanted to know that she felt the same. He was almost sure she did. She would give him a look that told him she did. Then immediately after, she would become slightly distant. Never cold, but almost shy and maybe a little uncertain.

A few times, he dared to kiss her, and she immediately responded, only to move away a few moments later. "Move" was the keyword. She didn't push him away. He took solace in that. That was something to note, he thought. She was, he noticed, no longer wearing her wedding rings. When she first returned to Detroit, she was still wearing them. His heart sank when she noticed him staring at them. "I still feel married," she'd said. "I don't understand the feeling myself, and I certainly don't expect you to understand."

But he did understand. He wore his wedding band long after his wife was gone. He'd lost her, but he still felt married to her. It wasn't until Rubye insisted he start going out with the gang that he finally took the gold band off and carefully returned it to the box that Sara had packed away after its purchase. He had actually felt better once he'd done that. He was no longer able to look at the ring on his finger and cry inwardly for Sara. He admitted that touching the ring and looking at it had made him feel sad. It made the loss of his wife more glaring. It made the loss feel so much more real. He hadn't wanted that feeling. He wanted Sara.

He had even tried to foolishly bargain with God. If you just return her to me, he'd prayed, I will be the best man possible. I'll do whatever you say, God. I will do whatever she wants. I'll even give up the police force. But, of course, it had not worked just as he knew it wouldn't.

Now he knew he would always love Sara, but he also knew he would wait for Shay. He would wait until she was ready, no matter how long. Maybe the absence of her wedding rings was a sign. At least, he hoped it was. She remained quiet while Sebastian's mind took him through the entire gamut of emotions he was feeling. Now she spoke.

"I do want to talk about it. But first, I want to find out what's going on with you. I saw some look of concern on your face when you picked me up. Surely, the FBI will have this third man in custody in no time, won't they? Is that what's bothering you?"

"Just work, and I guess I'm just a little tired." This time his smile was genuine. He was with her now, and everything was great. But for some reason, his experience with Sara kept nagging at him. He needed Shay to know what had happened.

"I'd like to reciprocate if you need me. I am a counselor, you know," she said, smiling.

"Well," he said hesitantly, "there is something that I need you to know about my relationship with my wife, Sara."

"I'm listening," Shay said softly.

"We'd been married for fifteen years when she died. For most of those years, my being on the police force troubled her. She was afraid something would happen to me. She was often paralyzed with fear. I tried to convince her that I'd be fine. But she wouldn't or couldn't shake it. Hearing about any police officer in the world getting injured or killed would set her off. She was often depressed and always frightened. She wanted, begged me to leave the force.

"After I made commander, I tried to convince her that I'd be okay. My job was no longer on the street but safe inside an office. She was okay for a brief period. But then, with the death of someone who had previously been my partner, she was just unable to cope. She cried all the time. And the end result was when she read about a mentally challenged man bursting into a police precinct, shooting up the place, and killing one officer before being taken down. Sara had to be hospitalized after that episode. So, as much as I loved police work and thought of it as my life, I knew I had to at least try to give it up to save Sara and our marriage.

“So, I finally used that engineering degree that Sara was always reminding me that I possessed and took a job with General Motors. Sara was ecstatic, but I hated every minute of it. I stayed there a little more than five months before; I just couldn’t take it any longer. I came home and told Sara I was returning to my position with the police department. She asked me how I thought I could quit for five months and then think I could just return to my old job.

“What she didn’t know was that my position had only been filled temporarily because even though Sara thought I had actually quit, I had only taken a leave.” He paused.

Shay placed her hand over his and urged him to go on. She could tell how difficult this was for him.

“When I told Sara that I had only taken a leave of absence which held my position for six months, she was angrier than I’d ever seen her. She accused me of lying to her, letting her believe I’d finally given up police work. She was screaming that I was a liar, and how did I think I could get away with placating her for five or six months before returning to the force. She accused me of not trying to make the position with General Motors work. I tried to take her into my arms to comfort her, but she grabbed her car keys and ran out of the house.

"It was raining that night. I stood on the porch as she jumped into the car and took off, tires screeching. I just stood there on the porch with the rain pelting me. I didn't even try to go after her. The crash happened right at the end of our block. A drunk driver in a truck broadsided her. The sound of that crash played over and over in my head for months and months. I was eaten up by guilt because I probably hadn't given the new job all I could. But most importantly, I felt I could have saved her. I should have gone after her.

"I never told this to anyone else other than Rubye, who finally convinced me that going after her would not have stopped the crash. By the time I would have jumped into my car, she would already have been at the corner where the crash happened.

"I got a phone call from a fellow police officer that night who also lived in the area and knew both Sara and me telling me about the accident. But I already knew it was her when I heard the crash. I actually ran to the scene and pried open her car. They had to force me out of the car. I had blood all over me, and I was just numb. And that's the way I've been ever since it happened until I met you." Sebastian stopped talking. He feared he'd said too much until she reached over and hugged him.

"I'm glad you had Rubye to help you through this," she said simply and smiled.

"Actually, my parents also came to stay with me during that time. They knew I was grieving hard. My dad is retired but still runs his barbershop part-time, so he was prepared to stay as long as I needed him until one of his main barbers fell and broke his leg. So, he had to return home. But my mom actually stayed another couple of months. The guys dropped by to help as well, but mostly to get my mom's home cooking. She used to run Elaine Crawford's café until she sold it a few years ago and retired. I'd love for you to meet her. She'd love you."

Sebastian took a long breath. He'd needed to get that out. He needed to let Shay into his life completely. And that meant sharing his feelings with her. Now, he turned to her.

"So, now tell me what's going on with you."

"I was just thinking how strong you were in a crisis as you talked. I don't want you to always see me as such a helpless type. I am strong, or at least I used to be. When I was married, I took on a good portion of the responsibility for building the business and running the office and our home. But I'm sure it's obvious to everyone that I've been back in Detroit for weeks without returning to work. I haven't even stopped in the office. I haven't so much as acted as if I was interested in what's going on there. And at the mere thought of returning to the business we...I built," she corrected, "I feel like a scared rabbit. I just can't be sure of what feelings returning to that office will elicit."

She paused, and Sebastian covered her hand with his. "You'll have to be prepared for whatever feelings returning elicits. But you'll never know until you walk into that building. And in the meantime, the worries and uncertainty that you're currently struggling with may be unwarranted. What if you return and find yourself laughing at your fears because you immediately take command like you did in the past?"

"I know you're right, and that's why I've decided to return."

"When did you decide that?"

"While you were talking." She laughed. "You are very persuasive, and you're right. It must be the detective in you. Why worry about something that might not happen?"

"What's the worst thing that could happen? So, you walk in and find that the bad memories rush in with you? It certainly wouldn't be pleasant. It is certainly not what I want for you, but I think that you need to find out. I'm always available to take that first step with you. I can and will hold your hand. Rubye will clear my schedule at the drop of a hat if she knows I'll be helping you. She really likes you." And so do I, he thought silently.

"I'll let you know. I might just need you."

She had no idea how much Sebastian wanted her to need him.

"I promise I'll be right by your side," he said. "One word from you, and I'll swoop you out of there and take you out and wine and dine you until you forget everything. Then we'll work out what the next steps are together." When she kept her head down and didn't immediately respond, once again, he hoped he hadn't gone too far.

When she lifted her eyes to his, he realized they were moist.

"That was the sweetest thing you could have said to me. You have been a big help. So, I'll tell you what. Why don't I definitely decide to return on Monday? No matter what, I will stay for a half day and wait for you to come and take me to lunch. If you can clear your schedule for the rest of the day, maybe we can go to Baker's Keyboard Lounge and listen to some jazz. Jazz always relaxes me. Then we can talk about how my day, or my half day, I should say, went at the office."

"That sounds like a plan." His broad grin let her know how much he liked that plan. "You know you always have options."

"I know," she said simply. Then hesitantly, "I've actually been thinking about my options. You are the first person I've shared that with. I want to make sure I'm thinking with a clear head when I make any decisions." She paused, and he waited patiently.

She took a deep breath. "Option number one, and actually, the last alternative, would be to sell my share in the business. Sam can certainly afford to buy me out and bring Angela in full-time and or hire someone new. Then I could just take an early retirement. Maybe even move back to Virginia." She stopped when she heard his sharp intake of breath.

That option scared Sebastian to death. Instantly, without his being able to help it, his eyes became moist. He lowered his head and said nothing, but not before Shay noticed.

"That would be the very last option, I promise you. And even so, it isn't as if Virginia is another continent away or something," she said gently as she absently circled his hand with her fingertips.

Even that small gesture aroused Sebastian. He stared at her fingers as they circled. He swallowed and took another deep breath. He wanted her so bad. Shay stopped, realizing what she was doing to him. She had not made love in years, but she was not oblivious to Sebastian's needs and feelings. And she had to admit she felt pretty aroused herself.

Removing her hand from his, she continued. "Now, let me tell you about some other options." He relaxed a little. He waited.

"I was thinking maybe I'd work from home and do online or virtual visits. Even though I'm sure you will think I'm running away and avoiding my problems.

“I don’t think that at all. I simply think you’re looking for alternatives that will work for you. If they work, and you continue to manage the career you love, you’ll be a success. It’s just like anyone who has in the past decided to work from home instead of in an office. These days that’s perfectly normal,” Sebastian reassured Shay.

At the end of the evening, as usual, Sebastian didn’t want to let Shay go. He never wanted their time together to end.

“How about stopping at an all-night diner for coffee or something?”

Shay laughed, knowing what he was doing. She actually found that she didn’t want the evening to end either. But she declined coffee that would just keep her awake.

Chapter 70

Shay disliked the fact that she had been nervous about finally returning to her office. The feeling made her feel weak. She had come so far and made so much progress over the last few months. She wanted nothing to mar what it had taken her months to accomplish. She was deathly afraid that returning to the office, which almost felt like returning to the scene of a crime, would have a negative effect on her newfound confidence.

But she knew it was time. She had been back in the Detroit area for more than three weeks without stepping foot into the office. She phoned Gwen with instructions and to get updates daily. She also spoke with Sam daily. Between him and Angela Nelson, the office was doing well. All their clients were being taken care of. But Monday was the day she had decided on, and Monday it would be.

Monday came far too soon, but Shay had always been a woman of her word. She had made a decision to return on Monday, and she would. She had notified both Gwen and Sam, and they were both ecstatic. Gwen knew personally the challenges Shay was facing regarding her return. Sam wasn't privy to the conversations between the two friends, but he sensed there was an issue when Shay did not return to the office immediately upon returning to Detroit.

Shay woke hours before her alarm went off. She dressed in a blue pinstripe pantsuit that she paired with a crisp white blouse. She slipped on navy blue stiletto heels and made sure her hair and make-up were perfect. She knew anyone who had not seen her since the incident would be looking closely to reassure themselves she was alright. Everyone at the office cared about Shay and had often checked in with her to check on her progress and to let her know she was missed.

Her phone rang as she was about to leave her condo.

"Hello, Sebastian."

"I was just calling to say good morning and to assure you that I will be available whenever you need me today. I don't care what time. I'm available for breakfast, a break, lunch, or dinner. I'm at your disposal."

"I know and feel both blessed and comforted that you are in my life. You've really been supportive. I promise I will call you the minute I need some air. Don't worry about me. I'm going to be fine," she said, more to convince herself than Sebastian.

Shay pulled into the parking lot of TRFG, turned off the motor, and sat for a brief moment. She took a couple of deep breaths and realized she'd be okay. Exiting the car, she walked into the building. She was met by Gwen, who greeted her warmly. Shortly after, Sam and Angela exited Sam's office. Sam couldn't resist hugging Shay. He and Angela both welcomed her back. The fact that they had both come out of Sam's office together looking slightly flushed was not lost on Shay. She smiled inwardly as she walked to her office. She glanced at Jeff's door. The office now belonged to Angela.

Hesitantly opening her office door, Shay stood in the doorway for a moment. Finally walking in, she looked around. She didn't know what she had expected. She had spent the last ten years in this office. Those ten years, in spite of everything, had been good years. It had felt good to enter the first time she entered ten years ago, and now, well, now, it still felt almost the same. The photo of Shay, Jeff, Pam, and Kimberly Alice had been removed, probably by Gwen. It had been replaced by a photo of Kimberly Alice, and Pam. Shay smiled. It was just like her friend to be sensitive. The office had even been freshly painted a bright yellow.

Shay walked over to her desk and ran her hand over the smooth dark cherry wood. She had purchased the desk from DuMouchelles Art Gallery during an auction. She had bid more than she had to because she really wanted that desk. Only to learn that the desk was so large and so heavy that movers charged twice their normal rate. The door and frame had to be removed to get the desk into her office. She rubbed it again lovingly as she sat down.

There were flowers on the desk. Reading the card, she smiled. They were from Sebastian, of course. The card read Welcome back to the city where you belong. Always, Sebastian.

Now, she looked around the room. The paintings she had selected remained on the walls. She noticed that one, which had been a gift from Jeff, was now gone.

Shay opened her calendar on her computer and was struck with an idea. She hastily picked up the phone and dialed Willa Raines's cell phone number. She hoped Willa's number had stayed the same even though she was now in Chicago.

Willa answered after two rings. "Hello, Dr. Jackson," she said happily.

"Hello, Willa. You sound wonderful. How are things going there in Chicago?"

"I am so glad you called. I often think of you and how kind you were to me. I'm doing great partially because of you. I think of some of our conversations, and I'm encouraged. I have a great position at a hospital here in Chicago."

"That's great. How are the kids?" Shay asked.

"They're doing better. They actually weren't really that attached to John. He rarely spent time with them. So, other than their picking up on my sadness, they've been well. Once I realized that I needed to perk up if not for me, but for them, things got better. And how are you, Dr. Jackson? I read about everything in the papers. I'm so sorry you had to go through that."

"Thanks for asking, Willa. I am much better as well. I don't have any kids to be strong for as you do, so I decided I needed to do it for myself. Life goes on is not just a cliché; it is really true. And life is what you make of it."

"And that's what I remembered about some of our conversations. You said several times that it wasn't the things that happened but how you chose to respond to them. It was my choice, and I understood that I always have choices, and it's up to me. For that, I truly thank you."

"I'm just glad you're doing well, Willa. What I said during our last conversation still goes. I'm here for you if you need me. I intend to start doing some virtual counseling. So, any time you need it, we can arrange to do it virtually."

"That sounds wonderful. I'll certainly let you know. Take care, Dr. Jackson."

"You as well. Goodbye, Willa."

Shay smiled. Talking to Willa felt great. Counseling is what I do, and it is certainly a big part of who I am. I can do this, she thought as she buzzed Gwen.

"Good news, Gwen. I want you to start scheduling a few clients for me as early as next week. I can do this," she said.

"I can't tell you how happy I am to hear that. We've missed you around here."

Chapter 71

Shay's next call was to Sebastian. She smiled at the phone. "I'm feeling great and ready for that lunch you promised any time you can get away."

"I'll be there," he said. She sounded good, so he, in turn, felt good. He had been as nervous about her return to work as she.

Everything seemed to be going well at the office. There were moments when she passed by Jeff's office when she felt a tiny twinge and a shiver go down her spine. However, Jeff's name had been removed from the door and replaced by Angela's. His name had also been removed from the stationery long before Shay returned. His business cards that had sat on the front reception desk were long discarded. Shay glanced at the spot where they used to be and refused to allow herself to react.

No one at the office had mentioned to Shay that some clients had been lost due to the media's constant commentary on the horrific murders, all attributed to the victims having visited TRFG. Shay was never informed that Sam had gone on TV to discuss what had happened and how the integrity of the business was their utmost concern. An agency had even been hired to promote the business, and a few months later, all was well. Sam's clients and Shay's had continued to be loyal. Sam had handled his clients as well as hers.

Some of Angela's loyal clients from her previous business had followed her to TRFG, as well.

During that time, Shay had deliberately avoided TV and newscasts after walking into a room and seeing a close-up of her being led into the police station after her ordeal. The TV in her bedroom at her parents' home stayed off for the duration of her time there. Her family, noticing the look on Shay's face whenever the incident was reported, followed Shay's lead and turned off any newscast on the TVs in the common areas of the home.

Chapter 72

After being back at work for two months, Shay finally breathed. Things had gone even better than she'd hoped. She had started out putting in half days at the office. Sebastian was always on hand to spend time with her once she concluded her work day. Shay thought it was really sweet that he constantly, but without being pushy, seemed to always be around when she needed either an ear to listen, someone to make her laugh, a companion to enjoy jazz with, or a shoulder to cry on. And once in a while she did cry.

Shay and Sebastian had just returned from the MGM Casino, which was near Shay's office. Sebastian had picked her up at her office.

Shay had worn a simple suit to work, but changed into a sexy little black dress before Sebastian arrived.

"Wow, you look stunning," He hadn't expected that. He thought she looked good in whatever she wore, but he appreciated that she had wanted to wear something special for their date tonight. Just saying the word date felt good to him. He was really on a date with this gorgeous intelligent woman.

There was no denying the attraction between them.

"You like?" she said as she twirled around for him.

The evening had gone well, as the times they spent together always did. Sebastian reluctantly drove Shay back to her parked car. He hadn't wanted the evening to end. He got out of the car and slowly walked around to open the car door. He noticed Shay staring at something on the side of the building. Turning to see what she was looking at, he saw a small plaque glowing in the dark. PARKING SPACE OF DR. JEFF JACKSON, the plaque read in large letters. He'd never noticed it before but realized it was more visible at night.

Sebastian grabbed Shay's hand and pulled her out of the car. She was visibly shaking and crying. He held her close for a few moments. He then guided her back into the car.

"I'm sorry. I shouldn't be acting this way. Seeing that just shocked me. Through tears she told Sebastian about the plaque.

"Jeff had it designed for those few times he would return to the office after dark. There was already a plaque there but it wasn't visible in the dark. Jeff had only returned once to find someone parked in his space. He found the trespasser, as Jeff called him and angrily told him it was his reserved space. The poor man apologized profusely and promised never to park there again. But Jeff wasn't satisfied with that. A few days later the plaque went up. I'd never seen Jeff so angry. He actually wanted to fire the maintenance man, but was satisfied with the new plaque."

Shay stopped and sniffed. Sebastian handed her his hanky. That's what my broad shoulders are for," he comforted her.

"You know, I guess I'm just spoiled. Between Gwen and Sam, every trace of anything in the office that could have reminded me of Jeff disappeared. They took the name off his door, the stationery, and the sign in the lobby. They even replaced the furniture in his office and even the artwork. I shouldn't fall apart just because I see a sign. I can't live my life acting as if Jeff never existed. He damned well did exist and I can't pretend that he didn't try to kill me."

Sebastian held her. "Please come home with me and sleep in my guest room. I can't let you drive all the way home like this."

"I can't Sebastian. Pam and Kimberly Alice are there. I found someone to walk Pam and feed them both because I knew we'd be out late, but I need to be there in the morning. Besides, I have no clothes and I have a client in the morning. I'm okay now.

"Okay, but I won't let you drive all that way this late without following you

.""But-" He put his hand up to silence her.

"Alright, but why don't we stop by your place and pick up what you need and you can stay in my guest room? You must be tired. I won't hear of you following me and driving all the way back here.

Sebastian was in agreement with anything that would keep Shay both safe and close to him for a bit longer.

Arriving at the condo, Shay went to tend to her animals while Sebastian walked around the first floor. Everything was immaculate and spacious. A balcony overlooked the lake.

Shay came up behind Sebastian. “You know I have gym equipment upstairs. Feel free to give up your gym membership and use this any time you'd like."

Shay's words bolstered Sebastian's spirits causing his heart to quicken at the same time.

“Would you like a drink or maybe some cocoa before turning in?" She asked

"I'd love some cocoa if I can have lots of marshmellows."

Chapter 73

Shay prepared breakfast for Sebastian. It was actually the first time she had prepared a meal in her spacious new kitchen. She had eaten out or ordered meals delivered most of the time she'd been back in Detroit. Her meals at home were usually just a sandwich or fruit in the evening.

Now, hearing Sebastian's footsteps on the stairs, she poured the batter into the waffle iron. Shay looked up as Sebastian entered the kitchen. He looked fresh.

Sebastian, on the other hand, felt anything but fresh. He had not gotten much sleep. He lay awake thinking of Shay in the same house, his thoughts consumed by bits of their conversation last night. Especially Shay's offer of the use of her exercise room. He thought of how cozy it had felt sitting in front of the roaring fire with Shay drinking the mugs of steaming hot cocoa. They contained, he remembered, almost more marshmallows than cocoa.

And now Shay was preparing breakfast for him. She looked great in the kitchen. She had on a colorful long dress, and her hair was pulled up with sexy little whisps falling down. He stared at her until she looked up.

“Good morning.” She smiled, motioning him to a seat at the table in the nook. They shared food and had a good conversation. Sebastian thought nothing could be better. They never seemed to run out of topics to cover. They talked about upcoming events, the weather, the news, and sometimes just comfortable silence worked for them.

“I forgot to tell you that I won’t be available for lunch today. I have a seminar to teach that was scheduled months ago. I almost forgot about it myself until a few minutes ago. I was going to ask you out to a fancy dinner at our favorite spot, but the seminar won’t end until around ten p.m. But I’m free tomorrow for lunch if you can clear your schedule.”

“I think I’ll be alright alone for one night, Commander. And yes, I can manage lunch tomorrow.”

Dropping Shay off at her office, where she’d left her car the night before, Sebastian headed to police headquarters and was aware of Rubye’s pleased smile when she noticed how happy he looked.

“I guess you had a good night, huh?” Rubye said with a devious grin.

“Yes, I really did,” he said, heading into his office. He was glad Rubye had not followed. He closed the door. He just wanted to take just a moment before starting work to savor all that had happened both last night and this morning. He didn’t want to get ahead of himself, but he felt as if he had been blessed twice in this lifetime to find someone to love.

Sebastian smiled and sighed happily before delving into police business. Christmas was nearing, and with it, the usual increase in robberies, shoplifting, and pickpocket crimes. He handled his duties efficiently. But in his free moments, the thought of Christmas had him wondering what Shay might like as a gift.

Shay had recently been working the entire day. Sebastian felt the absence of her calls that had him rearranging his schedule to meet her for lunch. He was, however, glad that she had adjusted. Her sudden tears last night had jarred him and caused him to realize she was still somewhat fragile and raw after her ordeal. He figured she would be for some time. But he knew and hoped she knew that he would always be there to provide help and comfort.

Slowly, his office door opened. He didn't have to lift his head to know who would dare enter the Commander's office without knocking.

"What is it, Rubye?" he said, still looking down at the report he'd been reading.

"Mr. Moore is here. He wants an update on the investigation of the robbery of his jewelry store and the homicide of his head clerk."

"Send him in."

Sebastian updated Mr. Moore on the investigation. Sebastian's detectives had made an arrest and were talking with several other suspects. Sebastian relayed the information to Mr. Moore, who seemed pleased. Mr. Moore insisted on getting his updates from the big guy, the head honcho, as he referred to Sebastian.

After that, Sebastian headed for the training room, where he'd be instructing a group of shiny-faced cadets until late in the evening. The department had sprung for a nice lunch and dinner for the trainees in between the sessions. He was right; the agenda that had been laid out for him continued on until 9:30 that evening. The trainees were excited and didn't seem to mind. Sebastian was a good and energetic speaker and never let the class become dull. He enlisted their input in such a way that multiple hands constantly went up.

As soon as he arrived home, he got out of his uniform. Quickly, he threw on a T-shirt and a pair of lounge pants. He picked up his cell phone and decided he'd make some cocoa first. Remembering how cozy it had felt as he and Shay sipped the chocolate drink, he had the urge.

Taking a few sips of cocoa, he relaxed and was about to dial Shay's number when the landline rang. He looked at the caller ID and was taken aback. Shay was calling him. He answered on the first ring,

"Sebastian, I'm glad you're home. I've wanted to share something with you all day, but I didn't want to disturb your work," she said.

"You can always call me. If I'm really that involved in something, Rubye will let you know. What's up, you sound excited."

"When can you get away tomorrow?" she asked.

"Probably not until late evening, I'm afraid. I have training scheduled again all day tomorrow and into the evening. I apologize; I thought I'd be available to you for lunch. I didn't know they had me scheduled for two full days."

"It's okay, I understand."

He could tell she was disappointed. "I'm sorry. Rubye put this on my schedule weeks ago. It's a new class of police recruits, and I always do the first day. Maybe I could go in on their last day instead," he said, not wanting to disappoint her.

"Certainly not, Commander. I will not have you rescheduling things for me." She laughed. "Just relax. This can wait," she assured him.

He figured it could, but he didn't want to wait to see her. But he supposed he'd have to.

There was something in her voice. Something that made Sebastian anxious. He couldn't tell if that anxiety was to lead to something good or bad.

"I did something yesterday that I've wanted to do for a while, but was afraid."

"What's that?" he said, wondering what it could be.

"I visited Jeff's Aunt Maggie. I had been thinking about visiting her for a while, but like with my fear of returning to work, I thought it might bring back memories that I didn't want to deal with."

"And how was it?"

"Well, first let me tell you that I owe taking this step to you."

"How so?" he asked

"Do you remember my hesitation to return to the office?"

"Yes, of course."

"Well, you more or less told me that I might just be worrying for no reason but that I'd never know unless I did it. So, of course, I did, and it turned out well. With Aunt Maggie, I was willing to try. She's such a sweet lady. I've taken over paying for her to stay at the facility. But that's not enough. She deserves to have visitors. And I found out that you feel the same way. Why didn't you tell me you've been dropping in to visit her?"

"I'm sorry I didn't tell you," he said. "I didn't want to bring up anything that would cause you to remember the past. When I visited the first time, I learned that she never had visitors, so I just dropped in whenever I had time. It was nothing."

"It was everything. She went on and on about Sebastian, the nice commander who visits all the time and brings her little gifts. You've been visiting for months. You started visiting her when I was still in Virginia. You even paid her last month's fees when the payments Jeff arranged ran out." Shay paused as her eyes filled with tears. "What a kind and caring man you are."

"Please don't make a big deal out of it," he said, sounding a bit embarrassed.

Shay wanted to say more but didn't want to continue embarrassing Sebastian. She had a lump in her throat and something more in her heart.

Chapter 74

Listening to Shay and Sebastian's conversation, George smiled. He didn't have to worry about his target having an overnight guest again. So, tonight it would be. It was time to grant the Doc's final wish.

George busied himself, getting ready. He'd been bringing the white truck and parking it near his apartment. He'd already put the signs on both sides of the truck. Jones Carpet Cleaning, they boldly proclaimed.

He was now ready to turn in so that he could be up bright and early. Around three a.m. would work, he decided. She'd be sleeping. Just as he sat down on his bed, his phone rang. He looked at the caller ID. Aunt Edna. He sighed. He really didn't want to talk, but he couldn't ignore his aunt. She'd been good to him. He'd probably be dead by now if she hadn't taken care of him after Gracie put him out.

He picked up the phone. "Good evening, Aunt Edna." She said something, but George couldn't understand her.

"Why are you whispering, Aunt Edna? Is something wrong?" he asked.

"I don't know," she said a little louder now. "The FBI just left."

George's heart pounded at her words. No. He couldn't go to prison.

"They were asking a lot of questions about Dr. Rogers. He's the newest tenant staying in the loft. They wanted to know exactly when he'd leased the space, who came to visit him, and things like that. They also asked me if I knew someone named Maverick Jones?"

George's heart continued to pound. "Did they ask about me?" he asked, keeping his voice level.

"Of course not. Why would they ask about you? Unless he called you for repairs, you've never even met him, have you?"

George's heart slowed. "No, I've never met him," he lied. "I just wondered because, based on TV, when the FBI investigates, they talk to everyone, even if they aren't involved, that's all."

"I guess you're right, but no, they didn't mention you."

Edna chatted on for a few more minutes and hung up when George told her he had another call coming in from one of her tenants. He hung up quickly.

"That bitch," he exploded. Pacing the room, he continued talking to himself. "The one time I let myself be soft with any woman other than Gracie, look what happens." He banged on the dresser. "The only person," he continued, "who knew about the loft and Maverick Jones was Gail."

He had intended to kill her but thought it would be okay. She was really upset when he told her that he and Gracie were getting back together. But she seemed to calm down when he forked over five thousand dollars of the money the Doc had given him. She'd even hugged him. She said she knew how much he loved Gracie and wished him good luck.

"It was all a lie," he said aloud, continuing to pace. "How could I have fallen for that dribble?" But apparently, he thought, she hadn't mentioned him, at least not yet. He'd take care of her, he decided, right after he killed Shay Jackson.

George pulled up to the condo at exactly three a.m. All the lights were out. He glanced across the street and noticed a light on, but the rest of the house was dark. Some folks leave a light on in one room, he decided. Anyway, if anyone noticed him, they'd just think he was picking up carpet to be cleaned as the truck indicated. He threw the carpet he took out of the truck over his shoulder. Dropping off and picking up, he decided.

George quietly let himself into the house. He'd had a key made when he'd been in there to bug it. He crept upstairs carrying the cloth he'd soaked in chloroform. She was sleeping soundly. He put the soaked cloth over her entire face. She was out like a light. He quickly wrapped her in the carpet and again threw it over his shoulder.

He placed his bundle in the back of the truck and headed for Southwest Detroit.

****

Elena watched the entire thing from between the cracks in her blinds. Why would anyone be picking up the carpet at this hour? Maybe the company just wanted to get an early start and had arranged it with the owner, she reasoned. Then she thought better of it. That didn't make sense. And there was something else bothering her. She'd seen that truck before. It said something about an alarm company. Yes, that was it, Smither's Alarm Company. She'd intended to look them up and possibly have an alarm installed on her house. She'd forgotten to take care of it.

She hesitated for only one moment before placing a call.

"Hi, Officer Grady. This is Elena. Is my brother still working the night shift?"

"As a matter of fact, he is. Hold on, and I'll get him for you."

"Elena, why are you up so early?" Police Commander Brad Graves asked his sister.

"You know, since I retired, I never sleep. I need you to let me know if this seems strange?"

"Okay, let me have it."

"Brad, you remember I told you a new neighbor had moved in across the street. I think you said she was a friend of your colleague and friend, Sebastian. Such a nice man he is. A few weeks ago, this white truck with a sign that said Smither's Alarm Company was at her house. I didn't think anything of it at the time. But this morning, what looked like the same truck but now with a sign that said Jones Carpet Cleaning pulled up. I couldn't see a license plate. The guy hops out, carrying carpet over his shoulder, and enters the house. A bit later, he comes out carrying the same carpet, but it looks a lot heavier this time. I know you'll think I'm crazy, but I swear it looks like there's a body in it. But even if there wasn't, don't you find it strange that someone would be picking up carpet this early in the morning and that the same carpet he took in is the carpet he's bringing out?"

"I sure do. I need to hang up and make a call. I'll update you later."

"Sebastian, wake up, buddy. I think something could be going on at Shay's house." Brad relayed what he had been told. "It may be my sister watching too many police shows, but in light of what happened to Shay before, I thought you need to know."

Chapter 75

Sebastian was up and dressing while on the phone. Once he hung up he dialed Shay's cell but got no answer. He immediately placed another call.

"Rubye, I know I woke you up, but I need you to get me a phone number and an address for Gail Brown. The woman Jeff Jackson hired. And I need it yesterday."

"I'm on it," she said, recognizing the panic in Sebastian's voice.

She called him back within minutes with an address and phone number. "The FBI," she said, "is still tailing Gail Brown. She'd had one visitor. A man named George Hayden."

"Rubye, get the FBI involved. I think someone has kidnapped Shay. I got some information from Brad, you know my friend and commander who works at the Fifth Precinct. I've called Shay's phone. It goes to voice mail. I don't think she has her cell with her. I'm on my way over to Gail Brown's place. I believe she knows something about this and she's going to tell me." He hung up abruptly.

Within five minutes, Sebastian pulled up in front of Gail Brown's apartment and banged on the door. The FBI tail followed him into the building. Gail opened the door, still groggy from sleep.

Sebastian didn't take time for formalities.

"Tell me what you know about Shay Jackson and who might have kidnapped her."

With wide eyes, Gail responded, "I swear I was coming in to tell you today that Dr. Jeff paid George Hayden to kill her if he failed. At first, I didn't believe he was going to do it. If I'd thought he really would especially after Dr. Jeff was dead, I would have told you. I swear I would have."

"Tell me now, everything you know. Where did he take her?" Sebastian said angrily.

Gail closed her eyes and thought. "The only place I can think of would be this abandoned factory in Southwest Detroit that he took me by one night. It's a real abandoned section of town. I don't know what street it was but there were no houses and the only thing that was there other than the factory was some burned out building. That's all I know. I swear." She was now crying.

Sebastian was out of the apartment and running to his car, while dialing his cell phone. He got the sergeant on the desk at the Fourth Precinct, where it sounded as if the factory would be located, and told him who he was and described the area Gail had mentioned. Within minutes, three police cars were on the way to the location and so was Sebastian.

Chapter 76

Shay was awake when she was dragged from the truck. She screamed and kicked at her assailant to no avail. George dragged her into the factory.

"You can scream all you'd like," he said. "No one will hear you. Everything in this area is abandoned for miles. There's no one around."

"Who are you and why are you doing this?" she asked tearfully.

"I'm fulfilling a promise I made to your husband to get rid of another cheating bitch."

Shay's heart pounded and her breath caught in her throat.

"I didn't cheat on my husband. I would never do—"

George slapped her hard across the face. "You cheated then and you're still cheating with the same man. You lying bitch. I've seen you. I've heard your conversations with him. So stop lying. I'm going to end your romance for good. In a minute, I'm going to actually fire up this old furnace and drop you right in. And later, I'll take care of your boyfriend."

Shay watched this unknown man in fear. His eyes glowed as he told her of his plans.

Chapter 77

At four-thirty a.m. there was almost no traffic. Sebastian looked at the speedometer. He was now up to eighty-five miles per hour. But at least he'd just received a call from the commander at the Fourth Precinct. Their officers had just located the abandoned factory and the white truck. They had the building surrounded and were about to break in the door when Sebastian pulled up.

George was taken by surprise when the officers busted in. He pulled out the gun he kept in his waist band. The first police officer through the door shot him in the chest.

Shay was sitting on the floor where she had fallen, stunned, after the slap. She was shaking when Sebastian found her. He took her in his arms and held her there until the shaking subsided a little. He looked at the bruise on her face and at Hayden. He was dead. Sebastian was sorry he hadn't been the one to do it. Tears ran silently down his face. He'd almost lost her again. He pulled her closer and just held her for a couple of minutes as the officers took charge.

Now, he gently lifted her up from the floor and carried her to his car. She was still wearing pajamas. He took the blanket he kept in the backseat of his car and wrapped it around her. She was sobbing, just as she had after the ordeal with Jeff. He drove straight to his house. It would be up to the officers at the Fourth Precinct to do the paperwork this time. He'd make a report later. But right now, he had to tend to Shay.

He carried her into the house and took her to the same bedroom she'd used before. He put ice on her bruised face and pulled the covers up. He'd given her a sleeping pill he'd kept around when he had trouble sleeping on and off. She soon drifted off. He quietly left her side for only a moment to step out and contact Rubye to let her know they'd found Shay and that she was with him. He guessed he wouldn't be training the recruits after all. He wasn't leaving Shay's side.

Sebastian, again in the chaise lounge beside Shay, turned when he heard her stir. She was once again sobbing. He tried to comfort her.

"I promise you it's really over this time. I won't let anything happen to you. I promise I won't." He smiled at her. "I'm going to start taking care of you by getting you away from the Detroit area for a few days. We'll go to your place and pick up some clothes and be on our way. I've cleared my schedule and yours too. I called Gwen. I also called Saundra. She's picking up Pam and Kimberly Alice."

Shay sniffed, trying and failing to smile. "I guess you've thought of everything. Except was this incident on the news? If so, I'll have to call my family again."

"No, we kept it off the news. Everything was done quietly."

"Thanks for that. I didn't want to have to explain once again being the victim," she said tearfully. "I'm going to stop crying and take a shower. I think I need to have something other than pajamas to wear," she said, looking down at her white pj's with cats all over them.

"I thought of that too," he said, handing her one of his shirts and a pair of his wife's pants that he had failed to get rid of when he cleaned out her closet. They were about the same size and height so they should fit, he thought. "We're going straight to your house after you shower and you can change then."

Sebastian and Shay spent the next three days in a two-bedroom suite at the Westin Hotel in Chicago. Sebastian wined and dined Shay for three entire days. They ate Garretts popcorn, Cheesecake Factory cheesecake, went on the architectural tour along the river, visited jazz clubs, strolled along the magnificent mile while holding hands, and did everything possible to take her mind off what had happened. He knew she was fragile. Who wouldn't be, he thought, after what she'd been through twice, now. But he swore again, to her and to himself, that she'd never have to go through anything like that again.

After a couple of days, Shay's resolve to put things behind her returned. She told him how frightened she'd been, but that she would be okay. He knew she would.

Returning home, Sebastian hesitantly left Shay at her condo and returned to his work. Shay returned to work as well. The pair had gotten closer and learned more about each other while in Chicago. Even though Sebastian had ached to make love to the woman who was sleeping in the other bedroom, he made no move to make that happen. He had been happy just to be able to spend so much uninterrupted time with her.

Chapter 78

After returning from Chicago, Shay met Sam and Angela at Mario's Restaurant, just a few blocks from the office. Shay was delighted to see Sam. He appeared to be doing well. All three embraced. He looked happy and healthier than he had since losing his wife. Shay had even noticed that Sam had not been using his cane as of late. All to which it was obvious Angela had been a significant contributing factor.

Shay smiled as she listened to Sam excitedly tell her how Angela often prepared dinner for him. Angela had brought homemade lunches for both of them daily. Angela had accompanied Sam to concerts.

Angela had played golf with Sam. And finally, how Angela and Sam were planning a wedding for next year with a honeymoon in Spain.

"Oh my, that's wonderful news. It is obvious that you two are good for each other. I can't tell you how deliriously happy I am that you two are together," Shay said, looking straight at Angela. "I have to confess that I was kind of worried about this man before you came back into his life."

Angela smiled. "Did you know that we dated in high school? We even went to the prom together. But we were young, and it wasn't really serious."

Sam interrupted her. "She wasn't serious. I was. She broke my heart." He laughed.

"Oh, stop," Angela said. "I was only sixteen years old, and he was eighteen. It seems like a lifetime ago. We went our separate ways. I married Willie, and Sam married Edith. We were both happy in our marriages and blessed to have found the partners we had. But now we are just as blessed to have found each other again," she said, smiling at him.

Sam sat smiling widely back as Angela spoke. It was clear he felt the same. Damn, they were exploding with happiness, Shay realized.

Their happiness was contagious. Stealing a bit of their excitement about life caused Shay to realize she had been holding back. She needed to get back to work. She was glad she had returned. Now just maybe, she needed to open up more to Sebastian. She didn't know what she was afraid of. Sebastian was certainly no Jeff. He didn't seem to have any secrets. He had opened up and shared everything.

He'd told her about his deceased wife, his guilt over her accident, and how he had not come alive again until he met her. She knew how close he was to Rubye and was glad he had her as a friend. He had already introduced her to his parents when they had come to visit shortly after her return to Detroit. He had also introduced her to his siblings. She had gotten along well with his two brothers and his sister. He seemed to want to share every fleeting thought and moment with her.

He texted her numerous times each day to tell her he was thinking about her and called any time anything remotely good or interesting happened. He gave her a play-by-play explanation of his life from childhood to the present. He shared his likes, dislikes, and fears with her. He seemed to like nothing better than to call Shay in the evening to tell her about his day and inquire about hers.

Shay discovered that she looked forward to his calls and his texts and to seeing him. But she had been keeping him at a distance. He never complained. He was true to his word when he said he would wait for as long as necessary. He never pushed her or asked for more than she was willing to give. Which she realized was really not very much. Each time she wanted to tell him how she felt, she refrained. She didn't want to encourage him. She didn't know why. But she realized now she needed to rethink her feelings for this big, kind, gentle teddy bear.

"What was I thinking?" she said aloud. "I love him." Once home, Shay dialed his number.

"I have a request," she said as soon as he answered. She could hear the smile in his voice.

Sebastian was taken aback. She rarely called him. "Anything. You know I'll do anything for you," he said

"Would you please come over and spend the night with me? I want you."

She said it so softly that he almost didn't hear her. Especially since he was already out the door and striding toward his car to get to her. He hadn't even thought to throw as much as a toothbrush into a bag in case she let him stay the night. He just wanted her to have lunch and dinner, read his silly texts, and listen to him on the phone. He hadn't dared to dream of a phone call from her like this one.

He broke every speed limit from Detroit getting to her. He pulled up to her condo and jumped out almost before the car came to a complete stop. He rang the bell but didn't have to wait. She had been watching for him.

She opened the door immediately, wearing only a short peach-colored nightie. His love was displayed on his face. She saw it as she pulled him in and held him close. He thought he would burst.

"I love you," she said, leading him to her bedroom. Two glasses and a wine bottle sat on the small round glass table in front of the sliding glass door leading to the balcony.

Sebastian was still smiling. He was actually a little nervous and extremely aroused. He sincerely thought that he might explode the minute he touched her. He wanted to please her, and having a premature ejaculation was not exactly what he was going for here. He had a silent talk with himself as he sat on one of the two chairs placed around the table holding the wine. *Calm down,* he told himself. *She called you. She won't change her mind. You love her. You'll do everything to please her. You can do this. After all, she just told you she loved you.* He couldn't believe she'd said that. But she had. There was no doubt how he felt.

She sat watching him. She had all the time in the world, and she could sense his struggle. She poured the wine. They clinked glasses and drank. He relaxed. She came around the table and kissed him on his neck. He pulled her to him. He wanted to talk about how he felt. She wanted to make love. They met in the middle of the bed. They made love, and then they talked.

"I'm serious," he said. "I love you enough that if you aren't sure about us, I can continue to wait. I don't want to rush you, and I don't want to ever hurt you. Shay, I need you. I want to be with you every minute. I want to share everything with you. I want to know that you are happy and safe," he said softly.

"I want to apologize to you. Don't think I haven't realized that I've run hot and cold where you're concerned. I know that, at times, I felt so close to you and responded as such. Then seconds later, I tried to distance myself. I want you to know that I was attracted to you from the very beginning. That attraction has only grown deeper. I was just scared and often confused about my feelings and whether I had the right to feel as I do about you. When I called you tonight, it was because I've finally come to grips with my feelings. No more denying how much I care for you. No more pushing you away. I'm glad I called."

"I knew you were afraid. I tried not to be pushy. When I was, it was because I just couldn't help myself. I was willing to take cold showers for as long as it took."

"Cold showers?" she laughed.

When you called tonight, I was going to call you in just a few moments, right after my cold shower." They both laughed.

"No more cold showers for you," she said as she rolled over on top of him, kissing him. She was obviously ready for more of him, and he wanted more of her for the rest of their lives. Kimberly Alice jumped up on the bed as usual and nestled in her usual corner, as Pam jumped up and went to the opposite corner at the foot of the bed. Thankfully, the animals had waited until the lovemaking session was over. Sebastian looked at both as he held Shay and smiled at them. "I'll love the two of you as well," he said softly.

Shay heard him and nestled closer. Sleep came easily in Sebastian's arms. "I love you," she said. "Oh, by the way, there is one last option that I wanted to run by you."

"What's that?" he said, kissing her forehead.

"Marrying you," she said as she watched the look of love and pure joy on Sebastian's face.

THE END

www.ingramcontent.com/pod-product-compliance
Ingram Content Group UK Ltd.
Pitfield, Milton Keynes, MK11 3LW, UK
UKHW021711190726
13853UKWH00001B/490